I LOST SIGHT OF THE AIRCRAFT IN THE TURN, WHIPPING MY HEAD AROUND AGAINST THE G-FORCE, TO TRY AND GET MY EYES BACK ON TO THEM, WHEN I HEARD TWO LOCATER BEACONS GO OFF ...

I looked around and down, and suddenly saw a blazing Tornado plough into the ground below us.

Flames flashed through the forest as the aircraft smashed through the trees, tumbling over and over before exploding in a massive fireball. The Tornado had obviously not been hit by a SAM missile – this was not Iraq – either an aircraft fault or human error had sent it catapulting from the sky. There was no sign of the crew, no parachutes or anything ... I put out a distress call on the emergency frequency: 'Mayday, Mayday, Mayday. Tornado Down' – words I had hoped never to hear again.

Flt Lt John Peters was born in London in 1961. He joined the RAF in 1980 as a university cadet and graduated from Manchester University in 1983. In 1987 he became a staff pilot at the Air Navigation School, RAF Finningley. In 1988 he converted to Tornado GR1s and was posted to XV Squadron, RAF Laarbruch in Germany; the squadron was subsequently involved in the Gulf War. After another tour on 31 Squadron at RAF Brüggen, he returned to England in 1993 to become an instructor pilot at the Tri-national Tornado Training Establishment, RAF Cottesmore, Leicestershire. He is married to Helen and has two young children, Guy and Toni.

Flt Lt John Nichol was born in 1963 in North Shields, Tyne & Wear. He joined the RAF in 1981 and trained as an electronics technician, subsequently serving in the South Atlantic in the wake of the Falklands War and in many other parts of the world, including Norway, Denmark, Kenya and Ascension Island. He was commissioned as a navigator from the ranks in December 1986. He and his pilot John Peters were deployed to Bahrain in December 1990 as part of Operation Desert Storm and were taken captive after their aircraft was hit and forced to eject over the Iraqi desert. The bestselling story of their ordeal is told in *Tornado Down*, also published in Signet. Following the Gulf War and the disbanding of XV Squadron, John retrained to fly the Tornado F3 air defence fighter based at RAF Leeming in North Yorkshire.

RAF Flight Lieutenants
John Peters and John Nichol
With Neil Hanson

TEAM
TORNADO

Life on a Front-line Squadron

A SIGNET BOOK

SIGNET

Published by the Penguin Group
Penguin Books Ltd, 27 Wrights Lane, London W8 5TZ, England
Penguin Books USA Inc., 375 Hudson Street, New York, New York 10014, USA
Penguin Books Australia Ltd, Ringwood, Victoria, Australia
Penguin Books Canada Ltd, 10 Alcorn Avenue, Toronto, Ontario, Canada M4V 3B2
Penguin Books (NZ) Ltd, 182–190 Wairau Road, Auckland 10, New Zealand

Penguin Books Ltd, Registered Offices: Harmondsworth, Middlesex, England

First published by Michael Joseph 1994
Published in Signet 1995
3 5 7 9 10 8 6 4 2

Photographic acknowledgements
The authors and publishers are grateful to the following for permission to
reproduce copyright photographs:
Cpl Paul Betteridge 19; British Aerospace Military Aircraft Division 13, 15, 16; Sgt Mick Coles 8,
10; Crown Copyright, Ministry of Defence 14; Quadrant/Tony Hobbs 23; John Peters 2, 11, 12;
Andrew Phillips 4, 5, 6, 7, 18, 20; Lt Christopher Ryan USAF 22; Geordie Smith 17, 24, 26;
S.A.C. Chris Weissenborn 9, 21.

Every effort has been made to trace the copyright owners, but if there have been any
omissions in this respect, we apologize and will be pleased to make appropriate
acknowledgement in any further editions.

Printed in England by Clays Ltd, St Ives plc

Contents

Contents

Acknowledgements

There are many people who should be thanked for their time and help during the production of TEAM TORNADO; the following are just a few.

Firstly and most importantly, our thanks go out to Neil Hanson for putting our endless ramblings into an eminently readable form. Thanks Neil, without you there would be no book.

Thanks also to Mark Lucas for making it all happen, and to the staff at Michael Joseph for putting it all together.

We are extremely grateful to all those who allowed us to use their photographs, especially Geordie Smith and Andrew Phillips. Andrew Bunce at British Aerospace found us many of the fabulous air-to-air shots.

Thanks finally to Steve Clarke at the Ministry of Defence who toiled more than we did to ensure that TEAM TORNADO was published on time.

Introduction

John Peters and John Nichol: There have been innumerable books about the forces; memoirs of everyone from Field Marshals to the lowliest of squaddies, accounts of skirmishes, battles, wars won and wars lost.

All those books have focused on the forces at war. War is what we continually train for and the reason why we have armed forces in the first place, yet it occupies only a fraction of the working lives of career servicemen. In the seventy-five-year history of the Royal Air Force, we have actually been at war for less than seven years of that time, and five-and-a-half years of that was on National Service, during the Second World War.

Tornado Down obviously struck a chord with many people, but it was the comment of one of our fellow air crew's wives that really started us thinking about writing this book: 'I've been married for ten years and I never understood what my husband did, until I read *Tornado Down*'. Even RAF airmen who do not fly, told us that they learned a lot more about our work from the book than they ever had during their Air Force careers.

We wanted to write a book that would set out the reality of Air Force life in peacetime as well as war in a way that, as far as we are aware, has never been written before. Our aim was to show the gritty reality of life on an Air Force squadron, both the glamour of fast-jet flying and also the dangers – more air crew are killed in training accidents every year than lost their lives in the Gulf War.

The modern Air Force is not about 'bull' and marching at all. Nor is it about Biggles and Carruthers reliving their exploits, while a forelock-tugging batman brings them cups of tea. The Air Force today is about computers and electronics and the application of ultra-modern, cutting-edge technology to one of the oldest human preoccupations of them all, self-defence against hostile neighbours. Even the most junior ground crewman today has skills and qualifications that would make the minds of his Second World War predecessors reel, while a degree in physics or computer sciences is of far more use to a modern pilot than a handlebar moustache.

The timing of this book is apposite, for the Air Force, like the other branches of the forces, is going through a massive upheaval following the end of the Cold War and in the aftermath of the Gulf conflict. The forces are being pruned more savagely than ever before, as the government seeks to collect the 'peace dividend'. Our strategic plans, our tactics, our role, are all being re-examined minutely as we adapt to this brave new world, in which the single, monolithic enemy has been replaced by a score of simmering trouble spots in every part of the globe.

One thing does not change, however. For all the incredibly sophisticated and expensive technology that is wrapped around today's air crew, a battle in the air still revolves around the skill, training, knowledge and courage of the human being at the heart of the machine. That human being, in turn, relies on a pyramid of people extending down into the darkest depths of the Air Force, the men on the ground, who get his machine into the air.

This book is a personal view of life on the front line. It follows a year in the lives of two ordinary air crew, a pilot and a navigator, returning to peacetime 'normal service' following the trauma, the terror and the elation of victory in the Gulf War.

I

That's it then

THE DISBANDING OF XV SQUADRON

John Nichol: I heard the rumble and was instantly awake, bolt upright, drenched with sweat, my eyes staring into the darkness. I waited for the flash and the blast wave that would rock the building to its foundations, shaking me like a terrier on a rat, before dumping me to the ground in a broken heap.

Seconds passed. Nothing happened. The low, bass rumble grew quieter, fading slowly into the night. As my eyes grew used to the darkness, I began to make out the contours of the room, a familiar outline, not of an Iraqi prison cell, but a bedroom in my parents' house in North Shields. The rumble was not an incoming bomb from a Tornado or an F-16, barrelling in over the rooftops of Baghdad to rain down high explosive, but the Tyne and Wear Metro train rattling past. The sound of trains passing in the night had often lulled me to sleep as a boy; now it awoke me from a recurring nightmare.

I was wide awake, my pulse racing, flashing back to the Gulf: our abortive bombing run, the wall of flak bursting around us, white-hot tracer buzz-sawing through the sky, the gut-wrenching explosion as the SAM missile ripped into the jet, and the ejection out of the blazing, doomed aircraft. Then came the capture, the beatings, the kickings, the torture, and the feeling of utter helplessness, trapped in my cell in Baghdad as bombs dropped by my own friends and colleagues rained down out of the night sky, falling with a shriek like the whistle

1

of a runaway train and a rumble that grew louder and louder until it ended in a blast that tore the night apart. Enough . . . I forced my thoughts away from that black hole.

After our release, we faced the first media barrage at the Baghdad Novotel, still not quite convinced that we were really free. Only when the plane lifted clear of the runway did we start to believe it, letting loose a ragged cheer of elation and relief. An even more massive media assault was waiting for us in Riyadh. While we faced the phalanxes of press photographers and TV crews, the SAS guys were discreetly slipped past the media cordon and put on to a waiting Hercules, well before we arrived to join them for the rest of the journey to safety, as the cameras once more whirred and the flashguns popped.

We changed planes again at King Khalid Military City, and were on a VC-10, heading for Cyprus, within minutes. The SAS guys sat on one side of the plane with their mates, and we sat on the other with ours. I ate chicken tikka masala and a lot of chocolate, drank a gin and tonic and chatted. The transition from a hideous nightmare of imprisonment to the absolute normality of crew room banter with my mates, had happened in just a couple of hours. Even then, I did not completely relax until we touched down at RAF Akrotiri in Cyprus. Then I really knew that the ordeal was over. I had an emotional reunion with John Peters and then raced to a phone, to let my parents know that, despite what they had been told by the newspapers, I was alive and safe.

We could not have had a better place to recuperate. Akrotiri is one little corner of paradise that the RAF has still managed to hold on to. We have lost Belize, Gibraltar and Aden, but Cyprus remains, the only decent place to go anymore. The hospital had a typically institutional feel, gloss-painted walls and bare concrete floors, but after the privations of the 'Built-more Hilton' – our last prison in Baghdad – it seemed like a home from home, and the feeling of clean clothes on a clean body was a luxury I had almost forgotten.

I had only to walk out of the back door of the ward to be on a balcony in the bright sunshine, where I sat for hours, watching the waves lapping onto the rocks. In the whole sweep of the shore, I saw only one person, walking a dog. I spent the time in silent contemplation, just sitting and being quiet for a while, thanking God that I was still here. The sheer normality of everything was the biggest shock of all, both to us and to the people caring for us. After seven weeks of deprivation and ill-treatment, everyone was expecting us to be complete nutters, but instead we were completely normal ... or at least, as normal as air crew ever get.

The SAS guys were also back to normal. One of them went off to find a few videos and came back laden with unwholesome family entertainment, including a few video nasties. The psychiatrist in charge of our rehabilitation tried to persuade them not to watch these, warning them of Post-Traumatic Stress Disorder and saying: 'You will do yourselves psychological damage'. The SAS man had the perfect riposte, however: 'It's alright, we were all barking mad before Iraq, so none of this is going to make any difference'.

John Peters went back to Germany on an executive jet, but we had to make do with a VC-10 the following day. We landed at Brüggen, where the Commander-in-Chief, RAF Germany, was waiting to meet us. After the formal greetings, we then had to take off and fly around the sky for forty-five minutes, even though Laarbruch was only a ten-minute hop away, to allow time for the C-in-C, RAF Germany, to drive there and greet us all over again.

A car whisked me away immediately for a very tearful reunion with my parents, whose first trip abroad in their whole lives was to come and welcome back the son who they thought had been killed in the Gulf.

John Peters: The jet landed at Laarbruch late at night. I came down the steps into a barrage of television lights and photographers' flashbulbs, to be reunited with the family that I thought I would never see again. The reunion with Helen was a moment that neither of us will ever forget, a prayed-for, and gratefully received second chance. Holding her and the children in my arms again gave me a joy that was almost too intense to bear.

Guy had altered a little in the months that I had been away, but Toni had changed out of all recognition, growing from a newborn baby into a toddler. She was only twelve weeks old when I left for the Gulf and I could not get over how big she had become. You expect to be saying: 'My, haven't they grown' when you go to visit your other relatives, not when you see your own children. I was very aware that I had missed a lot of Toni's early life.

There was a welcome home party my first night back at Laarbruch, but we left at about eleven o'clock to go home. As soon as I was out of the euphoric atmosphere of the party, I felt instantly exhausted. I fell into bed, but though absolutely shattered, I could not settle, the bed was just too comfortable after seven weeks lying on a concrete floor.

I got up the next morning, brushed my teeth, and put the kettle on. I wandered around the house and went out and stood in the garden, savouring the cool spring morning. Almost instantaneously the seven weeks of captivity in Iraq became unreal. Everything was frighteningly normal, as if I had just woken from a nightmare. The kids played in the lounge as if I had only been away overnight. Guy looked round, said: 'Hello Daddy', and that was it. I wanted to hug him and hold him, crushing him in my arms, but he just wanted to go off and play with his toys. Daddy was home, wasn't that perfectly normal?

The only reminders of my ordeal, apart from the near-skeleton staring back at me from the mirror, were the sacks of mail lining the hall. The station had been deluged with letters and cards for me, although one gift of some chocolate cherries fell foul of the zealous base security staff, who detonated the package on the runway in the mistaken belief that it contained a bomb.

The sudden return to absolute normality was more disturbing to me than anything more dramatic could ever have been. I went over and over the past weeks in my mind, reassuring myself that it had all really happened. I could still vividly recall being shot down, the orange flames, the capture, the brutal beatings and the horrific feeling of being bombed, but it was the personal, special moments that I remembered most: John and I in the desert with bullets pinging around our ears and the brief, but all-encompassing, glance we exchanged at the moment we decided to surrender, a look that could have been a last farewell.

I thought of the Joliet prison in Baghdad, when we manoeuvred our way towards each other and shared one moment of human warmth, John's reassuring hand on my shoulder, before we were again put into solitary confinement. The next contact was even more welcome, a hug at Akrotiri in Cyprus after our release – victory!

I remembered sitting on the bed in the military hospital in Akrotiri, having a beer with a mate, Rob Woods, and leafing through the newspapers. We had been up all night chatting, laughing and joking, forty hours without sleep, forty hours since release from captivity; I was free . . . alive. My face, complete with vacant look and goatee beard, peered back at me from a handful of newspapers scattered on the floor. Flattered that I was front-page national news, I was abruptly deflated by Rob, who, with a wicked smile, passed me the *Sun*. I was still front-page news, but only just, occupying only a tiny corner, almost squeezed out by a much more important story: 'Queen is Bitten in Corgi Fight – 3 Stitches After Dogs Turn Nasty – Exclusive'.

After the front-page stories and our momentary fame, Helen and I restarted our lives together. Like any couple that has undergone a traumatic event, we talked and tried to make each other understand what we had been through. It was not just my experience, my whole family had borne the pressure, and Helen looked as shattered as me, for she had been under a terrible stress. Helen and I wanted to talk about everything that had happened, but whenever we had time together it always seemed to be interrupted by someone calling round to see us. It was not that we did not like to see our friends, it was just that we needed some time for ourselves. We were trying to snatch moments together to tell each other our stories.

The strain we had both been under showed itself in an occasional flash of anger, usually over something quite trivial. On one occasion, Helen's parents, who were visiting us, had to sit stony silent and embarrassed as we had a few harsh words. Helen got angry with me and I got angry in return. I even swore at her, which is not a good thing to do, least of all in front of the in-laws. The flare-ups came and went quickly, and both of us gave each other time and space and talked whenever the house was not full of friends dropping in. Gradually we re-built our relationship, as we regained the weight we had lost – Helen had shed a stone while I was in the Gulf, I had lost two stones – and our resilience. The lines of stress and strain disappeared from both our faces. We were stronger, as individuals and as a couple, for what we had been through.

Like the broken sleep of a nightmare, however, the experience had left us both drained. I was weaker than I thought, mentally fine, but physically exhausted. Helen would beg me to rest. I had sat in solitary confinement with nothing to do for seven weeks except think about my freedom, if I ever regained it, but she was right. Even quite normal activities, like walking to the shops and back, left me worn out. Although naturally slim (or a 'weed', as John would say), I had lost all my muscle bulk.

Gradually I got back into Air Force routine. I no longer had my identity card and had to go to the guard room to pick up a temporary ID. I walked in and said: 'Hello, can I get an ID card? I've lost my other one.' Despite all the TV and newspaper coverage and the reporters camping just outside the camp gates, the guard did not recognize me and told me: 'You'll have to fill in a form first and I'm afraid I'm going to have to report this. Where did you lose it?' I was about to tell him, when the sergeant came in and saw me, and began explaining to the guard, in that friendly way that sergeants have the world over, why I did not have an ID card and why the guard was not going to be reporting the fact.

Everybody was given leave on our return from the Gulf, but when we got back to work, there was, not friction, but an understandable distance between those who had fought in the

Gulf and those who had been left behind. The unfortunate guys who had not been to the Gulf had really been messed about while we were away. They had been put into an amalgamated squadron – the 'leper colony' as they jokingly christened themselves – and had hardly been able to do any flying at all, because virtually every plane was in the Gulf. As a result, they were very frustrated. They had heard every Gulf War story there was to tell pretty quickly and you could see their eyeballs rolling up into the top of their heads if any of us started yet another Gulf anecdote. Initially we wanted to talk about it all the time, but we swiftly realized that we could not go on and on about it. We were back to normal and had to get on with our peacetime lives.

To help us to readjust, we were sent on a detachment to Decimomannu in Sardinia for two weeks. The whole squadron, those who had been to the Gulf, those who had not, and those who had only recently been posted to XV, all went together, as the squadron began to return to normality. It helped us to get used to peacetime flying again, but equally importantly, it stopped an unbridgeable divide growing between the men who had been to the Gulf and those who had stayed behind.

The 'Boss', Wing Commander John Broadbent, insisted that there were to be no Gulf flying suits, the beige desert war suits we had flown in over Iraq. We were all to wear our normal green flying suits and were to go out as a squadron, absolutely united. Those two weeks in Sardinia brought us back together and rebuilt the team spirit, the special bond which is the essential feature of a squadron. Ironically though, it happened just in time for the squadron to be torn permanently apart.

On our return to Laarbruch, we discovered that XV, and the other squadrons based there, were to be disbanded. What was left of the euphoria of victory instantly evaporated. We now found ourselves suddenly focused on much more prosaic matters, much closer to home. Gulf War anecdotes were the last things on anyone's mind now. Everyone was preoccupied with what might happen to them and their families. With all the cutbacks, jobs, particularly flying jobs, were very thin on the ground. We went through an endless stream of personal interviews with the flight commanders and had lengthy 'chats' with the Boss.

Gradually our futures were decided. I was to be posted to another front-line Tornado bomber squadron, 31, a few miles down the road at Brüggen, while John was to switch to the Tornado fighter, retraining back in England at Coningsby in Lincolnshire. With our worries eased, we all settled down to enjoy our final days on XV, accepting the inevitability of disbandment. The party atmosphere was contagious, from doom and gloom the mood swung to hilarity. XV had always had the reputation of being a 'fun' squadron and it was one that we were determined to maintain to the end.

When the end came, there were to be some emotional farewells as the 'family' scattered to the four winds. The mystique of an Air Force squadron is not quite like that of an Army regiment. There are squadron associations, but we tend to place them on the back burner, regarding that sort of thing as more of an old boys' preoccupation. As a result, the feelings generated when the squadron disbandment parade was held, came as a great surprise.

Gleaming Tornados stood in the corners of a vast hangar, decorated with the squadron crest on the wall and banners in Air Force colours stretching from the roof to the ground. Our Squadron Warrant Officer Pip Curzon, five feet two inches tall and five feet two inches wide, is an old style, archetypal Warrant Officer, a figurehead for airmen and officers alike. He had used all his powers of persuasion, cajoling, pleading, wheedling, threatening and, if all else failed, purloining – Air Force speak for 'stealing' – to obtain whatever was needed to give the squadron a proper send-off. We stood at attention, flanked by Air Force 'brass' and by past members of the squadron, as the pale blue standard with the squadron crest in the middle, and our battle honours down the sides, carried on a pole topped by a golden eagle, was paraded out of the hangar for the last time. It left a lump in all our throats. The noise of the band and the marching feet faded gradually away, leaving a silence that no one felt able to break. We filed out of the hangar like mourners leaving a family funeral.

Everyone understood why the disbandment had happened, the politics and economics behind it, but that did nothing to remove the feeling of personal loss, at leaving something that we all felt was special. We had been to war together. Many of the guys had repeatedly risked their lives flying missions deep into Iraq, and four of us had been shot down, John and I, Rupert Clarke, and one of the most likeable blokes on the squadron, Steve Hicks, who was killed.

Yet we had to leave all that behind and start again. Laarbruch continues as a RAF station, but it is now home to Harriers and helicopters, not Tornados. Like most people, when I think of Laarbruch or XV Squadron now, I remember mainly the good times; the comradeship, the sense of unity of the squadron, the challenge ahead, being part of something big. My memories of the bad times in captivity are crystal clear, but now distant. They are experiences I can recall in an instant, but I am marvellously separate from them. That life, those events, seem light years away – like a sepia photograph, another world, another person. If I sit down and put my mind to it, I can remember what my fear was like, the smell and taste of blood, the sound of my body being beaten, but I can only remember the experience, not the pain. Time dulls unpleasant memories.

My only reminders are the scrapbooks of photographs and press cuttings, and two trophies in the lounge. An anti-aircraft artillery shell, polished and mounted on a dark hardwood base, is inscribed: 'Iraqi 23mm Anti-Aircraft Artillery Shell Presented to Flight Lieutenant John Peters by the Officers and Men of XV Squadron, as a Reminder of the Events of 17 January 1991'. On another, larger, wooden plinth, is the back section of a pitot tube, taken from our downed aircraft. John Nichol has the front end, which is badly bent and distorted. I also have a photo album with pictures of various bits of the Tornado spread like a twisted and broken metal sculpture across the sand. My yellow Prisoner of War suit with the bold letters PW stitched on the chest, the last evidence of my ordeal in Iraq, is neatly folded in some dusty, half-forgotten cardboard box in the loft. As we stood in the canvas Red Cross tent on the Jordanian border, after our release from Iraq, I remember joking with one of the American PoWs, Bob Wetzel, that the PoW suits would be great for a fancy dress party. Somehow that idea does not appeal any more. The Prisoner of War suit has never been brought out since I came home, soon it will be just another family heirloom mouldering away in the loft.

The children remain blissfully ignorant of what happened to their Daddy, while he was away from them. Toni, now four, seeing the pictures of the Gulf PoWs, proudly points out: 'John Nichol' . . . 'Daddy' . . . stabbing emphatically towards the pictures with her chubby little index finger. Guy, now six, a little more aware but still mercifully ignorant of the reality, asks: 'Why did you look so unhappy, Daddy?' or: 'Why did you crash your plane?' He cannot help but pick things up here and there and I can sometimes see him trying to piece the puzzle together. One day, when he is older, he will ask me and I will explain.

The Gulf War was three years ago. The PoWs were a momentary front page story, but once covered, another story breaks and ours is quickly forgotten by the papers, although it will always be part of our lives. Helen and I have emerged stronger and closer for what we went through, but John Nichol and I are 'divorced' – the partnership has been dissolved. John Nichol, my nav, my back-seater, with whom I endured the ordeal in Iraq, the mate who nearly agreed to a suicide pact, blowing out each other's brains rather than be captured, the friend with whom I had shared so much, is now on another base, flying another jet. Our lives are now quite separate, and on the surface we have the standard Air Force friendship, picked up and dropped as the occasion permits, a quick long-distance phone call or a beer at some party somewhere, fitted in between our separate squadron commitments. Beyond that, we do have a special bond that will always endure. Very few friendships undergo the kind of test that ours has faced.

John Nichol: 'That's it then, that's the end of us.' John Peters
and I were standing outside the main gates of an Air Force base
in Germany. It was late at night and snowing heavily, a week
after the disbanding of XV Squadron. We had gone to war,
returned, and now the 'peace dividend' was being collected in
full. In the whole of our lifetimes, a squadron had never been
disbanded, yet now, in the space of a few days, three squadrons
had disappeared, including our own.

The two of us had been skiing in Garmisch, setting off the
morning after 'dining-out' XV Squadron. An old Air Force
tradition, a dining-out is a formal dinner, normally held to say
goodbye to one or two people leaving a squadron. In this case
an entire squadron of 200 people was being disbanded, never
to return. We are normally moved on to new squadrons
every two or three years, but the disbanding of XV Squadron
was far more emotional than the parting, say, of a group of
fellow students at the end of their three-year university course.
It was more like the feeling when half of a family is emigrating
to Australia. Some of us might meet up again from time to
time, talk on the telephone, perhaps spend an odd holiday
together, but to all intents and purposes, the family was splitting
up forever, never to reunite. The special bond we had forged
was about to be broken and it became a very emotional night.

There had been a parade and lots of pomp and circumstance
the previous week, with senior Air Force officers present as the
squadron standard, which people had given their lives to
defend, was paraded for the last time. That was the formal end
of XV Squadron for the serving officers; the true end was the
'dining-out' a week later.

We tried to push the sadness into the background as we met
for drinks in the Mess, along with most of the other station
officers, there to say goodbye to us, all dressed in our 'number
fives' – our best dress uniforms. After a number of apéritifs,
the Station Commander gave the order to adjourn for dinner
and we all wandered through into the dining room. This had
been decorated from floor to ceiling in squadron colours – pale
blue and red – with banners trailing from the chandeliers. The

walls were lined with a full-size image of a Tornado, which had been blown up from a colour photograph, keeping the planning room colour photocopier tied up for days. In salute to the squadron and in anticipation of the post-prandial mayhem to come, the white damask tablecloths had been removed and replaced by swathes of crepe paper, again in the squadron colours.

The most junior officers went into the dining room first, followed by the rest in order of seniority. We all stood behind our chairs and then, when everyone was in position, the Station Commander made his grand entrance and strode to the head of the table. After the padre had said grace, the Station Commander gave the order: 'Gentlemen, be seated'.

The air of strict formality was abruptly demolished, for the squadron practical jokers had been hard at work all day. Chairs were tied together beneath the table and every knife, fork and spoon had been painstakingly tied together with fishing line, which also looped through the candelabra, the cruets and around the stems of the glasses, before being tied to the chairs. As soon as the Station Commander gave the order to sit down, the whole room dissolved into total chaos as people tugged to and fro on their chairs, while cutlery and crockery flew in all directions. When order was just about restored, people unfolding their napkins prompted a fresh outburst as a fusillade of nuts and bolts cascaded across the table and dropped into our laps.

After a riotous dinner, we returned to the bar for further drinks, where the atmosphere could easily have turned a little maudlin. I had been ordered to ensure that the squadron went out with 'a bang and a flash' not a whimper, however, so after a trumpet fanfare to lure everyone out of the Mess, I set off £1,000 worth of fireworks. Rockets the size of champagne bottles took off like surface-to-air missiles, and for the grand finale, our squadron's war trophy – a four-barrelled Iraqi Triple-A gun – had been dragged down from its place of honour in front of the crew room and set up outside the Mess. The gun barrels were loaded with massive fireworks, which blasted off, sounding as if the gun was actually firing.

Unfortunately, due to a 'technical error', I had loaded the fireworks upside down. The display was unaffected, but the ends of the gun-barrels melted in the heat. Finally a set of lights lit up, saying 'Goodbye XV'. We walked back into the bar and that was it – XV Squadron was disbanded. In retrospect, it seemed appropriate that the squadron's war trophy had been melted down on the night that the squadron itself had ceased to exist. We ordered up a fresh round of drinks and sang the squadron song one last time. We had sung it on the morning of 17 January in the Gulf as we prepared to go to war, taking off on what proved to be a one-way journey into Iraq. The sound was awful, with half of us off-key or flat, but the volume and the emotion of it sent shivers down my spine.

There was not much more to be said. JP and I were setting off before dawn the next day to go skiing, so this was to be our last sight of our mates from XV. We did a final circuit of the bar, saying goodbye to the men with whom we had gone to war. It was the traditional Air Force farewell: a handshake and a terse: 'See you around'. Anything more emotive would probably have had us all blubbing like babies.

We left for Garmisch at 5 a.m. after going to bed at what seemed like 4.55 a.m. JP and I were last onto the bus, clutching pillows purloined from the poor fool who had lent us beds for the night. For a week, we skied and drank a lot, and talked a little. Then we caught the bus back north. We sat in silence most of the way and reached Brüggen, JP's new station, near the Dutch border, late at night. He would continue to fly the Tornado bomber, the GR1 there, but I had been posted to RAF Coningsby, in Lincolnshire, to begin learning to fly the Tornado fighter – the F3.

We unloaded his bags and his skis, and I just said: 'Well, this is it'. We shook hands and hugged each other and I got back on the bus. As it pulled away, I looked back and could see him standing there in a pool of light, with the snow falling around him. We would never again share a cockpit.

No longer mates flying the same machine, working together

as a team, from now on we would be foes, stalking each other in rehearsal for the deadly game of chess played out between fighters a mile above the earth and bombers only feet above the ground.

2

Business as usual

OCCUPATIONAL HAZARDS

John Nichol: It was only my second sortie since being shot down in the Gulf. The first, a training flight with an instructor pilot, was nothing more than a get-you-back-into-the-routine flight. This one was to be my first normal sortie; after all the highs and lows of war in the Gulf, we were back to peacetime work, business as usual.

We took off on a cool May morning, in typical weather, with cloud down to about 1,500 feet, forcing everyone to stay at low level. The horizon was hazy, but there was still good visibility out to about ten miles. Anything beyond that was lost in the haze, which hangs in the air above any heavily-industrialized area. The sortie we were flying was a 'two v one', a standard practice sortie in which two Tornados fight a third, simulating attack by an enemy aircraft. We took off as normal and cruised out over the river, gazing down on the barges trundling to and fro. They would travel no further in a day than we would in a couple of minutes.

The two of us flew 'abeam' of each other, side by side and about two miles apart, scanning the skies for the 'enemy'. The first time we were attacked, we saw the aircraft coming from a long way off, and simply pulled a hard turn to avoid him, turning away and running out of range, before continuing our track to the north. As we came round a corner, we were on hyper-alert, settling down again after the turn, but checking

15

behind each other for danger and looking ahead, scanning the sky, knowing that the other aircraft must be nearby. He had not 'tapped' – intercepted – us for five or ten minutes and the classic time for an attack is when you have just made a turn and are having to search a whole new area of sky.

Sure enough, we picked him up, straight ahead of us and about four miles away, coming right down the middle of our formation in a classic head-on attack. There is nothing we can really do to counter a head-on attack, except to widen – spread further apart – and put on speed. If we attempted to turn and run for it, we would just be presenting the hottest part of the aircraft, our exhausts, to his heat-seeking missiles. All we could do was blast straight past him as fast as we could go. He came burning in toward us and flashed straight through the middle, beginning a hard turn to try and drop into our six o'clock, for a missile shot: My pilot, Bruce MacDonald, threw our aircraft into a hard right turn to face him, the G-force plastering me to my seat.

I lost sight of the other aircraft in the turn and was whipping my head around, against the G-force, to try and get my eyes back onto him, when I heard two locater beacons go off. The locater beacon starts up either because someone has ejected or, quite often, because someone in the cockpit has pulled the operating handle by mistake. I called to Bruce: 'Someone is going to get a major bollocking for setting those off', but as we continued our turn, I looked around and down, and suddenly saw a blazing Tornado plough into the ground below us. Flames flashed through the forest as the aircraft smashed through the trees, tumbling over and over before exploding in a massive fireball. The Tornado had obviously not been hit by a SAM missile – this was not Iraq – either a bird strike, an aircraft fault or a human error had sent it catapulting from the sky. There was no sign of the crew, no parachutes or anything. My heart was pounding and there was an acrid taste of bile in my mouth. I thought: 'My God, they're dead.'

Bruce immediately put our aircraft into a climb to 1,000 feet and began circling over the crash site, as I put out a distress call on the emergency frequency: 'Mayday, Mayday, Mayday. Tornado Down' – words I had hoped never to hear again.

One of the listening emergency centres called us up immediately, asking: 'What assistance do you require?'

I gave them the position of the crash site, and said: 'There's a Tornado down, there are two people on board.'

'OK, scrambling search and rescue now.'

A friend of mine was flying over one of the weapons ranges a few miles away at the time and was listening to the emergency frequency, as everybody does – it is standard procedure in case something happens and you can be of some assistance. He told me afterwards that when he recognized my voice putting out the 'Mayday' call, he said to his nav: 'Hell's bells, John doesn't need this all over again'. I could only heartily agree.

We had still not seen any trace of the Tornado crew, no parachutes, no bodies, nothing at all, and we were all the more convinced that they were dead. It was a sickening feeling, circling like carrion crows above a carcase. Then our radio crackled into life. The other member of our formation had spotted a white and orange parachute tangled in the branches of a tree. A minute ticked agonizingly by, before one of the crew of the downed Tornado called up on his locater beacon, which also enables you to talk on the emergency frequency.

'We're OK. My mate's injured. He's dangling from a tree and I think he's broken some ribs, but he's alive. I'm on the ground and I'm alright, except that I knackered my back a bit when we banged out [ejected].'

I was almost crying with relief. 'Search and rescue are on their way, thank God you're OK.'

A couple of minutes later, the rescue helicopter came in, picked the two men up and took them off to hospital. We flew back to base, concentrating grimly until the jet was safely landed and we had taxied back to 'the line' outside the hangar. As I climbed out of the cockpit, I began to shake with the release of tension. I was swept by wildly differing emotions, elation that the two men had survived, horror that I had witnessed another Tornado crash, another fireball, another ejection. We were back to business as usual all right, and the business of flying fast jets to their phenomenally powerful limits remains fraught with risk. Even in peacetime, danger and death are never far away. It is a marked contrast to most other branches of the forces.

Soldiers on tours of duty in Northern Ireland serve a nerve-jangling apprenticeship in war, but there were many in the Falklands and the Gulf who had never seen a dead body, nor had a friend or colleague die. Being involved in a real shooting war was not something that they had experienced or ever anticipated and it proved a brutal rite of passage. Even though the Falklands had been the Air Force's only direct involvement in an armed conflict for forty years before the Gulf, the risks and accidents in our routine training prepare all of us, in some way, for the impact of war. Emergencies happen with monotonous regularity – bird strikes, fuel problems, trouble with the landing gear, engine problems, electronic problems. Sometimes you are lucky, but there have been plenty of occasions when a crew finds that its luck has run out. You do not spend long in the Air Force without losing friends or colleagues. It is perhaps one of the reasons why we are better prepared for war; we are the men who go out in the morning and may not come home at night.

John Peters: Emergencies are just an occupational hazard for air crew, so routine that we almost get blasé about them. We will be sitting around in the crew room, when the tannoy blares out; 'State Two. Tornado, ten miles, engine vibration.'

We know that the crew will have an amber caption showing on their emergency warning panel. They will already have dumped fuel and will be dealing with the emergency as calmly as they can. Unless it is a jet from our own squadron, the normal reaction is simply to carry on drinking our coffee and struggling with the *Telegraph* crossword. Somebody is working hard, in a potentially dangerous situation, but we expect them to sort it out and land safely. There may be a good tale to tell afterwards, but it is an everyday occurrence; we have all had emergencies, we all expect to have more, and none of us ever expects the worst.

It is very different when the worst actually happens. In training, none of us ever really believed our instructors when they told us how many mates they had lost, but by the time you have joined a squadron, you quickly become used to death. We never really get hardened to it, we simply get accustomed to the idea, and we all have an unstated, but unshakeable belief, summed up in six words. 'It will never happen to me'. You could not do the job otherwise.

It was only the first friend I lost, the first funeral I attended, that affected me badly. I went all through my training with Andy Mannheim. He was twenty-five years old and flew Jaguars. When a crash occurs, the 'jungle telegraph' is frighteningly quick, but the press can be even quicker and the RAF is always desperate to contact the next-of-kin first, before they discover the news from a journalist or by hearing it on the car radio. Andy had been involved in a head-on collision with a Tornado, in a valley in the Lake District. The accident report declared the cause to be 'an operational hazard', stating that, because of the contours of the valley walls, even if he had seen the other aircraft, it would have been humanly impossible for him to have avoided his fate. His only 'memorial', apart from a gravestone, is that the valley now has a one-way only flow arrow on the low-flying chart, like a one-way street for cars.

At first I did not believe that he was dead. Later, memories of our last meeting flashed through my head. I found myself looking at old photos; of him standing proudly next to his clapped-out old wreck of a VW Beetle, of Andy and his wife Vicki in my local pub on their last visit. They had only been married for four months. Helen and I had been at their wedding at the RAF church, St Clement Danes in London. It was a memorable day. I was one of his guard of honour, as he and Vicki stood together under an arch of swords. They had hired a red London bus to take all the guests to the reception, where Andy, who had French relatives, did half of his light, witty speech in French. He taunted both families, as it was the day of the France–England rugby international. We did not receive the wedding photographs until after his death.

I remember lying in a bath that evening, talking to Andy as if he could hear me, wishing him the best. The worst part was having to talk to Vicki over the phone; what could I say, why could this not have been a mistake? Words stuck in my throat and what I said sounded stilted. After putting the receiver down, I chastised myself for sounding so tongue-tied and lame.

The funeral was not what I expected at all. I met all my old mates, now just established on squadrons after three years' training, and it was really great to see them, even though the reason for our meeting was so sad. There were so many people that the church was too small to hold us all. Inside, the murmuring and shuffling turned to silence as the pallbearers, all in dress uniforms, carried in the coffin. It was covered by a union jack, with Andy's peaked service cap placed on top. The pallbearers returned to their pews. I glanced across at one of them, whose face was pale and tense, betraying his strained self-control.

Vicki sat sobbing in the pew across the aisle. As the music played, Helen and the other women alongside me started to cry. I clenched my jaw, thinking that I must be strong, I must not let the uniform down. Helen was gripping my arm and I was digging my fingernails into my palms, every sinew in me straining not to cry. I stared ahead, fixing my gaze. I wished that I was in the crowd, instead of isolated in the front row. I kept repeating to myself that I was in uniform, and I must not cry. I whispered, rather than sang the hymns.

The speech from the squadron 'Boss' remembered Andy as I knew him, a good pilot, a good bloke and an excellent squash player (annoyingly I never managed to beat him), but he had not an ounce of rhythm and was a hopeless dancer. The memory raised a smile, but what a loss, what a waste of a life. A poem was read, 'High Flight' by Pilot Officer J.C. Magee, celebrating the spirit of individuality that is the absolute essence of flying. Unless you fly, you can never understand.

Oh, I have slipped the surly bonds of Earth
And danced the skies on laughter-silvered wings:
Sunward I've climbed, and joined the tumbling mirth
Of sun-split clouds – and done a hundred things
You have not dreamed of:
Wheeled and soared and swung
High in the sunlit silence.
Hovering there
I've chased the shouting wind along and flung
My eager craft through footless halls of air;
Up, up the long delirious, burning blue
I've topped the windswept heights with easy grace.
Where never lark nor even eagle flew;
And while, with silent lifting mind I've trod
The high, untrespassed sanctity of space,
Put out my hand, and touched the face of God.

It was the first time I had heard the poem, but then, it was my
first funeral. At the end of the service, I was drained and my
head ached from the forced self-control. As I turned to join the
queue leaving the church, I saw that there was not a dry eye in
the house. What a fool I had been. I will always regret not
crying then, because the moment was forever lost. I should
have cried, for Andy and Vicki, but I was too concerned about
self-control and being in uniform.

I had to attend another friend's funeral only three months
later, but by then I was already baptized in loss. The succeeding
funerals are never the same as the first one; like the rest of my
peers, I had already become conditioned to accept that it can
happen to any of us, at any time, even though we remain
convinced that it never will.

Helen Peters: I heard about the crash on the lunchtime news –
a Jaguar was down, in a collision with a Tornado. The Tornado
crew were safe, the Jaguar pilot dead. As soon as news of a
military jet crash comes over the radio, a cold hand clenches

your heart. You list in your head all the people you know who fly that type of aircraft and give yourself all sorts of reasons why it could not possibly be any of them: 'They couldn't be flying there', 'They are in Germany', 'Aren't they on holiday this week?' although deep down inside, you know that it could be your friend who has died. When the identity of the victim is announced, there is a brief elation if it is not someone you know, followed immediately by a sense of shame that you are celebrating your friend's survival, when someone else's husband, friend, father, son, has been killed.

When John came home that night, the victim's name had still not been announced, but John had not even heard about the crash, so we assumed that it could not be anyone we knew. I served up supper and we were just sitting down to eat when the phone rang. We had the normal jokey argument about who should answer the phone; I lost. As soon as I answered, a voice said: 'Helen, it's Julie'. Then I knew. I had spoken to Julie, the wife of a Harrier pilot; a couple of days before. There could only be one reason for her call now. 'The Jaguar crash – it was Andy.'

I immediately thought of Vicki and what she was going through. I saw pictures in my mind of us all, only four months before, at Vicki and Andy's wedding, a lovely day full of humour. When we all piled on to the red double-decker bus outside the church, a group of Japanese tourists started clicking away with their cameras, as if the boys in blue and the guard of honour had been put on especially for them.

We had been planning to spend a few days on the Broads with Andy and Vicki, but it would never happen now. We had even spent a lovely evening with them, discussing the name of the first child they hoped to have. Their little boy, Oliver, would now never be born. Vicki had resigned from a good career with Marks & Spencer to be with Andy. He was posted to RAF Coltishall, entailing a move to Norwich, where there were no openings with Marks & Spencer. We forces wives have to make these big decisions to be with our men, but what was the point? She had given up her career, her lifestyle, everything, for four short months. I am sure she has never regretted it though. She would have felt worse if she had lost Andy without ever having been his wife.

We travelled down to Coltishall for the funeral later that week. About ten miles from there, a black RAF car came up behind, driven by some friends, Nige and Kath Tyson. We were waving, flashing our lights and saying how good it was to see them, when we remembered just why we were all on the same piece of road, travelling in the same direction.

In church, no one quite knew how to behave. We were all looking to each other for a lead. I was trying to be strong, but as soon as Vicki was led in, I was in floods of tears. I desperately wanted to go to her and comfort her. She was dressed immaculately as always, but looked so pale and drawn, as if she was not really there, just a ghost. She was leaning heavily on Mark, the best man at their wedding and their closest friend, and gripping a single rose tightly to her breast, her knuckles showing white. The coffin was carried in. Two of the bearers were desperately trying to hold back their tears, with no free hand to wipe their eyes or hide their grief. How can you accept that someone so full of life lies dead inside that coffin?

Andy died on 17 June 1987. Our son Guy was born on 3 October 1988. A new life, Vicki is his godmother.

3

The freedom of flying

BITTEN BY THE FLYING BUG

John Peters: I cannot remember a time when I did not want to be a pilot. Since I was a small boy, all I ever wanted to do was fly, even before I really knew what flying was about. I joined the Combined Cadet Force at school and did a flying scholarship from there.

You cannot hold a pilot's licence until you are seventeen years old and I qualified for mine when I was seventeen years and three months. Ironically I did not learn to drive a car until I was twenty, so I was zipping around the skies long before I was let loose on the roads. I went to Compton Abbas airfield and learned how to fly a Cessna 150. To get your pilot's licence you need thirty-five flying hours. As part of the scholarship, the Air Force gave me thirty of them, but I had to persuade my dad to stump up for the other five.

Back home, as a 'reward' for my father's generosity, I took him and my mother flying and flew some of his friends around as well. When I look back now, it makes me break out in a cold sweat, because I was flying these people around the skies and I know now how little I really knew about flying then. It was a bit like when you pass your driving test and go screeching around the roads, thinking you are God's gift to the motor car, but really knowing nothing about it. Of course John tells me that he still breaks out in a cold sweat every time I fly, because I still know nothing about it!

I then did a 'Test in Advance' through which I got an Air

Force cadetship, which meant that they sponsored me through university, where I did my degree and was a member of the University Air Squadron. The cadetship committed me to the Air Force for the duration of a 'Permanent Commission', sixteen years, although I do have an option to leave after twelve years, which is coming up in two years' time.

Several people have asked me why I stayed in the Air Force after what happened to John and me in Iraq, but quite apart from any contractual obligations, what happened in seven weeks does not change a lifetime. If I had given up flying it would also have been proof that they had won. My whole train of thought while I was in captivity was: 'I must not change. They can do anything to my body, they can even bugger me or put a knife up my backside – my biggest fears in captivity – but however bad it gets, I must not have changed when I get out of here.'

When I did get back, all I wanted to do was fly again. Fast jets are unique and the thrill of flying them has never left me. Skimming over the grey waves of the North Sea, plugging the burners in and pulling the stick back to raise the nose twenty, thirty, forty degrees, I go soaring up into the sky as the altimeter winds up to 20,000 feet. Then I roll the aircraft upside down to see the whole of the east of England laid out below me, from Newcastle, down through Flamborough Head and the Wash, to East Anglia and beyond.

The freedom of flying is pure joy; it is like a drug. The poem I first heard at Andy Mannheim's funeral says it all. There was no doubt that I was going to remain a pilot, but it was not just a question of whether to stay in the Air Force; I also had to decide whether I wanted to remain on a front-line squadron. I did actually sit down and think about becoming a Qualified Flying Instructor at the back, out of the front line. The more I thought about it, the more I realized that it would be wrong. I told myself: 'No, you're either in the military or you're out', but I had to be sure that not only could I do it myself, but that if someone else got in trouble, he could rely on me. I knew the answer was 'Yes', and that is why I stayed in the front line.

*

In the Air Force you spend your career changing squadrons, but you do become very loyal to your current squadron, especially your first operational squadron, even without the added bond of going to war together. The unity and loyalty you feel to the squadron with which you went to war is something no one can ever replace, or reproduce in any other situation. In common with 16 and 20, the other Laarbruch squadrons, XV returned from the Gulf to a disbandment parade. I was fortunate to be offered another front-line tour, moving to 31 at Brüggen. Normally you are posted individually, but a deluge of ex-Laarbruch air crew pitched up at Brüggen together that spring. The squadrons there were justifiably proud of their own war record and initially the 'WEWAL' – When We Were At Laarbruch – stories, went down like a lead balloon. It took a couple of months for the irritation to die down.

Luckily, the Tornado world is a small one, and I moved down to Brüggen with some good friends, including 'Lunty' – Chris Lunt – the mate whose aircraft would not work on the fateful day, 17 January 1991, when John and I set off to fly our mission into Iraq. Lunty was there to meet me in Amman, Jordan, on the day of my release from gaol in Iraq. 'Humpo' – Mike Humphries – a navigator on XV who was to become a good friend, was also posted to Brüggen, as was Jack Calder, a stocky Geordie navigator from 17 Squadron; for some reason, all the navs seem to be Geordies. Jack and Bob Brownlow were the reserve crew hastily called out to replace John and me, after we were shot down over Iraq. They went on to complete eighteen missions, but I am still not sure whether they are grateful for the opportunity we gave them ... Squadron Leader Steve Randles, who led our first training sortie in the Gulf, had become the Squadron Executive on 31 and Squadron Leader Bertie Newton, a rotund, gentle character, was also at Brüggen. The last time I had flown with him was when he was a nav instructor at Finningley. Now he was a Flight Commander on 31, with twenty-one war missions, including a Mention in Despatches for his services in the Gulf.

I already knew virtually all the guys on 31 Squadron and they warmly welcomed all of us, but even so I was surprised how long it took us to settle in and feel at home at Brüggen; even the children felt it. I did not think that kids formed strong relationships with other children at such a tender age, but Guy, who was only four, really missed his friends from Laarbruch, and his sense of loss surprised me. It was neither the people nor the place that I felt were wrong, it was just the circumstances. It was part of the readjustment we had to make after the war, having to establish ourselves at a new place, make new friends, with all the pressures involved with the 'stigma' of the 'Oh, the guy on TV' syndrome.

At that time, not much was known about the PoW situation and everyone gave me plenty of banter about it – and crew room banter is as quick-fire, harsh and uncompromising as it comes. It is very much a case of 'book a sentence' if you want to take part in the conversation. No one can ever be 'a personality' on a squadron, there are just too many of them already. I was swiftly nicknamed 'Number 6' after Patrick McGoohan's character in the TV series *The Prisoner*. Just the same, virtually everyone sneaked up to me on their own when we were drunk in the bar on a Friday night, and gingerly broached the subject.

John Nichol: I did not grow up with a great sense of vocation, thinking: 'One day I will join the Air Force'. I was always going to leave school when I was sixteen, even though pupils at my school were expected to stay on to do A levels. I was not academically unsound – I got nine O levels – but I had no intention of staying at school.

I loved maths and physics and developed a big interest in electronics and technical things, and I knew from about the age of fourteen that I wanted to leave school as soon as possible and become an electronics engineer. I applied for a job with virtually every electronics firm in the country. Despite the recession which was going on then – some things never change

– I was lucky enough to be offered two jobs and was on my way home from an interview for a third one with the Electricity Board in Newcastle, when I passed an RAF recruiting office. I looked in the window, saw some glossy brochures and thought I would pick one up, not with the remotest intention of starting a military career, just to have something to read on the bus journey home.

When I walked in, a friendly RAF recruiting sergeant sat me down at a desk and we chatted for a while. He arranged for me to come back for an interview the following week. The next week I spent four hours in the office, doing lots of interviews and aptitude tests, and by the end of the day I had signed on the dotted line and become a member of Her Majesty's Royal Air Force. That recruiting sergeant was wasted there: he could have made a fortune as a salesman.

A couple of weeks later, I was marching round the parade ground at RAF Swinderby, being shouted at by a drill sergeant, and thinking: Not much electronics going on here. I did six weeks of recruit training at Swinderby, which is like any other RAF base in Lincolnshire, but worse, and was then sent to RAF Locking in Weston-super-Mare, or Weston-super-Mud, as we preferred to call it, a seaside town which was a place of wonder and delight to a seventeen-year-old allowed out after dark.

I did eighteen months of vocational training, learning to be an electronics engineer, and then went to the Tactical Communications Wing at Brize Norton in Oxfordshire, where I began my real RAF career, providing communications for RAF squadrons which had been deployed into the field. When helicopters or Harriers or Hercules transports flew out into their deployment bases, we would drive out in our Land Rovers, stick up a few aerials, hammer a few stakes into the ground, fix up some bits of wire, bulbs and batteries, tie them together with electronic string and allow the squadrons to communicate with anyone, anywhere in the world.

The job got me meeting air crew and looking at the different way that they lived their lives, which is what decided me that I wanted to fly fast jets too. Although not by any means unique, it is quite an unusual transition to make. By far the most common route into being an officer, the way taken by 95 per cent of people, is to come in after taking a university degree.

It is much harder for someone to come from the ranks. Instead of just going to the Selection Centre and doing a number of tests, you first have to be interviewed by your immediate boss, and then your squadron boss. If they both think that you might have the capability, you are put forward to a Station Assessment Board, where you march into a room to be confronted by three senior officers, a Wing Commander, a Squadron Leader and someone from the specialist area that you want to join.

I was interviewed by them for two-and-a-half hours, after which they wrote a report grading my eligibility to be commissioned. If you passed that hurdle, the next step was to see the head honcho on the station, the Station Commander. He interviewed me for another two or three hours and then he graded me, ruling on whether I could go forward to join everyone else at the Officer and Air Crew Selection Centre, where the university graduates make their first appearance.

We spent three-and-a-half days there. The first two were taken up with medical exams, aptitude tests, and hand–eye co-ordination tests. If you passed them, you moved on to the next stage, leadership tests. First you are put into discussion groups, and by this time you do not have a name, you just have a number stuck to the chest of your denim overalls. The members of the assessing board throw topics for discussion at you and then sit silent in the corner, making notes and deciding your future, while you stand around with a group of total strangers, discussing something you know absolutely nothing about.

The next stage sees you given a problem to solve. Mine was to get six people from one side of a massive hangar to the other, without touching the floor. There were logs, ropes, tyres, a number of bars and planks, and I had to organize my team to get across, using this stuff, without touching the 'shark-infested custard' as the yellow-painted floor was known. Once more, the assessors stood in the corner, watching us and evaluating my leadership qualities from the cack-handed way I went about things.

After that we had to go into interviews with specialists, lasting for anything from an hour to five hours. They question you relentlessly on what you want to do in the Air Force, why you want to do it, what you know about the Air Force, your interests, your knowledge of current affairs, and so on.

'Why do you want to become air crew?'

'How many helicopters does the Air Force have in Hong Kong?'

'Which squadrons are ground-attack squadrons?'

'Which ones are fighters?'

'Why do you think the Arab–Israel conflict has reached its present state?'

My answer to most of them was 'Pass', but they just swooped from one topic to another, with no apparent pattern, constantly probing. If you know something, they ignore that, instead they probe until they have found something you do not know about, and then probe even more, trying to make you become flustered and make mistakes. After all of that, you have to sit and twiddle your thumbs for six weeks until you finally get a letter telling you whether you are in or out. I was in.

I have never even thought of leaving the RAF since I joined, for two very good reasons: one, I love the work I do, and two, even if I did not, my contract would keep me in the Air Force. Non-commissioned personnel can 'buy themselves out' of the services, but as a commissioned officer, that option is not open to me. Whether I like it or not, and luckily I do, I am in the Air Force until I am thirty-eight or 'until Her Majesty no longer requires my services'. Her Majesty always used to require our services until our engagements had expired, but the cuts in the armed forces now mean that is no longer always the case. A lot of people have been made compulsorily redundant, something that we thought would never, ever happen in the forces.

Because I was commissioned from the ranks, I do not have

the option that some people, including JP, have, of leaving the Air Force after a set amount of time, normally twelve years. Nor would I really want to leave. To be honest, despite all the skills and the training, as a navigator in the Air Force, there are not a lot of jobs that I could do on the outside anyway. People say: 'Why don't you just go to the airlines?' but airlines do not employ navigators, they have a microchip that does the navigation.

'Navigator' is really a misnomer in the Air Force, because that is not really what we do any more. We are 'Weapons Systems Operators' instead, and there is not much demand for weapons systems, nor their operators, in your average High Street. The old joke just about sums it up: 'What do you say to a navigator who has left the Air Force? "Two Big Macs and a large fries, please."' There is nothing else to do.

The decision to switch to fighters was almost made for me. Defence cuts meant that the Air Force was losing four GR1 squadrons, three of which were from Laarbruch, my station in Germany. As a result, there were just no flying jobs around. Most of the guys with whom I had been to war were put into ground jobs, which was a travesty. Incredibly experienced people were being given 'gash' jobs and air crew bums were going on to seats at office desks, simply because there were just too many bums for the available cockpits.

I was offered a transfer to helicopters or fighters, or a switch to training potential officers at the Royal Air Force College at Cranwell. It took me all of a nanosecond to think through those options. The thought of training spotty-faced youths at Cranwell did not appeal at all and, after the adrenalin rush of fast-jet aircraft, nor did the idea of putt-putting around the sky in a helicopter. I chose fighters, but in retrospect it has probably not been a good move, because I am merely average at what I do now, whereas before I was an experienced GR1 navigator. After thirteen years in the Air Force, I am now a new boy on the squadron and have to start clambering my way back up the ladder.

I went to the Tornado F3 OCU – Operational Conversion Unit – at RAF Coningsby in Lincolnshire, to learn an entirely new craft. A veteran of the Gulf War and of hundreds of training flights, I found myself forced to forget virtually everything I had learned in my Air Force career and start again from scratch. Fortunately, I was not the only grizzled old-timer in a class of fresh-faced youths; I started my fighter training alongside people at all levels of experience and from a whole spread of backgrounds. Some had flown the aircraft before, but had been in ground jobs for five years. Some had come from a completely different background, from bombers in my case, but there were others from helicopters and transport aircraft. Some guys already came from the fast-jet, air defence world, but had been on the Phantom, and were retraining to fly the F3, and there were also a number of *ab initios*, guys starting from scratch, fresh out of basic training.

The mix of backgrounds worked very well. There were guys who had immense airmanship – the catchword we always use – not in terms of firing missiles or dropping bombs, but of knowing the rules of the air, safety and what to do in difficult situations. They could pass on that experience to the rest, but even the guys who had just come through training had all the basic skills wrapped up and could pass them upwards to the rusty ones, who had forgotten some of the basics.

Coningsby is one of many RAF bases which have apparently been deliberately located in some of the most windswept, inaccessible and disembodied corners of the country. The wind comes knifing through direct from Siberia, what northerners call a 'lazy' wind, which cannot be bothered to go round you and so cuts straight through you instead. I did my training in summer. God knows how anyone survives a winter there.

The Fenland soil was drained by Dutch engineers 300 years ago, but has yet to dry out, to the delight of the thunder bugs, the little black flies that make every summer evening a misery. Among the mists and the smell of stagnant water, the delicious aroma of chicken shit wafts on the breeze from the battery

The freedom of flying

farms, dotting a landscape as flat as the airfield itself. The fruits of the jet-black earth, potatoes, carrots, greens of every shape and size, and the sweet and sour smelling sugar beet, are piled high on farm trailers lumbering to and fro.

The Mess in which I spent my sleeping hours and many of my waking ones is right at the end of the runway. When I was flying nights, scarcely had my head touched the pillow when the first takeoff of the day took place, prompt at eight o'clock in the morning. Four Tornados would go into reheat three yards outside my window, shaking not just the windows, but the whole building, which rocked to its foundations. When the jets were taking off, it was impossible to talk or even think in the Mess and the vibrations frothed up our beer on the bar. To add to the joys of being stationed there, the nightlife around Coningsby is nonexistent, just a transport café on the A17 and that well-known nightspot, Sleaford. The absence of attractions was probably a good thing in retrospect, for the course was difficult and relentlessly intense.

We started with four weeks of very basic air defence techniques, spending the first week just 'flying' a computer dot around a screen. You begin with your dot and an enemy dot doing 300 knots towards each other. You have a displacement between you and you aim to turn at the precise point that enables you to roll out one mile behind the other guy, in his six o'clock. That is the absolute basis of air defence, called 'the turn key'. As well as the standard 180 degree intercept, we also learned the ninety, where you approach at right angles and again turn to get in his six o'clock. It sounds incredibly easy, but never having done air defence before, I found it was actually very difficult to do.

After a week of that, we started the basics of the 'ground school' – how the Tornado systems work – the hydraulics, electrical and fuel systems, and so on. It all ends up at a trigger that you pull to fire a missile, but it is very important that you know how the aircraft works, not in the detail that a technician would need, but the working knowledge that you must have to

33

fly the aircraft. The F3 is not that different from the GR1, so I did not find that phase particularly difficult, but a few of the other guys were struggling, because some of the systems are incredibly complicated. We were also going into the flight simulator every day, with the staff throwing in every single emergency that we could ever have dreamed up and a few that we could not, to ensure that when we went into the air for the first time, we would already have seen and dealt with any possible emergency in the simulator.

If we were in difficulties with any part of the course, we had to do a lot of reading in our own time to catch up, because our knowledge was constantly and rigorously tested. It is not enough to know that the hydraulics normally operate at 270 bars pressure, for example, you also have to know what happens when it drops to 110; what valves will close, and what systems will be unavailable to you. If my right-hand hydraulic system fails, I know that certain other systems will also have failed. I will not have any nose-wheel steering on the runway when I land, and that means that there is little point in trying to travel the length of the runway. Instead I am going to slam the plane down, take the approach-end cable and stop in a matter of 200 feet, so that I do not have to worry about steering.

We then went on to the flying school part of the OCU and again began with the absolute basics. The first sortie was a familiarization sortie. I went up with a very experienced pilot, who simply showed me around, saying: 'This is the local area, this is how we get into the airfield, this is how we get out, these are some points of interest, this is what you should avoid, don't go anywhere near this, this is worth a look, nip down there and have a look at that.' The next time up, I just did a few basic things with the aircraft systems, as rudimentary as: 'Turn the radar on. That is what the picture looks like when the radar is on. There is a target, put that in' – very, very basic stuff.

The next sortie was a 'one v one' under complete control from one of the radar units. I was tracking the other plane on the radar, but they were telling me exactly what to do: 'Increase speed fifty knots, come right thirty degrees, descend 6,000 feet, start the turn now, roll out now'. They talked me round into a firing position to engage the target. From then on, the control systems were gradually degraded, so that I had to do more and more on the radar myself.

My unfamiliarity with air defence caused me a few more problems along the way. We were practising one v ones at medium level, just coming down the line, turning behind the guy, ending up in his six o'clock to take a shot at him. I had just about managed to get that off pat when the demonic instructors introduced one v ones with evasion. All that happened was that the bomber made one thirty degree turn off course, but the first time it happened, it completely blew my mind. I was scrabbling about, thinking: 'Oh my God, what do I do now, how do I get back on to course?' and I finished up saying to myself: 'I just cannot do this, I cannot understand what I now have to do.'

Somehow I began to get the hang of it and after working my way through all the permutations of one v one, I began again on one v two. Then it was down to low level – much more dangerous, much more difficult, because not only do you have radar handling problems, you also have to monitor the pilot's actions. It is no use getting a perfect intercept if you fly into the ground straight afterwards.

Then it was two v two back up to medium level, then down to low level, then bringing in some external targets, some bombers, which were much more realistic. I learned it all out over the sea, then came in over land and started it all again, building up once more from one v one. The last exercise was two v two, two co-ordinated fighters, with the fight led by the student – me – over Wales.

The reason I had such difficulties with air defence when I first started the course, was because it is so different from flying GR1 bombers at low level, or 'mud-moving'. Bombing is pre-planned. You get in to work three hours before your take-off, get out your maps, protractors, compasses and pencils and start throwing paper all over the crew room. The computers are whirring, steam is coming out of people's ears, but eventually, at the end of those three hours of planning, you have a cassette with the mission flight plan and a fully planned map with all the targets marked. You go out, put the cassette into the system and fly the mission as planned.

Air defence is completely different from that. You go in half an hour before you take off and do your thinking in the air. It is much more flexible, more reactive, and I had quite a bit of difficulty getting to grips with it. I had to spend a good few extra sessions in the simulator, but eventually the penny started to drop.

I ended the course facing two bombers who could do what the hell they liked; speed up, slow down, dive, twist, turn, loop, put me on the beam, but it had somehow all come together and I knew what was needed to make the intercept. It was a huge transition, but in the end, it all happened very quickly.

4

A monument to the Cold War

RAF BRÜGGEN

John Peters: RAF Brüggen lies a few miles from the Dutch border on the plains of northern Germany. If its presence on German soil is a monument to the Cold War, its massively reinforced gatehouse and bristling security owes as much to a threat that orginates much nearer to home, the IRA.

Brüggen sprawls over thousands of acres of pine forest and grassland, but any local children – or more sinister intruders – approaching the perimeter fence set in the sandy soil among the pine trees, will be detected and apprehended before they have got fifty yards. Every vehicle entering the camp is stopped and searched and fully-armed guards patrol incessantly. Although the fence is topped with razor wire, the glimpses of neatly manicured playing fields through the trees offer no clues to the real purpose of one of Britian's handful of remaining overseas bases. The main gate is the most visible sign of the British military presence, with a large concrete plinth emblazoned 'Welcome to Royal Air Force Brüggen'. A more guarded welcome is extended from behind the newly built red brick walls that siphon all vehicles towards the automatic barriers. Within the walls are slits hiding ever-watchful eyes and gun muzzles.

British forces abroad have always been insular to some degree, but the added threat from the IRA has turned us in on ourselves even more, with good reason. A plaque in the Market

Square of Roermond, the Dutch town just over the border, com-memorates two Australian holiday-makers who were misidenti-fied as British servicemen and killed by the IRA. No one travels outside the relative security of the base without checking under their car for bombs every time they return to it. Some people keep such journeys to a minimum and a few rarely leave the base.

At the barrier the RAF policeman checks my ID. There are security spot checks and I am singled out and directed into one of three brightly lit, roofed bays for inspection. We come to a halt over the frog-eyed lights that are inlaid in the road surface to illuminate the underside of the car. Guards open the bonnet and the boot, search the interior of the car and check the underside with mirrors before allowing us to continue, past the guard post, with its security glass, closed-circuit TVs and German interpreter. Like Alice in *Through the Looking-Glass*, we enter Little England, leaving Germany behind.

Helen Peters: The IRA threat is a definite pain about living on a squadron in Germany. We probably should think about it more, even when we are living in the UK, but we tend to get a little bit more blasé in the UK because there are so many other targets. It comes down to the question of whether you are really important enough for them to bother with. If they are going to risk their lives trying to plant a bomb, surely they will be aiming for a bigger target than a serviceman's wife and family? Nevertheless, in Germany, where we are slightly softer targets, we do tend to be a bit more cautious, and always check under our cars when we are off base.

We are more conspicuous in Germany too. I am sure the IRA terrorists are not stupid and it does not need a Sherlock Holmes to work out where the bases are situated. People driving around in British cars or with British number plates are automatically conspicuous too, but even if we had German plates, the IRA would only have to go into the local towns and sit in a café, looking for people getting out of a German-plated car, but speaking English.

When I take my children shopping, they say 'Are we going to the NAAFI, Mummy?' – the forces' supermarket. Children whose parents are not in the forces do not refer to the NAAFI, they would say 'Asda' or 'Sainsbury's' or something. Those are the things that give you away immediately, even though you do not mean them to. If the terrorists are doing their homework, I am sure they can spot us a mile off.

John Peters: The runway is the heart of RAF Brüggen, and its *raison d'être*, a mile-long strip of concrete, surrounded by coils of razor wire. At each corner of the runway are the squadron sectors, each guarded by a further ring of steel. A taxiway enters the squadron site, branching out into smaller arms, which each end in a HAS – a Hardened Aircraft Shelter – a concrete and steel bunker, housing a single aircraft. The huge steel HAS doors trail 'skirts' to seal the floor gap and block attack by napalm.

Each HAS was designed to withstand a high-explosive direct hit, but having seen the results of Allied bombing in the Gulf, the squadrons are now a little less optimistic about the strength of the shelters. The HASs all face in different directions, so that the weak points – the entrance doors – cannot be destroyed in a single pass by enemy aircraft. Around the circular concrete 'pad' outside each HAS are mounds of earth and concrete, further screening them from attack. Within each squadron's sector, like a spider at the heart of its web of HASs, is the hardened building known as the PBF – the Pilots' Briefing Facility – from which the squadron operations are processed and planned.

A series of fuel and weapon dumps is scattered around the operational areas, ensuring the station's continued ability to fight, even if bombs destroy one or more of the dumps. The weapons stores and other sensitive areas are also ringed with razor wire and manned by armed guards. Keep walking when ordered to stop and the next sound you hear will be the snap of the breech of an automatic weapon. Ignore the second request to stop and the next sound you hear will be your last.

Another steel fence and more armed guards separate the runways from the Combat Operations Centre, the Intelligence Room and all the other operations that keep the base functioning in peacetime and war. The COC is a high-security, doubly reinforced concrete monolith. It is from here that the Station Commander, Group Captain Rob Wright, would direct his station's war. A two-storey Operations Room, lined with perspex boards, continually updates him on the state of the station, its aircraft, engineering facilities and security, and the vital tasks being undertaken. All the key facilities are duplicated elsewhere on base, ensuring that we will continue to function even if a group of buildings is taken out by an attack.

When not in the air, I spend most of my working day in the Pilots' Briefing Facility, a squadron-scale version of the Combat Operations Centre. Whereas John took a fork in his career and had to start again almost from scratch, I have continued on the same track, still flying bombers, albeit with a new squadron, at a different station. With my increasing experience and seniority have come increased responsibilities, as a formation leader, night warlord and authorizer. A squadron authorizer, as the name suggests, authorizes the day's flights to take place and organizes them. It is complex work; you have to know the rules – and there are bucket-loads of them – but the job is really just an extension of the rules you follow when flying your own sorties. What the Air Force looks for in flying is your safety brake. The authorizer must ensure that the sorties flown are within both the general safety limits and within the individual capabilities of the crews. You want people to be punchy and aggressive, but always with an eye on safety. There is no point in dropping your bombs on the target if you run out of fuel; you still have to get your aircraft home.

The authorizer is the one who should be able to take a cool look at a situation when everyone else is running around getting wound up and everything is going pear-shaped, and say: 'Hold it, this isn't going to work, let's knock it on the head'. Above all, the authorizer's signature confirms that people are briefed and cleared to fly their sorties and if something goes wrong, you are massively beholden to your signature. Air crew are the most severe critics of our own profession, and while the pilot who makes a mistake will be given a hell of a time, the person who authorized the flight will have an even worse one. An investigation will probe every aspect of the sortie, with the authorizer facing a gruelling interrogation about his reasons for allowing the flight to take place.

The job of warlord is to direct the squadron at war, from ensuring that the mission plans are actually feasible, down to the most prosaic details, like making sure that the air crew are fed and transported out to the Hardened Aircraft Shelters on time. During exercises there is a lot of pressure on the warlord. As soon as the air crews have briefed, we are dispersing them to the HAS areas, because we do not want them all stuck in the same place a moment longer than necessary, since it is possible we could lose all the air crew in a single attack.

The vast majority of 31 Squadron congregates in the crew room where, amongst the mementoes, photographs and log-books of old heroes, is a rather less military collection of artefacts, a 'Gop' cabinet containing tasteless souvenirs and plastic tourist tat, collected by squadron members on their detachments abroad. The one inflexible rule is that nothing must have cost more than £1, but otherwise anything goes. A Tower of Pisa containing a small orange light rubs shoulders with a 'jumping' Statue of Liberty and a pair of miniature Mexican maracas. Next to the cabinet sits 'Ariellies the Bear', the squadron mascot, a battered teddy bear equipped with the full range of Air Force uniforms, including a flying suit, 'number ones' – dress uniform – and even a full set of tropical kit.

Ariellies the Bear is now closely guarded, following a most unsavoury incident a couple of years ago, in which he was kid-napped and held for ransom. The men on 14 Squadron had recently bought a battered old Trabant car as a present for their Boss, and spent days labouring to repair, clean, paint and polish it. The sight of this apple of 14 Squadron's eye, sparkling in the sunshine, proved too much for some of the guys from 31, who promptly hijacked it, driving it off to a secret hideaway in a cloud of noxious fumes. The response from 14 was swift and brutal; Ariellies the Bear disappeared from his perch, leaving no trace but a blood-curdling ransom note, signed 'A FREND' (sic). After the intervention of our Boss, a truce was declared and a hand-over arranged. We met on neutral territory and traded mascots, like two spies being exchanged at Checkpoint Charlie in the depths of the Cold War: 'Don't try any tricks. We're not letting go of the Trabant until we get our hands on the bear.'

Ariellies the Bear was borne aloft in triumph, back to his place of honour in the crew room, where he has remained ever since, unmolested by other squadrons. Other mascots have not been so fortunate, some suffering grievous indignities. Arriving at work one morning, 16 Squadron, which had a live goat as its mascot, found that a rival squadron had shaved off the goat's beard, while 43 Squadron – the 'Fighting Cocks' – were subject to a far more witty raid.

One of their aircraft was left for a night 'on the line' outside the hangar of another squadron, whose mascot is a tiger. When the 43 crew went back to their aircraft the next morning, they discovered that the fighting cock on the tailplane had been painted out. In its place was a painting of a pile of chicken bones and a trail of tiger paw prints, leading all the way down the fuselage and out to the end of the wing.

Some squadron rivalries are even more intense. For fifty years, IX Squadron and 617 have argued about which of them was responsible for the sinking of the German ship, the *Tirpitz*, during the Second World War. A metal bulkhead retrieved from the ship reinforces the claims of whichever squadron happens to hold it at the time, rather like possession of the Stone of Scone used to legitimize the Scottish crown. As a result, the bulkhead has changed hands a number of times, following daring, SAS-style raids by the other squadron; flying in to a neighbouring base under cover of darkness, commandeering transport to sweep them in and out of the rival squadron's lair, and using subterfuge, bluff and sheer force of numbers to carry off the prize.

When they last retrieved the steel bulkhead from 617, IX Squadron thought that they had solved the problem once and for all. They embedded it into a reinforced concrete wall in the crew room, even weaving the steel reinforcing rods of the concrete through holes in the bulkhead. Nothing but nuclear war could have shifted it, or so they thought. Not to be so easily deterred, 617 mounted a raid a few months later. They appeared in the crew room armed with jack-hammers, diamond-tipped saws and angle grinders and demolished the entire wall, before carting off the bulkhead once more in triumph.

The 31 Squadron crew room is an oasis of calm and tranquillity compared to this, although an occasional black cloud of discord does form. Sharing a crew room is a bit like sharing a house when a student. The same problems invariably arise; no one ever does the washing-up. A teetering pyramid of crockery piles up in the sink, alive with every fungus and bacteria known to mankind. We endured three months of this and then decided to employ a squadron cook. The money came out of our own pockets, but it was well worth the investment, not just because there was always a hot meal waiting when we got back from flying, but because we no longer had to bicker about whose turn it was to attack the pile of moss-encrusted dishes in the sink.

We also all contribute to the squadron newspaper fund. Every morning, a pristine copy of the *Telegraph* appears in the crew room, along with an assortment of 'comics' – the *Sun*, the *Mirror* and a couple of other tabloids. When the papers are thrown away the next morning, the *Telegraph* remains almost equally pristine. The only time it is opened is to photocopy the crossword. Meanwhile fights break out over the comics, with everyone desperate to immerse themselves in sex, scandal and soap opera. Such is the intellectual might of the men of 31!

With tidily mown grass between the concrete ribbons of the taxiways and pine woods surrounding the concentric rings of razor wire, the squadron sector can seem a tranquil place, with nothing breaking the silence but the birds singing in the trees and the air crew arguing about whose turn it is for the *Sun*. Then the doors of the HASs rumble open and the scream of Tornado engines tears the silence to shreds, bringing the abrupt reminder that the purpose of this peaceful-looking place is war.

A further fence separates the 'working base' from the rest of Brüggen, which has the look and the population of a small town. There are banks and shops, including the NAAFI supermarket in the town centre and pubs and clubs – the Messes where the Air Force's officers and men drink, as they work, by rank – and some of the similarly segregated living quarters.

Most of the single men live in barracks-style blocks, a few still instantly recognizable to veterans of National Service, although the Air Force is gradually replacing the 'barracks' with units in which even the lowliest airman will have his own private bedroom. Our married quarters are out in the 'suburbs', a mile from the centre of Brüggen, but still inside the perimeter fence. We live on a road that could be on any suburban housing estate in England – semi-detached boxes or terraces of three, standing in the shade of conifers and oaks. At Christmas virtually every house has a tree outside, decorated with white lights. It is a beautiful sight as you drive home after dark.

The house walls are stuccoed and painted beige, a colour as beloved of the forces as pink is of Barbara Cartland. The quarters are standard Air Force design, the same as on my previous station at Laarbruch and, indeed, all the Air Force houses that I have ever lived in: lounge, dining room, kitchen, three bedrooms, bathroom, attic and cellars. The rooms are bland; magnolia walls, beige carpets and unobtrusive curtains, usually coloured beige as well. Somehow the individual taste of the occupants manages to turn these identical dwellings into very different homes. Apart from the colour scheme, the only other ubiquitous features are the duty-free cars – almost always Volvos – and the banks of dustbins, four per household in environmentally sound Germany, one for paper, one for glass, one for refuse and one for biodegradable material.

The children play freely on the grass in front of the houses and in the road, for no one drives fast. It is a tight-knit, almost old-fashioned community, of a type that seems to have disappeared from England. The only friction tends to be caused by the first man to mow his lawn in the spring, forcing all the others to cut theirs as well. At weekends people wash their cars, mow their lawns and have barbecues. On weekday mornings the men are waved off to work by their wives and children. It could be Anytown, Anywhere, except that all the men are in uniform and all the inhabitants share the same occupation – the business of war.

That community of interest can be a blessing in wartime, when a wife can draw on the support of others in a similar position to her own, but the base is also a world in which husbands are never completely off duty and wives and families are always subordinate to the exigencies of Air Force training.

While bases in the UK can even look quite twee with their grandiose, two-storey Station Headquarters, in Germany all the buildings, including the Station HQ, are camouflaged and single-storey, painted dull, matt, operational green, and everywhere is surrounded by barbed wire and razor wire. Even outside the base, almost all the civilian roads throughout Germany have yellow speed limit signs for the tanks and troop convoys, erected not by the military but by local government. Had the Cold War ever turned hot, the battle between NATO and the Warsaw Pact would have been fought on this north German plain. Central Europe was earmarked as the battlefield, with the inner German border the frontline.

Even though the Cold War is over, Brüggen remains a prime target for Britain's enemies in a war, or in a terrorist campaign. Armed guards patrol constantly around the operational areas of the base, holding the quick-release leads of their 'attack' dogs, but even in the residential areas there are regular guard patrols. There is a jarring contrast between the sight of people in bathing trunks, watering the garden while their children play happily on the grass, apparently as safe as in any community, and the guards in green uniforms, carrying automatic weapons. They patrol in pairs, one either side of the road, just like a patrol in Belfast. Despite the apparent tranquillity, you are never far from the ugly realities.

5

Casual visitors not encouraged
RAF LEEMING

John Nichol: My base at Leeming in North Yorkshire is a stone's throw from the A1, a few miles south of Scotch Corner. The turning is signposted from the A1, but casual visitors are definitely not encouraged. As soon as you turn off the public road into the mile-long approach road to the station, a sign warns: 'This is a prohibited place within the meaning of the Official Secrets Act'. The warning is reinforced by the new gatehouse, where those without passes will be turned back. I drive through that gate every morning, but I am still halted, and my pass scrutinized carefully, every day, before I am allowed to proceed. While the guard checks my credentials, I stare down the barrel of a rifle issuing from the slit of a concrete pillbox. The menace of the rifle is only partly eased by the reassuringly banal sight of the guard's spectacles, glinting in the gloom of the pillbox.

As in Germany, the base security has been stepped up enormously in recent years, in response to the IRA threat. The guard room used to be in the middle of the base and visitors could drive right up to it before being challenged. Now the whole base is ringed by barbed wire, and if the outer perimeter fence is as much a symbolic as a genuine barrier to intruders, there is nothing symbolic about the inner barriers of razor wire and steel chain-link fences illuminated by blinding floodlights, nor the dogs and armed police patrolling constantly.

46

The station's buildings sprawl over an area of several acres, linked by a maze of roads on which newcomers to the squadron can often be glimpsed, driving in circles, forlornly looking for a familiar landmark.

Routine operations are carried out in drab, two-storey brick buildings which would blend into any postwar industrial estate. The operational functions are contained in hardened concrete blockhouses, scattered in a rough circle around the huge monolith of the War Operations Centre. The drab green camouflage paint of the hardened buildings singles them out at ground level, but makes them near-invisible from the air. The other squadrons stationed at Leeming house their Tornados in Hardened Aircraft Shelters, but we have none of them, for we are a rapid deployment squadron; if there was a threat of war or any military involvement, we would not be at Leeming, but deployed to a forward base. As a result, our aircraft are normally stored in a single cavernous hangar, housing as many as twenty Tornados – a mind-boggling sight, £500 million of taxpayers' money under one roof.

My squadron at Leeming, XI (F) Squadron, is divided into two Flights. The division is primarily for administrative purposes, but it is also good for morale, because there is tremendous competition between the Flights. When we go to Cyprus for gunnery practice, for example, the whole squadron – lock, stock and barrel, ups and goes out to Akrotiri, where we park ourselves in the sunshine for four weeks. We spend every single day there flying against an aircraft towing a huge banner and we use our guns – basic, First World War, Biggles-type stuff – to hose the banner down. The bullets from each aircraft are painted a different colour and competition is fierce, both between different squadrons, and within our own squadron, between A and B Flights, and between the individual crews.

As soon as we get to Cyprus, the air crew are auctioned off to the ground crew. We all stand up in turn on a chair and are sold to the highest bidders, who have us as 'their' crew for the month. If we win the gunnery trophy, our proud owners get a prize as well. It is just a way of getting everybody involved, from 'the Boss' – the Squadron Commander – right down to the guy who puts the petrol in the jet.

When we are back at Leeming, one Flight is on days and the other on nights. On days, Met brief is normally at eight in the morning, unless there is a special mission, when we might get in at half past six. The whole Flight files into the briefing room for the Met brief, when the Michael Fish of Leeming comes down with his tales of lies, lies and more damned lies about what the weather is going to be like. In fact he is probably right ninety-five per cent of the time, but we always seem to remember the days when he gets it wrong. After the Met brief, the squadron authorizer takes over. The authorizer is one of the senior flight lieutenants, who is in charge of the day-to-day running of the squadron, sitting behind the Ops Room desk and co-ordinating who is going off to do what. The authorizer gives a briefing, including the state of the airfield, the specific weather on the airfield and which runway and diversion we are using.

We always have to have the fuel to do our mission and come back with what we call FOG – fuel on the ground. That might be 1,000 kilograms of fuel left in the aircraft when the wheels touch the ground, a lot more still in the tanks than most light aircraft and helicopters have when they take off, never mind land. We would burn off their total fuel capacity in a single takeoff.

We need the spare fuel so that if we cannot get in on our final approach because an aircraft crashes in front of us, or some other problem, we have enough fuel to go off to our specific diversion. Normally we use Teesside, because it is the closest to Leeming, but it depends on the weather and the wind. Occasionally there will be a strong crosswind at Teesside, ruling it out as a diversion, in which case the FOG goes up and we use Coningsby in Lincolnshire instead. If something happens once we are at Coningsby, we are in deep trouble because we only ever hold enough fuel to go to our one specified diversion.

The authorizer also does the 'emergency of the day'. Every

single potential emergency – an engine fire, an oxygen failure, an electrical failure – is covered in the flight reference cards which we always carry. There is no divergence, no room for improvisation, it is written on the cards in precise, detailed steps, and that is the way it must be handled. The initial steps to counter each emergency are covered by a 'bold face drill' – a drill laid out in a bold typeface on the cards – that the pilots must know by heart and do without even thinking. If there is an engine fire in flight, for example, the bold face drill is:

> Throttle.
> High pressure cock – shut.
> Low pressure cock – shut.
> Fire button – press

Once the pilot has carried out the bold face drill, the nav then gets out the relevant flight reference card and goes through what may be as many as another sixty steps, but the bold face ones are the ones that we must know by heart, because they are the ones that will save the aircraft. In a big emergency like a double hydraulics failure, the aircraft will go out of control within a second unless we act immediately, which is why we must know those drills by heart. So the authorizer, as part of his daily brief, will say: 'OK, emergency of the day today is an engine fire in flight'. He will pick someone out and say 'Right. What is the bold face for that?' and they have to know it. If they do not, they are in serious trouble.

After the briefing, everyone shuffles off back into the crew room, the kettle is put on, the toaster fired up, and the day really starts with us chewing the cud in the crew room, which has a bit of the atmosphere of a rather tatty lounge bar in a suburban pub, not inappropriately, considering the thousands of bottles and cans of beer that have been consumed there down the years. There are plenty more to come; the squadron beer fridge is always kept well-supplied – and securely locked, preventing any wandering visitors from helping themselves.

The walls are lined with squadron trophies: propellers from aircraft shot down in combat, a Japanese flag captured during the Second World War, and a mass of photographs of squadron members past and present. A rectangular 'bar' dominates the middle of the room, although it dispenses nothing stronger than tea or coffee until the day's flying is over. Each crewman has his own personalized mug and his own idiosyncratic choice of sandwich filling in the fridge. An indiscriminate gourmand could assemble a peanut butter, tuna, goats' cheese, baked bean, egg and onion sandwich from the half-used containers scattered inside.

The padlocks on the beer fridge notwithstanding, the crew room is a warm and welcoming place, where we spend many happy hours indulging in the second favourite occupation of air crew – banter. Perched on the bar stools or lounging in the armchairs, we put the world to rights while fastening mercilessly on any minor blemish or imperfection in each and every crew-mate's personal and working life. A navigation error when flying, a new car, a new hairstyle, all are grist to the banter mill. No quarter is expected, asked or given, this is definitely the last place on earth to wear that 'interesting' pullover that Aunt Mabel knitted you for Christmas last year, or to confess to a belief in reincarnation or the virtues of colonic irrigation.

While we are chatting and brewing up, the guys who are leading the first mission of the day will be on the phone to the big air defence control centres, Boulmer in Northumberland, Buchan in Scotland and Staxtonwold down by Flamborough Head somewhere, teeing up exercises. Every day we go off and: 'Fly today as if we were going to war tomorrow', as the Boss never fails to remind us. Normally the exercise is just a one v one – two fighters going up and pitting their wits against each other, using the same tactics as if they were part of a group of ten fighters, facing a hundred Russian aircraft coming down the Icelandic Gap. Sometimes one of our jets will simulate being a bomber, flying low and fast over the sea with the other guy trying to intercept him – cat and mouse.

The other big part of the squadron's daily routine is training the new guys, who come on to the squadron every month.

Although they have passed out of the OCU – the Operational Conversion Unit – they still have to be trained by the squadron to combat-readiness, when they are declared to NATO as fully operational air crew. That can take anything from one or two months if you are already an experienced air defence navigator or pilot, right up to six, nine or even twelve months if you are an *ab initio* – someone starting from scratch.

A lot of squadron time is taken up with training its *ab initios*, also known as 'convexies'. An experienced crew leads an inexperienced crew around, starting with one v one intercepts, on a set sequence of forty to fifty trips that they have to fly before they are combat-ready. Some of those trips are pretty simple, but some are dauntingly complex. Hooking up to a tanker in broad daylight for midair refuelling is nerve-wracking enough the first time you do it, but attempting the same manoeuvre in darkness and thick cloud is something else again. Try driving down the M1 at 500 miles an hour, after dark, during a downpour. Once you have got the hang of that, turn your lights off and try to touch bumpers with a petrol tanker, trundling along in the slow lane somewhere in the darkness ahead; you will soon get the flavour of it. Even that does not quite duplicate the bowel-loosening feeling of refuelling in combat conditions, when there might be four planes trying to refuel simultaneously; not only are you trying to touch bumpers at 500 miles an hour, so are three other maniacs.

A typical squadron day might start with a convexies trip, flying one v one. Two aircraft might then go off to do electronic counter-measures training with one of our Canberras from Wyton, using up the first four or six aircraft. There will then be a break till lunchtime when the next six or eight take off. Four might go off to do a trial or a missile firing down at one of the ranges, another two or four might do 'affiliation' training, after phoning up to get some bombers, Jaguars or Tornados, with the F3s forming a Combat Air Patrol against them. In late afternoon we normally put up another convexies trip, if the weather is good, to train the guys to fight over land, and then we get into the night wave because they also have to learn to fly and do intercepts at night, all on the radar. There could also be another big mission, doing night flying with bombers, perhaps with AWACs and fighter support.

There is no consistent pattern to my work. Some weeks I fly every day, others I might only fly on three. In some months I have just ten hours' flying in my logbook because I have been on a course or on leave, but in others I put in forty hours. On Tactical Fighter Meet in Denmark we flew twice a day for a fortnight, putting in big missions and long hours, having already flown every day for the preceding two weeks in preparation.

I also regularly have the sheer joy of taking my turn as station duty officer. After working all day, the lucky officer gets to be on duty all through the evening, and on call throughout the night as well. The duty starts at six o'clock, attending the ensign lowering ceremony which marks the official close of the station for the day, though the RAF does not stop for the night just because most people have nipped off home.

There are constant problems: water pipes burst in the married quarters, fire alarms go off around the place, fights break out in the social club, signals and electronic mail pour into the station, some of which have to be actioned immediately, while some can be held until the next working day. We also still have defaulters, people who have been charged with minor misdemeanours, on 'jankers'. They are not allowed off station and have to do time-consuming tasks like tin-bashing, or sweeping the roads, with an inspection by the duty officer at ten o'clock at night. As duty officer I am allowed to sleep, but even in the quiet hours of the night, I am regularly woken up. On one duty I had the unfortunate experience of having to tell somebody that one of their relatives had died. All those sorts of tasks fall on the station duty officer. I am on call throughout the night, and the next morning I am expected to go straight back on duty, ready for the Met brief.

Fortunately for me, this type of duty is rare as the ground administration officers deal with the day-to-day personnel management. Not being directly in charge of airmen means that air crew tend to be much more familiar with their ground crew than some of their counterparts would accept. We know most of the ground crew by their first names, and the relationship is more like that of an extended family than a master and servant.

This does not mean that there is a lax attitude to discipline, it is just a more mature approach, although the different nature of how we fight in comparison to, say, an Army officer, also means that we do not need to be so rigid. Soldiers in the Army are trained killers, and officers need to use their men's skills to achieve definite objectives. The men are expected to follow the officers' lead into battle, obeying the commands of their superiors without question.

In this highly technical, computerized modern world, the need for skilled, technologically literate engineers has closed the officer–man distinctions. In the close-knit world of an Air Force squadron, the need for self-discipline and competence at work to achieve the best results overrides any need to enforce regimented discipline. Ultimately, air crew lead only themselves to war. The ground crew wave us on with a cheery 'Have a good trip, Sir!'

The book in which we enter the fault reports is called the 'Form 700' and it is the *This Is Your Life* of the aircraft; everything that has ever gone wrong with it is written down there, I tend to wander in and write in the book: 'The radar is bust', and the ground crew will sigh, smile patiently and say: 'Well Sir, what's wrong with it?' My reply is usually: 'I don't know, you're the bloody technician, it just won't work', but gradually, with all the patience and tact of doctors talking about a prostate problem, they will coax out the essential information to make the diagnosis, and then go away and fix it. They always blame us for breaking the aircraft, of course, sometimes with justification, but it is an indication of the friendly way that the Air Force goes about its business. It is a much more relaxed way than the Army way, but it is still very professional and the job still always gets done.

*

John Peters: People still tend to have a strange, National Service image of the forces, imagining that we all live in barrack blocks and have a very regimented lifestyle, spending all our time marching up and down. The reality, in the Air Force at least, is very different. I have only marched once since I finished my officer training, at an annual Formal Inspection, and I only wear my smart blue uniform when I do my turn as station duty officer, or at the Battle of Britain cocktail party. The rest of the time, all I ever wear is a flying suit.

Sometimes we have to work early or fly at night, and we are often away for a week or two at a stretch, making a total of three or four months a year, but apart from that it is a normal lifestyle, a routine Monday to Friday, eight to five job. We even have weekends off. It is not a restrictive atmosphere at all, far less so than most factories or offices. It is all down to self-discipline. If you wanted to spend the whole day sitting around the crew room drinking coffee, you could, no one is going to ask you what you are doing, although there is too much work to do for anyone to sit around for long. We now have far fewer operational strike/attack squadrons than we had before the Gulf War, but the workload has remained much the same.

With budgets trimmed tighter than ever, our lives are ruled by statistics: hours flown, weapons, fuel, low level, high level, evasion – everything we do requires a form to be filled in, proving how much we can achieve, at how little expense. Sadly, the greatest savings appear to be made by cutting down the time we spend in the air; even in my short time on the front line, my flying hours have been noticeably pared down. We are trusted to discipline ourselves to a great extent, but we are expected to have done the necessary preparatory work to fly the next mission, or pass the next test. If you have not, that is when the questions about why you failed and what you were doing when you should have been working will start. It is all done on results; we are trusted to discipline ourselves, but we have to produce the goods.

As air crew, virtually every piece of information we handle every day is classified 'secret', and certain things are covered by higher security classifications, but the secret side of our work sounds more glamorous than it actually is. There are cupboards full of classified books on the squadron, but we need to have read those books in order to do our job correctly. People might think that classified information is bound to be really interesting, covering deep, dark secrets and RAF skeletons dangling in the closet, but the truth is that there is absolutely no strain in keeping official secrets, because they are as boring as hell, instantly forgettable. Each book may be classified, each page of each book may be classified, numbered and recorded, but there may be as little as one word in that whole book that makes it classified.

The checks on classified documents arc meticulous in the extreme. Somebody on station has the daunting and most important task of checking and counting every single page of every single classified document, including the flyleaves, title pages and blank pages, at least twice a year. Just as nature abhors a vacuum, so the Air Force abhors empty pages in classified documents; even the blank pages are stamped with the words 'This page is intentionally blank'.

6

Four long days and sleepless nights
TACTICAL EVALUATION

John Peters: 'RED, RED, RED, AIR ATTACK RED.'

The warning blared out over the tannoy and the alert board on the wall flashed 'Red', as the siren began to shriek. There was a mad scramble for our gas masks. RAF Brüggen was under attack from nuclear, biological or chemical weapons.

I pulled my mask over my face, shouting: 'Gas, gas, gas' as I did so, to purge any possible gas residue from the mask with my exhaled breath. I pulled my NBC – Nuclear, Biological, Chemical – hood over my head and my navigator and I automatically checked each other's seals. We also donned our 'tin hats' – made out of Kevlar these days, but old habits die hard – although we were inside a hardened building, protected by a thick carapace of ferroconcrete, walls can still be breached, as the Gulf War TV pictures of bombs sailing through air vents amply demonstrated.

As I breathed in, the stink of fuller's earth and rubber filled my nostrils and the mask tightened on my face. There was a dull thwack as the outlet valve opened and closed. My breathing sounded as loud and laboured as a deep-sea diver's. I peered out through the eye pieces, gazing down long, dark rubber tubes at my colleagues, now remote and unrecognizable behind their masks, identifiable only by the name, rank and blood group stencilled in thick black lettering on the front and back of their NBC suits.

The siren's continuous, wailing ululation finally died away, but every telephone seemed to be ringing at once as reports poured in, information rattling and ricocheting around the station. We would have to carry on working in the NBC suits until the air raid was over and the monitors had completed all their checks, ensuring that no trace of radioactivity or poison gas had penetrated the area, sealed by airlocks against the outside world. Our masks and NBC suits also isolated us from each other; despite the integral voice piece on the gas masks, we had to shout to communicate at all.

The suffocatingly claustrophobic suits made even the most routine task ten times more difficult, but in a contaminated environment they are the difference between life and death. I grew hotter and hotter and the mask began to stick to my face and skin. I could feel sweat trickling down my neck and an irritating tingling around the edges of the mask. Stale sweat and traces of riot gas, mementoes of old exercises, were being rubbed into freshly shaved skin. The temptation to remove the mask and scratch the itch was almost overwhelming, but had to be resisted. Until the all-clear call, 'Clear in the Hard' – the hardened building – was made, to remove the mask, even for an instant, could end in death. I sat and sweated instead. This was only the first morning of TACEVAL – Tactical Evaluation – there were four long days and sleepless nights to go.

Individual pilots reach combat-readiness by performing a set number of sorties, covering every aspect of their work. TACEVAL is NATO's solution to the rather more complex problem of testing the combat-readiness of entire squadrons and stations. A multinational team of 150 assessors had appeared at Brüggen the previous day, to begin a one-week examination of every aspect of the operational, support and survival-to-operate readiness of the base while under enemy attack. Every function of the station, not just our ability to mount bombing raids, but ground defence, engineering, air defence, medical treatment of casualties, even cooking and waste disposal, is assessed and everyone is tested, from the Station Commander to the lowliest kitchen hand. The test of survival-to-operate readiness is how we react to situations that we might face in a real war – aircraft returning with battle damage, communications being disrupted, buildings damaged or destroyed, people being killed. Many other NATO bases had been mobilized to attack Brüggen, so that the local air defences were thoroughly tested, while we were engaged in the most nightmarish form of combat that any serviceman can face; nuclear, biological or chemical warfare.

It was an horrendous premise, but not an unrealistic one. We could have faced chemical weapons at any time during the Gulf War, and indeed we expected to do so. Nor is Iraq the only potential user of such weapons; there are several countries in the world that would use – and have used – a chemical agent without a second thought.

The transition from cosy domestic bliss to the nightmare of chemical war had been abrupt. The alarm clock dragged me out of my dreams at 4.50 a.m. I kissed Helen, who was still fast asleep, rolled out of bed and crept through to the bathroom, closing the door soundlessly to avoid disturbing the children, both painfully early risers. After a quick wash, I dressed in my war suit, which carries a badge of rank but is devoid of all other insignia and distinguishing marks, making us anonymous, grey men, in case of capture. I tiptoed downstairs, and standing in the hall, I put on my shoulder holster and picked up my webbing belt, from which dangled a gas mask, haversack, water bottle and field bandage dressing. As I fastened the belt, the gas mask clanked against the radiator and instantly I heard the patter of tiny feet. My sleepy-eyed daughter Toni tottered downstairs, looking for her morning Weetabix. I whispered 'It's not morning yet', and carried her back to bed, her face pressed into my shoulder holster. Back downstairs I hung the chin strap of my 'tin hat' over the water bottle and pulled my NBC hood over my head. As I closed the front door, I could again hear Toni padding along the corridor upstairs; Helen would be pleased. I jumped on my bicycle and pedalled off to war.

I cycled past the Officers' Married Quarters, rows of stucco houses, gleaming ghostly white in the moonlight. An odd bathroom window threw a beam of light into the dark, signs that others were preparing for the long day. I passed a solitary man walking home after his night shift, his face pale and drawn beneath the remnants of camouflage cream; we nodded, but did not speak.

I pedalled on through the 'town centre' towards a blindingly bright pool of yellow light illuminating a roadblock. A sign-board warned: 'You are now entering the exercise area'. A guard stepped out of the shadows, an SA-80 automatic rifle cradled in his arms. As he approached, his mate covered me from the sandbagged emplacement at the side of the road. I fumbled for my ID and we exchanged a few words, our breath fogging in the cold night air.

Beyond the roadblock, I parked my bike near the 'Soft' – the air crew administration building and crew room – and walked towards the operational enclosure. 'Halt. Stand still!' An aggressive voice challenged me from behind a steel gate, set like a portcullis in the massive concrete entrance. If I continued to walk forward, the guard would cock his rifle and after a second challenge, I would be shot. 'Give the password.'

I gave the password and produced my ID and the sector pass, allowing access to this specific area. As I was about to hand them to the guard, a friendlier voice said that he would vouch for me. The gate clanged back and alongside the guard I saw the smiling face of Geordie, one of the squadron engineers, just recognizable despite his disruptive pattern suit, cam cream and Kevlar helmet. We had moved to Brüggen from Laarbruch at the same time and found an empathy as we established ourselves on 31 Squadron.

As the night sky began to pale into dawn, I entered the 'Hard' – the Pilots' Briefing Facility. 'Soft' and 'Hard' refer to the skins of the building. The less vital buildings are soft-skinned – built from ordinary bricks and mortar, but the nerve centres of the functioning squadron are housed within a hard skin, tough enough to survive a high-explosive direct hit. The heavy steel entrance door of the Hard is protected by a re-inforced concrete tunnel. The only break in the concrete and steel is an intercom grille, highlighted by a day-glo orange arrow and a caption ordering: 'Speak here'. After again identifying myself, I heard a metallic clunk as the door was unlocked by unseen hands pressing an unseen button.

I slowly turned the steel wheel at the centre of the heavy door and hauled on the dead weight to get it moving. As it swung slowly open, pressurized air rushed out past me. I stepped inside and dragged the door shut, leaving myself trapped in an airlock between two huge steel doors, illuminated by a red light above my head, as I was again spied on by eyes behind bulletproof glass. I gave my name and reason for being there and was identified as friend or foe before the red light turned to green, signalling me to open the inner door. Dot, one of the Squadron 'Squippers' – Survival Equipment Technicians, who look after our flying equipment – had vouched for me, allowing me to enter the inner sanctum. It was early summer, but it might as well have been mid-winter. Cocooned inside this windowless concrete maze, I would not see natural light for the next thirteen hours.

Although the hub of the operational squadron, the Pilots' Briefing Facility, is a hardened operations building, the squadron is also expected to survive and operate even if the area becomes contaminated by attack from nuclear, biological or chemical weapons. The precautions taken to prevent the slightest trace of radiation, biological or chemical agent penetrating the building are rigorous in the extreme. The air inside the Hard is maintained at a higher pressure than the ambient air, so that any leaks will be from inside to outside, rather than the other way round. By preventing leakage of contaminants into this armoured shell, we are able to relax the individual NBC protection for those who work inside.

Air crew entering from outside may themselves be contaminated by toxins and to reach the heart of the Hard, in which the air is fully filtered, we first have to pass through contamination control, moving through airlocks from the operational enclosure to the outer sector of the Hard, the Liquid Hazard Area, then into the Vapour Hazard Area and finally through another airlock into the Toxic-Free Area. Just inside the airlock, I was issued with my handgun, a Walther PPK, by the Shelter Marshal, who sits in front of the air-conditioning control panel, constantly scanning the pressure gauges and LEDs. I walked down the corridor, raising a wry smile as I passed the closed door to the toilets on my right; Lunty always stood up at the end of all pre-Exercise briefs, like a priest shouting fire and brimstone at his congregation, ordering everyone to have a crap at home before coming to work, as otherwise the working environment became hell. Those willing to risk the wrath of Lunty discovered that even the toilets provided no sanctuary from Air Force discipline. Sitting in the cubicles, you are confronted by posters, pasted to the doors by Flight Safety Officers determined to catch air crew during their most reflective moments. Most people disappear into the smallest room clutching a newspaper or a magazine, but air crew are expected to read exhortations to 'Check your pins', which some lavatorial humorist had changed to 'Check your piles'.

At the end of the corridor was another code-locked door leading to the heart of the building, the Operations Room, controlling the squadron's fighting capability. Consoles lined with telephones, field lines, radios and computer screens face a wall of perspex boards, covered in chinagraphed writing, ever-changing information like the runners and odds chalked up in a bookmaker's, except that no bookie's is ever lit like the Ops Room. Harsh, stark fluorescent light illuminates every corner, so bright that the figures in the room cast no shadows and their features look strangely flattened. All the figures hunched over the consoles were busy, constantly receiving, exchanging and reacting to information: the Ground Defence Commander, Elaine Stewart, responsible for the protection and security of the squadron's sector; the Senior Engineering Officer, Squadron Leader Dave Robinson, organizing the rearming, fault rectification and battle damage repair of the Tornados; the 'Floorwalker', who deals with all incoming 'tasking' – the missions we are to fly – assessing and co-ordinating the mission planning; and the 'Warlord', the man who runs the air war from the ground. The duty Warlord was a Squadron Leader, John Scholtens, for in the Air Force, the ultimate 'Boss' of a squadron – in our case, Wing Commander Ian Hall, the officer commanding 31 Squadron – is expected to lead from the front, in the air, dropping bombs.

Cocooned in steel and ferroconcrete, strangely remote from the real world and yet immediately reactive to it, the Operations Room is the nerve centre of the squadron. Beyond it is the planning room, its walls plastered with maps and information. One whole wall is lined with shelves of maps; another, screened by a curtain, houses the classified weapon and electronic warfare data, required for everyday planning. In the centre of the room are planning tables and computerized magnetic map plotting tables.

Both operations and planning could wait a few moments. My first port of call, as always, was the crew room, where I grabbed a mug of tea (NATO standard – milk, one sugar) and a traditional Exercise breakfast of an Egg Banjo from the hotlocks – the large Thermos boxes in which hot food is transported from the central kitchens to the squadrons. The food, in individual tinfoil dishes with cardboard lids, is of low-grade in-flight catering standard and the secret is to pick a meal from the centre of the hotlocks, which may have remained at least slightly warm. An Egg Banjo – a congealed, rubberized fried egg and a slice of ham in a greasy sandwich – is never hot by the time it reaches us, but still tastes absolutely bloody marvellous at this time of the morning.

Still munching my breakfast, I made my first business call of the day, the Intelligence empire, where Louisa Burden, our Squadron Intelligence Officer, updated me on the state of play, the current political situation and the ground order of battle, pointing out the type and positions of friendly and enemy forces. On the map behind her she indicated the forward lines of the battlefield with chinagraphed attack and counterattack arrows.

Next came the air scenario, highlighting fighter activity and new missile threats. There already seemed to be an impenetrable wall of missile systems behind the enemy front line, with rows of interconnecting, overlapping circles, indicating the range of each system. Louisa pointed out the significant electronic developments, such as areas of radio and radar jamming, and gave me her assessment of all this information. With my mind reeling from information overload, I returned to the Ops Room to check in and phone the 'Met man' for the weather report and review the day's tasking.

Just like a TV weatherman, our Met man covers the general weather systems, with warm and cold fronts, but he also gives us visibility, cloud structure and low-level winds, and specific reports on our routeing and expected target weather. Each airfield also broadcasts its actual and forecast weather. The information is abbreviated into a colour-coded system, so that a glance at the 'Smartie Board' – the weather map covered in multi-coloured pins, like Smarties – gives us an immediate impression of the weather, without having to plough through the reams of reports continuously spewing from the Ops Room teleprinter. A blue smartie is best – excellent flying weather – whereas a red smartie is rotten – low cloud and bad visibility.

Perfect wartime weather for the Tornado would be with cloud on the deck, hiding us from the multitude of visually laid air defence systems and denying the fighters visual intercepts. The Tornado has the kit to know exactly where it is, whatever the weather, and our Terrain-Following Radar enables us to fly hidden in a blanket of cloud. The only way the defenders can then find us is by radar, which will be detected by our RHWR – Radar Homing and Warning Receiver – and can also be jammed.

Even with the most modern defence systems, we can still remove at least fifty per cent of the threats against us by going in at low level at night and in bad weather, which decreases radar range and obviously affects visual systems. In the Gulf one or two radar-guided guns fired in the air and all the other visual systems fired where the tracer of those guns was going.

In bad weather, the defenders cannot even see the tracer to align and fire their weapons. In wartime we aim for that kind of weather and go straight down into it, but in peacetime we are not allowed to fly in cloud at low level. We fly to a minimum visibility of five kilometres, which, at a cruise speed of eight miles per minute, is still only thirty seconds' flying time.

Mission planners always want the maximum range from the aircraft, leaving minimal combat fuel, whereas the pilots who actually have to fly the missions always want the reverse. If we are attacked, we want to be able to plug in the burners, hit maximum power and burn fuel at ten times the cruising rate, giving us maximum speed to get the hell out of trouble, but then still have enough fuel left to hit the target.

We also have to determine which weapon will be most effective against the target and the part of the target we should attack. Destroying the acquisition radar of a surface-to-air missile system, for example, will prevent the missiles being fired, even though they might still be sitting unscathed on their launchers.

Our other problem is timing. We have a set TOT – Time On Target – and if we miss that, because of being 'bounced' – attacked – by fighters or whatever, we may have to switch to a secondary or 'dump' target. If we go in late on the original target, there may be other of our aircraft dropping stuff from high level, which would be falling around our ears as we went in on our bombing run. We plan to take account of every possible variable, which is a tremendous mental pressure, but in theory whatever actually happens on the mission, we should have a contingency plan to cover it. No one sets out to be a hero, but the wise man plans not to be a hero at all. He just wants to fly along the 'black line' – the safest route he can find – drop his bombs and come home.

The mission was already hard enough, but now came a fresh communication designed to make it even more difficult. The Exercise War had escalated. The new threat assessment was that chemical weapons could be used against us. Scarcely had we absorbed the warning than the sirens began to wail.

*

Going to war in a chemical environment is a nightmare. Even the simplest task becomes deliberate and laborious. A slight mistake, even an intake of breath, and the unseen, unselective enemy will kill in a few seconds – simple chemistry with simply deadly results. The airfield can be poisoned with many toxins, some short-term, some persistent, delivered by bomb, artillery shell or missile, and running the gamut of horrendous effects, from choking, blistering or incapacitating to killing by attacking the skin, the lungs, the eyes, the blood or the nervous system.

Nerve agents such as Tabun, Sarin or Soman, are undetectable by smell or taste and enter the body through inhalation (the lungs), absorption (the eyes and skin) or ingestion (in food or water). The agent interferes with the nerve messages to the muscles, causing them to contract involuntarily. The initial symptoms are a running nose, increased saliva, tightness of the chest and dimmed vision (through the pinpointing of the pupils). The very final events of life are vomiting, involuntary bodily functions such as uncontrolled defecation and the eventual cessation of breathing – death, to the less medically minded of us.

Blood agents such as Hydrogen Cyanide or Cyanogen Chloride can smell of bitter almonds or peach kernels. They are fast-acting, highly volatile and lethal. The agent enters the bloodstream by inhalation and causes death by disrupting the blood's ability to carry oxygen. Initial symptoms are dizziness, rapid breathing, headache, nausea and convulsions.

Choking agents enter the lungs by inhalation. They are quick-acting and lethal, but are non-persistent and can be identified by smell. The phosgene-based gas smells of new-mown hay and is colourless, whilst the chlorine-based gas has a swimming pool smell and is yellow-green. Symptoms are shortness of breath, followed by unconsciousness. The agent affects the ability to breathe by attacking the throat and lungs. The body produces fluid to protect the lungs against the agent, but the lungs ultimately fill with the fluid, effectively drowning the victim.

Incapacitants include drugs such as Quinuclidinal Benzilate

and LSD, which was developed by the US military as an incapacitant before being appropriated as a psychedelic drug by the 1960s counter-culture. The official description of the effects of this type of agent states that the victims 'temporarily undergo physical or mental disability' – an unplanned 'trip' involving intoxication, poor co-ordination and unstable behaviour, rendering them incapable of operating their equipment or firing their weapons effectively. Flying a jet under the influence of LSD would make for a stimulating, but very brief, flight.

Blister agents originate from the mustard gases used in the First World War, but have subsequently been 'developed'. They come in the basic formula and in a number of increasingly hideous variations, cause the most distressing symptoms, but are not necessarily fatal. Even these 'damaging', as opposed to 'lethal' agents can seriously affect an army's capacity to wage war; half the troops can be occupied in treating the blisters of the other half. The blister agents cause inflammation and blistering of the skin, the eyes and the breathing passages. They can be detected by smell – of garlic, geraniums or fish – and are relatively slow-acting, though the speed of action depends on agent type, entry route and dosage. The agent may be inhaled, absorbed or ingested, and damp areas of the body such as the armpits and groin, are particularly vulnerable. Tiny droplets cause large blisters to erupt on the skin and if these burst, the fluid seeps onto other flesh, causing further blistering. Saddam Hussein has used these agents against his own population, both the Kurds and the Shiah Muslim 'Marsh Arabs' and with the Iraqi Scud missile threat in the Gulf, our NBC drills became second nature. We were subjected to gruesome pictures of Saddam Hussein's Kurdish victims during our Ground Defence Training, some with the whole of their backs bloated into a huge blister, the yellowed flesh drum-tight and filled with fluid and pus. Those horrendous images rammed home the awful reality of such agents; without protection, there is little hope of survival, and there can be few nastier ways to die.

The only way to survive such an attack is to wear full NBC protective clothing. The NBC suits and hoods, with gas masks or air crew respirators, will protect us in a chemical environment, and we also have access to drugs designed to counteract or at least minimize the effect of chemical agents. No NBC protection is provided for our wives and children at Brüggen, or any of the other front-line stations. This is not because of callous RAF indifference to their fate; they have no need of NBC protection because in times of tension, or at the first sign of impending hostilities, all families and non-essential personnel are instantly evacuated to the UK, leaving the base on a complete war footing.

If there is a threat of chemical attack, we immediately begin taking our NAPS tablets – Nerve Agent Pre-treatment Sets – as we had to do throughout the Gulf War. Everyone carries a bubble pack of pills, taking one every eight hours. The effect is to boost our resistance to the effects of nerve agent by several times the normally lethal dose. Even if we are contaminated before we can don our protective clothing, or the NBC suit is holed by shrapnel or a bullet wound, there is still a way to survive contamination with a nerve agent, although the cure – the 'Combo Pen' – is almost as unpleasant as the agent itself.

The Combo Pen looks like a fat, squat fountain pen. You take a firm grip on it and then push the black 'snout' of the pen hard into the fleshy part of your thigh. That action triggers a thick, one-inch needle, firing it deep into your leg, where it releases atropine – also known as belladonna, or deadly nightshade – directly into your blood stream. We are told to lie down on the floor before using the Combo Pen, because that is where we will be anyway after we have used it. We can take up to three of them and with the NAPS tablets and other pre- and post-treatment, although we will still need intensive medical attention, we can survive many times the normal fatal dose of nerve agent. We must be absolutely certain that we are contaminated, because if we do not have nerve agent poisoning, the intended 'cure' may kill us instead.

Chemical warfare may sound like something out of a science fiction comic, but it is all too real. We took the threat of chemical and biological warfare from Iraq very seriously during the Gulf War, and despite the UN attempts to dismantle Iraq's weapons of mass destruction since then, if we are ever forced to return to the Gulf to confront Saddam Hussein once more, the threat of chemical attack will still be very much on our minds.

The threat of chemical attack was only one of our worries; we were under heavy pressure. Reports poured in over the telephones and the radio, voices muffled by the masks, updating us on the situation. One of our HASs had been hit and there was a UXB – an unexploded bomb – on site, effectively trapping two aircraft and two full ground crews in the HASs, slowing the rearming and turnaround of our aircraft for the next mission and limiting rectification of minor faults from the previous sortie.

We now had just three crews left to service all the aircraft. The area around the UXB was cordoned off as the bomb disposal teams assembled. One aircraft was undergoing battle damage repairs and was not available for three hours, leaving only six serviceable aircraft.

The fuel bowser, used to refuel our aircraft, had been trapped across the other side of the airfield by an incursion of terrorists on the ring road. Squadron Leader John Scholtens struggled to find solutions, a phone in each hand and an ever-growing list of problems on the computer screen in front of him.

The squadron had just received two more tasks – missions – each taking two or three hours to plan. The weather had also taken a marked downturn, with the cloudbase down to 400 feet with drizzle below. The recovery fuel state – the minimum level of fuel with which we must return from our sortie – had increased markedly, limiting our range of operations. As a result, one of our previously assigned targets was 'weathered out'. In actual wartime it would have been a perfect target for the Tornado, but it fell outside our peacetime weather limits.

The engineers were pressing us for the weapon load for the mission and a takeoff time. Fully arming a war jet with two AIM 9L Sidewinder missiles, 360 rounds of armour-piercing and high explosive bullets, five 1000 lb bombs, chaff and flares, takes manpower and time. Station Operations also needed to know the departure time and the expected time of return so that Air Traffic Control could deconflict us from other missions and make our air defences aware that we were friendly aircraft, not enemy bombers on a hostile mission.

I started briefing the planning crew of Rich Gibby and 'Brains' – a.k.a. Damian Wyatt. Planning a mission normally takes at least ninety minutes; wearing gas masks and NBC suits was not going to make it any easier. Navigators have difficulties communicating with pilots at the best of times, and the distortion of talking through hoods and masks would add a further layer of incomprehension. The routeing out to the target was mercifully straightforward, with the Time On Target bracket in mid-afternoon, tea time for the unsuspecting defenders. We elected to arc around the target and attack down-sun, to allow better 'visual acquisition' of the heavily camouflaged target.

We decided to use CBUs – Cluster Bomb Units. The Tornado carries four, and on release, each 'bomb' bursts open to release a shower of 147 bomblets that rain down on the target. A shaped-charge warhead penetrates armour, while the fragmentation of the weapon is lethal against soft-skinned vehicles . . . or soft skin. Each Tornado covers an area the size of a football field with the weapon's destructive 'footprint'. As a sting in the tail, we elected to send in the last aircraft with five bombs with variable fusing. From our base hundreds of miles away, four Tornados would release 2,205 bomblets and 5,000 lbs of high explosive on the target inside thirty seconds.

We made the final preparations for the mission, going through 'sterilization', the removal of all personal documents and possessions. Rings, wallets, talismans, even pictures of wives and families, anything that could be useful to an enemy was taken from us and sealed in plastic bags. We completed the planning and received our final intelligence update and the day's codes, but until the all-clear, we were stuck in the Hard, with no clear passage out to our aircraft. Finally the tannoy crackled into life: 'Hostiles clear', the air raid was over.

We removed our tin hats, but not our masks; until the integrity of the building had been checked, a laborious and time-consuming process, the risk of NBC contamination remained. When the monitors complete their checks, ensuring that no trace of radioactivity or gas has penetrated the area, the call of 'Clear in the Hard' is gratefully received, with everyone tearing off their masks and gulping down the relatively fresh air of the Ops Room – providing Lunty's toilet-training instructions have been obeyed.

We are luckier than the guards outside, who have to continue wearing their masks long after we have removed ours. There is no filtration plant for the outside world and the guards have to wait until the last trace of chemical agent has cleared the area. Depending on the type and persistence of the agent used, this can take anything from two hours to two days. The chemical agent precautions apply to everyone; military police must patrol in their NBC suits, the engineers must prepare our aircraft wearing them.

The departing air crew left the sanctuary of the Ops Room, crowding out into the corridor, dressed in NBC suits and gas masks, tufts of hair sticking through the rubber straps. The suits, worn over long johns, are made from grey-green interwoven felt, with the texture of a rough dishcloth, and a charcoal liner that blackens the underclothes. This shapeless overall is tied at the waist with a cord. Bootees of the same material cover our feet and our hands are encased in black rubber gloves, like thick washing-up gloves. These are stretched tight over our wrists and taped down with black carpet tape to form a seal with the NBC suit. I collected my kit and followed the other crews, with my navigator, Humpo, at my side. With the gas mask on, peripheral vision is much reduced. We moved along the corridor like robots, swinging our heads from side to side to see beyond the narrow tunnel of vision from the visor.

Squeezing out of the airlock, we passed into the 'contamination' of the Vapour Hazard Area. Spare gas masks were hanging on the walls next to the airlock leading to the outer sector of the Hard, the Liquid Hazard Area. Alongside the masks were our AR5s – air crew airborne respirators – arranged in neat, named rows. The AR5 allows us to operate in 'dirty' conditions and is the finest available, but is still very hot, cumbersome and physically draining to wear.

An oxygen mask, compatible with the Tornado's systems, is attached to a wide, single visor, allowing the greater peripheral vision that is essential for flying fast-jet aircraft. Two air tubes enter the mask, giving us the look of *Star Wars* stormtroopers. One tube provides air to breathe, the other gives an air flow across the visor to stop it misting up. All of this is sealed in an outsize black rubber hood which covers our head and extends into a cape covering our shoulders and falling half way down our back. Under the cape is a bellowed collar, like a car inner tube shaped into a Tudor ruff, to allow unrestricted head movement. Should you feel airsick while flying in a contaminated environment, the recommended practice is to lift the mask from the face without breaking the neck seal, vomit into the collar and then continue flying, with puke swilling around your neck.

Until we complete the transit to the aircraft and connect ourselves to the Tornado's systems, we carry a respirator known irreverently as the 'whistling handbag', which forces air through three filter canisters into the mask. When switched on, it hums loudly. The noise of the whistling handbags, combined with the constant din of the air-conditioning system, renders us all practically deaf. Dot, the Survival Equipment Technician who works permanently in the Liquid Hazard Area, has to wear ear defenders to prevent permanent damage to her hearing.

Before passing through the airlock from the Vapour Hazard Area to the Liquid Hazard Area, I grabbed my AR5 and forced the neck seal apart. When I was ready to put it on, I glanced at Humpo, took a deep breath, closed my eyes and nodded once. Humpo immediately stripped off my gas mask and stuffed my head into my AR5, while I kept my eyes closed and my mouth shut. Humpo moved quickly around me, adjusting the seal and ensuring a snug fit and then tapped me on the shoulder. I purged any gas residue from the mask with a shout of 'Gas, gas, gas' and opened my eyes. Then I repeated the drill for him. With a thumbs-up and a nod, we picked up our whistling handbags and shuffled through the airlock into the Liquid Hazard Area – the changing rooms where our flying kit was hanging. Once we have flown in a contaminated area, the kit is kept permanently outside clean areas. Each person has a pedestal from which our G-pants and lifejacket are usually dangling, while our helmets perch on a ballcock at the top. The G-pants are skintight and fill with compressed air whenever you are 'pulling G', holding your thighs, calves and stomach in a boa constrictor-like embrace which prevents the blood from draining from your brain under the G-force.

During exercises, our flying kit is kept in impersonal black bags, to speed evacuation of the building if it proves necessary. The pedestals which usually sprouted flying kit stood as bare as winter trees, with just a single black chrysalis dangling from each one.

The roar of the air conditioning was deafening, reverberating from bare metal, with nothing to mute the noise. The galvanized steel ducts hang from exposed steel girders, the building is clinically, crudely functional. The only colours in the sea of grey steel are the black and yellow warning stripes marking out the barriers between the 'clean' and 'dirty' zones. Our reflections stared back at us from mirrored walls, not of glass because of the risk of flying debris in a bombing raid, but stainless steel, polished until gleaming. Around the room, pairs of pilots and navigators helped each other to don their flying kit. Painfully slowly, I picked up my kit, following the step-by-step instructions fixed to the wall, although they were already imprinted on my mind from constant repetitions.

The total weight of the NBC suit and all the other kit is around forty pounds and it is stiflingly hot. The Tornado has air conditioning, but we have to reach the aircraft before we can take advantage of that. In the early days in the Gulf, air crew preparing for the worst in full NBC kit were nearly passing out from the heat on the way out to their jets. Luckily the start of the war was delayed until the cooler weather of mid-winter, and in any event, the threat assessment was rapidly downgraded to allow us to fly without the encumbrance of the NBC kit.

There was no escape from wearing the full kit this time, however, and the only way to change into it is slowly; try to do it in a hurry and you merely get hot and very frazzled. In the rubber gloves my hands were hot and sweaty, and my fingers were like bananas. Buttons could not be coaxed into button holes and laces took minutes to tie, even though Humpo helped every action, like a parent dressing a child. At every move, the hoses from the whistling handbag were annoyingly in the way and had to be pushed aside.

The airflow across the visor keeps it demisted, but there is no cooling system for the rest of the body. I sweated uncontrollably, my hair matting against the helmet. I could not scratch my itchy head and was reduced to jerking the helmet to and fro, trying to kill the itch. An itch on the nose was slightly easier to deal with, because the AR5 has what is known as a 'nose occluder' – a lever on the outside of the helmet which moves two bars on the inside to squeeze your nose, so that in flight you can clear your ears when descending.

On the other side of the helmet is an anti-drowning connector attached to the air pipe, so that if you end up in the sea you will not find yourself sucking salt water, instead of air, into your lungs. During training we are forced to jump into a swimming pool to simulate ejection into the sea, countering the entirely natural fear of drowning with this huge rubber bag over our heads, by proving that the anti-drowning connector really does work. It will only work if you are still conscious when you splash down, however. The life jacket and survival dinghy inflate automatically and the survival light and radio beacon are also automatic, but the anti-drowning connector is not. Despite its name, if you are unconscious when you hit the water, you will drown.

The changing room was packed, with not a square foot unused, but I was grateful we were not on deployment somewhere. In the Gulf, we had to use 'Porton Liners' – double-skinned tents, erected inside cargo containers or concrete block-houses, and again divided into LHA, VHA and 'clean' areas by airlocks. Eight of us had to get into and out of our NBC suits in a space no more than eight feet by four, and we were expected to remain in the 'living quarters', barely more than twice the size, eating, sleeping and using the toilet, as long as the threat of chemical, biological or nuclear attack remained.

Humpo and I worked together, dressing each other and checking each other in slow motion, giving a thumbs-up and a pat on the back after each stage was completed, looking and acting like astronauts before a moon walk. One of our last acts was to pull rubber 'galoshes' over our flying boots. They would be removed just before boarding the aircraft, to prevent the risk of contaminating the cockpit. Finally I clipped on an intercom box, used to talk to the ground crew, though we can both plug into it for a cosy chat with each other as well, linked together like Siamese twins. After a final thumbs-up, we passed through the last airlock to continue the transit towards our jet. We took out our guns and emerged from the entrance of the Hard between heavy concrete screens, placed to block a sniper's line of fire.

Outside, buckets of fire belched smoke, simulating the fires left by exloding bombs, and troops armed with machine guns crouched at every corner, ready to clear our route; air crew are valuable people and every care is taken to protect us. There is no need for the enemy to go to the trouble of maintaining a layered air defence system if their special forces are able to kill or disable our pilots with a single bullet before we have even reached our aircraft. We did not run, but moved fast towards our armoured transport, past sandbagged gun emplacements, taking care to walk only on the concrete, not the grass, in case 'green parrots' – tiny minelets that can blow your foot off – had been dropped.

Our transport sped us to the Hardened Aircraft Shelter and we struggled up the ladder into our Tornado, each step torture, our bodies dragged down by the weight of the hood and the NBC kit. Even when settled in the cockpit, I was still aware of the hood. Its weight made my neck and shoulders ache, my head movement was restricted and my senses felt dulled. I could not even hear the engine noise, nor catch movement out of the corner of my eye. What was normally an almost instinctive glance at a switch or instrument had to become a deliberate head movement.

The feel of the flying controls was also less sensitive inside the rubber gloves, which felt more like boxing gloves, and it was easy to get disorientated; yet within this cumbersome survival suit, we were still expected to carry out the most delicate and intricate tasks. I glanced at the detector strip on my NBC suit. Just like workers at Sellafield, we wear patches on our protective clothing that instantly show the extent of any contamination by nuclear or chemical weapons.

The engines fired up, the blast doors rolled back and we taxied out bang on schedule. All the gates leading to the runways were closed off with barbed wire, and guards in NBC suits dragged the barricades apart, closing them off again behind us. We had allowed the minimum time to taxi to position and take off, not a second was wasted once we were outside the protective embrace of the HAS, for an aircraft on the ground is a sitting duck if another raid comes in. We moved out to join our four-ship, all radio-silent, lined up in pairs then blasted down the runway and off into the sky, our minds already fixed on the target.

Ahead lay a rendezvous with a tanker for mid-air refuelling and then a hostile mass of fighters and radar-guided missile systems, through which we somehow had to thread our way, like space invaders advancing down a screen. Close to the target were more missiles, including hand-held heat-seeking missiles – I knew only too well from the Gulf how effective they could be. Over the target airfield, there would be everything from missiles and Triple-A belching flak into the sky, to troops just lying on the ground, firing their guns into the air.

The mission was long and very arduous. Even with a fighter escort, we were 'bounced' – attacked – by fighters and scattered to the four winds three times, regrouping only to be bounced again. Somehow we threaded our way through the fighters and the maze of missile systems and hit the target bang on time, screaming in low and then soaring over the top in the classic 'loft' attack, which we were flying in the Gulf when hit by a SAM missile.

The return to base was complicated by a further 'bounce' from enemy fighters, and we finally landed back at Brüggen sweaty and dog-tired. Even after the blast doors of the HAS had rolled shut with a dull clang, we knew that we still faced an hour of hard work before we could reach the sanctuary of the Toxic-Free Area at the heart of the Hard. While I was still winding the engines down, Humpo had already clambered out of the cockpit to complete his first task back on solid ground, phoning through his mission report to the Combat Operations Centre.

On our return from the 'dirty' zone, the precautions to prevent even the faintest trace of a potentially deadly agent being carried into the key areas of the base are exhaustive and exhausting. First we had to face a security check in case we were not exhausted air crew returning from a mission, but enemy Special Forces, seeking to infiltrate the Hard. Having satisfied the guards, we began decontamination. The list of steps which we had to follow, posted in bold capitals on the wall inside the first airlock, seemed endless, and there was a further unending sequence to complete before we could pass through the Vapour Hazard Area as well. Each step is laid out in minute detail, so that even the most exhausted or battle-scarred pilot will not make a mistake that could cost him his life.

At the entrance to the Liquid Hazard Area was a tray of fuller's earth. I stood in the tray and shuffled my feet through it, stamping off the excess, as if coming in from the snow on a winter's day. We removed all our flying kit except the AR5 in the Liquid Hazard Area and then entered the Vapour Hazard Area to remove our AR5s. The safety equipper put my gas mask on and, eyes closed, I was led to a tray of fuller's earth to decontaminate my hands before adjusting the mask and drawing breath.

We moved on to an area divided into 'dirty' and 'clean' zones by a metal bar one foot high, striped in black and yellow – the Air Force warning colours used on everything from NBC contamination areas to the handles of the Tornado's ejection seats. The safety equipper stood behind the bar and as my NBC suit was gradually removed, I decontaminated first one leg and then the other, hoisting the clean leg over the bar into the clean zone. After stripping off all my other kit, I held my rubber-gloved hands behind me, the last bits still in the dirty zone, and the squipper peeled the gloves off. By the end, I was again pouring with sweat and the charcoal-lined NBC suit had left black stains on my white underwear and tinged the rest a dingy grey.

We were wearing our NBC suits when shot down in the Gulf, because the air raid sirens, warning of incoming Scud missiles, had sounded shortly before our scheduled takeoff. As a result, we were still wearing them five days later and had badly chafed arms, legs and bodies, and were tinged grey all over. Unable to wash, we remained that colour for the next seven weeks.

We passed through the final airlock to enter the Toxic-Free Area, the clean zone, with two other crews, six men squeezed together in a space the size of a small cupboard, as the air was purged for three minutes before we were allowed to continue. As it was purged, we rubbed our arms, legs, torsos and hair, to disperse any lingering traces of contaminants that had somehow survived all the previous stages of decontamination. The angry young men of war returned from airborne heroics to enter the Ops Room clad in vests and long johns.

A red weal stood out angrily around my nose and cheeks where the mask had been. I put on a fresh NBC suit and sank down in the crew room with a cup of tea, praying that there were to be no further surprises from the TACEVAL assessors that day. I had already been at work for ten hours and still had three more to do.

*

7

The margin between life and death

EVERYDAY EMERGENCIES

John Nichol: We were already travelling at over 160 knots when I realized that something had gone terribly wrong.

We had lined up on the runway on a beautiful June morning, and gone through the final checks, just as I had done a thousand times before, a set of twenty challenges and responses between navigator and pilot, covering every function of the aircraft, from the emergency power system to the arming of the ejection seats. The noise of the Tornado's twin jets rose to a scream as my pilot, 'Swirv', wound up the engines through maximum dry power and into reheat, the afterburners blasting out flames as the plane bucked and strained against the brakes.

The final checks complete, Swirv released the brakes and rammed the throttles forward. With the engines bellowing on full power, the Tornado's acceleration pinned me to my seat. From the moment the pilot releases the brakes, a Tornado fighter on full combat power will climb to 30,000 feet in less than two minutes. This was a routine takeoff, on a routine mission to 'tap' – intercept – some bombers over Northumberland, but the thrill of that awesome surge of power was still as great as it had been on my very first flight.

'Forty knots.'

'Sixty knots.' As we flashed down the runway, I called out our speed to Swirv, while both of us scanned our instruments and the warning panel for any sign of a problem. Takeoff is the most critical time for any aircraft, weighed down with a full load of fuel, a mechanical problem or the loss of an engine can be fatal.

'Eighty knots.' We needed to have 100 knots on the clock before we crossed the cable like a tripwire across the runway, which can be hooked to stop a malfunctioning aircraft either on its takeoff run or on landing, just as the cable on the flight deck of an aircraft carrier stops a speeding jet in its tracks.

'100 knots. Cable.' The first hurdle cleared. The runway controller huddled in his battered caravan, gave us a wave as we passed, reassuring us that nothing was dangling from the aircraft or had fallen off.

'120 knots.' Despite the weight of fuel, we were rocketing forward now, towards the next crucial speed marker, 135 knots. Beyond that, we would only stop for a catastrophic emergency.

'130 knots.' I scanned the warning panel and the instruments again, all were clear.

'135 knots.' The final hurdle now was 155 knots, takeoff velocity. Once beyond that speed, the pilot has only to 'rotate' – pull the stick back – and the Tornado will get airborne.

'155 knots. V-rotate.' We were committed to takeoff.

'OK. Rotating' replied Swirv, pulling back on the stick. I felt the Tornado angle slightly upwards as the nose wheel lifted and then . . . nothing. The nose had lifted, but the main wheels were stuck to the ground as if glued to it.

'160 knots.' Sweat prickled my neck. We were still increasing speed, blasting down the runway like a runaway train and apparently with as much hope of getting airborne. It was too late to abort the takeoff; we were going far too fast to stop. The cable at the departure end of the runway was useless to us; at this speed, the momentum of the aircraft with its full load of fuel would just rip the cable out of the ground. If we did not get airborne, we would go straight off the end of the runway and crash. At a speed of over two hundred miles an hour, if the impact did not kill us, the detonation of thousands of gallons of aviation fuel, ignited by two white-hot Tornado engines, certainly would.

'Swirv, what the hell's happening?'

'I don't know. It's OK.'

The next few seconds seemed to last for hours. We are trained not to panic in emergencies, to take deep breaths and think clearly. So far the training was working – just. I was still checking the instruments and calling out our speed, and Swirv was acting as if a failure to leave the runway was an everyday occurrence, but just the same, the last way to describe our predicament was 'OK'. We were well past the point of no return and had still not come off the runway.

'170 knots.' We were hurtling along, at 190 miles an hour now, with 3,000 feet of runway left and the main wheels still stuck to the ground. I tried again.

'Swirv, what the . . .' but before I could get the rest of the sentence out, I looked out of the side of the cockpit and saw the cause of the problem. We had no flaps; they had spontaneously retracted during the takeoff run. As a result, there was no curvature on the wing, and without it, no lift was being generated to get us off the ground. I felt sick.

'It's not OK at all. We've got no flaps, for Christ's sake.' Swirv selected the flaps again and again, but still nothing happened. He said nothing in reply; there was nothing useful that either of us could say.

'180 knots.' I was willing the jet into the air with every ounce of my being, but it was as earthbound as a racing car – and travelling even faster. The wheels stayed glued to the ground. It was pointless even thinking about braking, our only hope lay in more speed not less. We had to keep accelerating right to the very last inch of concrete in the hope that our sheer velocity would generate the lift that our flaps had failed to produce.

'190 knots.' We were 1,000 feet from the end of the runway now, and at the speed we were travelling, that was precisely three seconds away. Swirv began to curse the jet with every swear word in the book, threatening, cajoling, demanding, pleading with it to get airborne.

'200 knots.' I stared dully at the instruments, as our speed rose even higher, thinking: Not me; not again.

I could see the grass at the end of the runway just ahead. If we reached it before we got airborne, we were dead. Then I felt a bump as the wheels finally dragged themselves off the concrete, right at the end of the runway. The margin between life and death had come down to about fifty feet – one sixth of a second.

We were airborne, but not yet safe, for a fence was looming up. Agonizingly slowly, each second seeming to last a minute, the Tornado rose, skimming the fence and the runway lighting stanchions as we limped skywards. Swirv's four-letter monologue faltered and died with a final emphatic expletive. We lifted our landing gear and remained in the 'circuit' around the runway at 1,000 feet, while we again tried selecting the flaps, again without success; they had completely failed. I had practised the standard emergency procedures in the flight simulator until I was sick of the sight of them, but I was grateful now for the endless repetitions. This was only the second time I had faced a real emergency, and this time at least there was no SAM missile and the Tornado was not a fireball about to explode.

We still faced an emergency, but after what we had just gone through, the problems of getting down again seemed almost trivial. Without the use of flaps, we would have to land very fast. Normal landing speed is about 150 miles an hour, but we would be coming in at over 200. The wind was also very strong and blowing straight across the runway, making it difficult to control the aircraft on the approach to landing in normal circumstances; without flaps it would be impossible.

Returning to Leeming was out of the question. We flew down to Coningsby in Lincolnshire, where there was less wind and an into-wind runway. It was an unexpectedly early return to the base where I had done my training to convert to the Tornado fighter, the F3, a few months before. We circled until we had dumped all the spare fuel, getting the aircraft weight down as low as possible. In theory we dump fuel only in specified areas, but in an emergency, we have to dump it wherever we happen to be. Swirv threw two switches to open the pipes and 300 kilograms of fuel a minute began pouring out of the top of the tail fin, vaporizing on contact with the air. When the fuel load had been reduced to the minimum, Swirv closed the dump pipes and made a straight-in approach to the runway.

The airfield emergency services were all on stand-by and I could see the ambulances, camouflaged Land Rovers with a Red Cross painted on the roof, and the fire engines, manned by firemen in their fire-resistant 'space suits', positioned from one end of the runway to the other. If anything went wrong, they would be alongside the aircraft in seconds.

The cable engagement team was also ready, in case we had to take the cable. We were too fast to take the cable at the start of the runway – we would have ripped it out of the ground and torn the plane apart – but the cable at the departure end of the runway was a get-out clause for us, if things got really hairy.

We came in at over 210 miles an hour, which is extremely fast when you are only used to coming in at 150, but Swirv got us down onto the runway safely, even though the nose wheel was bucking and shaking furiously. We heaved two very big sighs of relief as the thrust-reverse buckets deployed, the engine noise inside the cockpit rising to a deafening roar as the thrust from the engines rebounded from the buckets, help-ing to slow the plane. The airframe was vibrating so hard that it felt like it was trying to shake itself apart, but we slowed to a halt before the far end of the runway, without needing to take the cable. From limping airborne with noth-ing in hand at all, we had got down again with a bit of runway to spare.

Almost before we had come to a stop, the engineers were swarming all over the plane. They took it apart, put it back together and took it apart again, but despite six hours of checks, they could not find a thing wrong with it. They were not happy, because they could not reproduce the fault, but this is a classic syndrome of any modern high-tech jet. The flying controls of a Second World War aircraft were physically connected by rods to the flaps and the other control surfaces, but in the modern 'fly-by-wire' system, the controls are connected to a computer and the computer operates the equipment. Finding a fault in a Tornado is far less simple than looking for a broken con-rod in a Spitfire. For that, all you need is a mechanic with an oily rag; to troubleshoot a Tornado, you need degrees in electronics and engineering and a brain the size of a planet, and even all that still might not be enough.

We flew the aircraft back up to Leeming that afternoon, and this time, although my heart was in my mouth as we began the takeoff run, the flaps behaved impeccably and we got airborne with several thousand feet of runway to spare. After we landed at Leeming, the engineers there put the aircraft up on jacks, connected it up to simulate flying and 'flew' it around for hundreds of hours without ever being able to find what had happened. It has flown again many times since then and never gone wrong at all.

John Peters: Even in the most dangerous mechanical or electronic emergency, you always feel that you have a chance of controlling it, using the skill and experience you have acquired. There is no conceivable fault or combination of faults that you have not already faced and dealt with in the simulator. A collision with another aircraft is not something for which you can prepare in the simulator, however, and near misses and crashes are far from rare.

Not long after John's flaps emergency, a Tornado from my own home base, RAF Brüggen, was in collision with a civilian helicopter during a low-level training flight over the Lake District. The crippled Tornado managed to make an emergency landing, but unfortunately the two men in the helicopter were killed instantly, as it spiralled out of control and crashed. The Tornado crew never even saw the helicopter, believing that they had actually hit a bird. Accidents like this bring the dangers of flying fast jets into vivid focus, especially if they involve a friend or acquaintance. To list the chain of events leading to an accident is always frightening, because it shows how narrow are the margins within which we operate, but we have to learn the lessons without allowing ourselves to brood on what has happened. We learn to accept it and almost instantly continue our work.

A Tornado and a civilian aircraft approaching each other head-on will have a closing speed of about 725 miles an hour. Aircraft flying head-on are much more difficult to spot than from above or below, and even if both pilots detect the other aircraft as soon as it becomes recognizable, the maximum distance between them, even in perfect visibility, will be just two miles.

Having identified the tiny speck in the sky as another aircraft, the pilot must then decide that it is a potential collision risk, choose a course of evasive action and allow time for the aircraft to respond to the controls. That will take a minimum of ten seconds and during that time, the distance between the two planes will have shrunk from two miles to one fifth of a mile. This is the case in perfect visibility and assuming that the pilots are alert and looking forward. In marginal conditions, neither pilot would be likely to detect the other one soon enough to take any worthwhile evasive action at all.

With the exception of the airspace around airports and heavily populated areas, where military aircraft are strictly regulated, low flying can take place anywhere in the UK, in a band from 2,000 feet down to 250 feet. The only flying permitted below this minimum height is in the military restricted areas in Scotland and Wales. Civilian aircraft flying below 2,000 feet are well aware that they risk colliding with a fast jet flying at 600 miles an hour.

Civilian aircraft passing through those height bands anywhere else are also at some risk, and low cloud can often give them little choice but to fly at those heights. Military and civilian air authorities do exchange information on flights, and do everything in their power to keep their aircraft out of each other's way, including imposing one-way systems on some bottlenecks where, because of terrain and heavily populated areas, fast jets are funnelled into a corridor perhaps as narrow as a couple of miles. Despite their best efforts, however, it is simply impossible for Air Traffic Control or anything else to remove the risk of near misses and collisions altogether.

There is no such thing as ATC – Air Traffic Control – during low-level flying for us. It is not the same as flying along the well-defined 'motorways in the sky' that civilian aircraft use. When we are flying around valleys, hugging the earth, ATC radars cannot see us at all, never mind deconflict us from other low-flying jets.

The Tornado may be a powerhouse of electronics and computers, but the best flying technology in the world is not worth a spent match without the man with his hand on the stick and the throttle. Our motto is: 'Look out. He who sees, kills', but it could equally be: 'He who sees, lives'. Our formations are designed to maximize self-defence and mutual protection, but the most important precaution of all is to keep your head 'out of the cockpit'; you actually have to learn to survey the sky. What with the HUD – the Head-Up Display – and the assorted cockpit ironmongery, that is not as easy as it sounds, and your head is always nodding from side to side as you scan the sky, changing your focus from near to far, but the keenness of the human eye is the best protection against accidental collision, just as it is against attack by an enemy in visual range. 'See and avoid' remains the only guaranteed way to fly safely.

8

One hundred and eighty!

ARMAMENT PRACTICE CAMP

John Peters: It would be perfect weather for a dream holiday, eighty-five degrees, brilliant blue skies and a roasting breeze that provides no relief from the heat, but it is no good at all for work. Once airborne, the air conditioning kicks in and things cool down, but sitting sweltering in a metal Tornado, holding for takeoff at the end of the runway at Decimomannu in Sardinia is not at all pleasant.

We go to Decimomannu – 'Deci' for short – to practise air combat, but on a very limited scale. Air combat is something that 'muds' – bombers – engage in only as a last resort. Our aim is to drop bombs on targets, not get embroiled in fights along the way. Our most important detachment at Deci is Armament Practice Camp, covering the full range of our weapons 'events' – different kinds of bombs and different methods of dropping them – matching the wide variety of targets and defensive systems we can expect to find at war.

I keep the canopy raised until the last possible moment, when an Italian voice clears us for takeoff. The dreaded two minutes begin as the canopy comes down, producing an immediate greenhouse effect. My body is instantly awash with sweat, trickling down my spine. I cannot use the aircraft's air conditioning during takeoff because it would bleed vital air from the engines, robbing them of a small percentage of their power. In the ambient temperatures of Sardinia in July, the aircraft

1. John Peters and John Nichol on one of their last flights together on XV Squadron. John Peters signs the Form 700 that releases the Tornado into his care.

2. XV Squadron partake of a few drinks before their final disbandment, some sporting their newly presented Gulf War medals. John Nichol is in the third row, Mike 'Humpo' Humphries is in the first row on the right.

3. XV Squadron's final photograph together before disbandment is a tongue-in-cheek look back to the days of dogfighting and handlebar moustaches. John Peters is seated ninth from the right, John Nichol kneels at the centre of the picture. Rupert Clark, another Iraqi prisoner of war, is fifth from the right and seated in the right-hand chair is Wing Commander Andy White, the Squadron Commander.

4. John Peters wearing the all-in-one air crew Nuclear, Biological and Chemical warfare suit. The felt-like cloth is lined with black charcoal. Black rubber gloves protect the hands.

5. Air crew leave the safety of the Toxic-Free Area dressed like this – NBC suit, rubber gloves and standard issue gas mask.

6. With the AR5 on, now protected against any vapour hazard, air crew continue to the Liquid Hazard Area. An extended visor allows for increased visibility for flying. One air tube supplies breathing air, the other forces air over the visor to keep it clear. On the nosepiece is the U-shaped lever that operates the nose occluder.

7. Half an hour later, fully dressed for a mission in an NBC environment. Covering the NBC suit is the flying suit, then shoulder holster, then life-jacket. Now almost unrecognizable, John Peters carries the 'whistling handbag', the portable ventilator that forces air through several filters before being fed to the mask. Covering the flying boots are oversized rubber socks that are removed before entering the aircraft so as not to contaminate the interior.

8. RAF Leeming on exercise; one airman gives first aid to his unlucky mate, his actions hampered by the cumbersome charcoal-impregnated NBC suit. In the background, airfield battle damage repair crew carry out repairs to the runway following an air attack; in this case filling in a bomb crater.

9. Fire and rescue crew demonstrate how to douse the flames of a burning aircraft.

10. Crash and rescue crew simulate the rescue of an incapacitated pilot from a burning Tornado F3.

11. Harp Lake, Goose Bay seen from the navigator's seat. The mirror-like surface of the water is given perspective in this photograph by the height of the aircraft. At low level, the perfect reflection of the sky in the water makes it all too easy to confuse the two, especially when flying at 600 miles an hour.

12. On exercise at Goose Bay, 31 Squadron practice covert evasion techniques. Chris Lunt takes to the ground for camouflage, while Rich Fewtrell cunningly disguises himself as a tree. Sunglasses are, of course, an essential part of any airman's survival kit!

engines need all the thrust that they can produce. The takeoff run is longer than usual, and after lifting off, we still have to complete all the checks – Gear Up, Flaps, and so on – before I can throw the switch to bring sweet relief as the air conditioning blasts a cold wall of air over me.

We climb out of Deci and follow the routeing to the Frasca range, heading north-west from the southern plain, over the patchwork of olive groves and vineyards, with specks of white buildings punctuating the terracotta landscape. The range is on a plateau set on a peninsula, a finger of land jutting out from the mountains that fringe the western coast of the island. We soar over the mountains, still lush green from the spring rains, and shimmering with heat haze, then fall towards the sea, crystal blue and sparkling in the sun. We must forget the beauty, however, for this is work. The pace begins to pick up. We call the range, check the parameters, speed and height, and our time and spacing from the other aircraft of the formation.

Green symbols glow in the HUD – Head-Up Display – in front of me, visible even in the glare of the sun. A speck in front is another aircraft, fifteen seconds – two and a half miles – ahead, but even at this distance, his jet wash causes slight turbulence. The range at Frasca is 255 feet above sea level. Over the sea we fly at 500 knots and 405 feet altitude, but approaching Frasca, skimming in over the cliffs, the height suddenly drops from 405 to 150 feet, the planned pass height over the target, giving an instant ground rush with fifteen seconds to go to target.

The aircraft ahead clears the range after completing its bombing run, radioing: 'Two, off hot', to signal that the range is free for us.

I call: 'Three, finals hot' – on my final approach to drop bombs – for clearance to attack.

The targets come into view, specks scattered across the plateau, barrels and painted circles for the bombs, white screens for the strafing runs. The 'bombs' we drop are dummies, painted bright blue with black noses which collapse on impact, detonating a small charge to give a puff of smoke and flame, showing the accuracy of the raid for the Sid Waddell of Deci, marking our scores and ready to give the perfect shots 'One hundred and eighteeee!'

Each sortie is forty minutes long, allowing a four-ship formation only twenty minutes on the range, in which each must drop eight bombs and fire up to fifty rounds of ammunition at the strafe target. Every bombing pass involves a different target and a completely different event: a front or back seat bomb – controlled by the pilot or navigator – a dive, a laydown, a loft, a 'pop' manoeuvre, using a slick or retard bomb.

A 'laydown' attack, for example, is a straight and level attack at 150 feet, the classic attack from low level, beneath the enemy radars, giving the defences little time to react. The forty-five degree dive, by contrast, brings us in on a screaming dive like a Second World War Stuka, dropping from 15,000 feet. It is extremely accurate and very effective where there is no SAM threat, keeping us outside the range of Triple-A systems until the last moments of the attack.

The retard bomb has a parachute, which deploys to slow the bomb's fall, giving us time to put some distance between ourselves and the blast as it detonates. Slick bombs are the same bombs without the parachutes and are used in loft attacks, where we fly in fast and low, then pull up sharply at a pre-determined distance from the target, extracting the maximum energy from the speed of the aircraft and the slingshot effect of the sharp climb to loft the bomb in an arc onto the target. With the onboard computer calculating the exact moment of release, it is a devastating weapon against an airfield or a command bunker. The enormous terminal velocity of the bomb drills it several feet into the ground before it explodes, ripping and buckling a huge area of concrete to put a runway out of action. Against hardened facilities, the tremendous kinetic energy drills the bomb deep into the reinforced concrete before the high explosive rips it apart.

After practising all these attacks using the full kit and computers of the Tornado, we then progressively degrade our equipment, simulating kit failure, to the point where they become 'reversionary events', dropping bombs in more old-fashioned ways, effectively a steel sight and a squinting eye. The dialogue between pilot and nav, front and back seats, is staccato, with scarcely a wasted word.

'Range is coming down.'

'Yes, I've got the target. Late arm and stick top to live.'

'Height's good, speed's good, timing's good.'

'We're cleared in hot.'

'Great. Target's slightly right – now nudge it left – that's the target.'

'Yeah, I've got it now. Lock on.'

'It's locked, it's looking good, Filming.'

'Right, committing, committing . . .'

The green symbol in my HUD marches towards the computer mark over the target and BOOOMF! the bomb comes off, we pull away and immediately go into an entirely different 'event'.

When I push the button, I say; 'Committing', rather than 'Bomb's gone' or any of the Second World War kind of stuff, because although I commit the attack when I press the weapon release button, the bomb does not come off immediately. I commit the attack about three or four seconds early, leaving the computer weapons system to do the rest, releasing the bomb at the precise time, height and speed it has calculated to hit the target.

'Reversionary bombing', on the other hand, involves dropping a bomb without the help of the computer, either by eyeballing the target in the front seat or by using a raw radar return in the back. I, or the nav in the back, who also has a button, hit the 'pickle button' – the firing button – and the bomb comes off immediately, just as in pre-silicon chip days. It means that if you are going to war and all the computer equipment in the aircraft goes down, you can still drop a bomb with reasonable accuracy. If nothing else, there will at least be secondary damage to the target; you are still throwing some high-explosive into the target area and with luck you will hit it.

Although we can go through virtually all our weapon 'events' at other European ranges, Deci is the only place in Europe

where we are allowed to do the 'reversionary loft', because it is
prone to quite large errors. Without computer guidance, the
correct moment of release is not easy to find and the reversionary loft becomes a real 'drop and hope' event, prone to considerable inaccuracy.

As we come off target, I make the radio call: 'Three, off hot'
and check the fuel, as the next member of the formation begins
his bombing run. When you call: 'Off hot' as you complete your
bombing run, there is nothing worse than hearing the range
controller reply: 'Nothing seen'. If you hear that, you begin to
sweat, because it either means that the range controller is as
blind as a bat, or, more plausibly, that you have not dropped
your bombs where you thought you had.

The next event is a forty-five degree dive-bomb. I plug in the
burners to climb to 15,000 feet. We rocket to height, no longer
glued to the terrain, but soaring over it, hovering high above
the peninsula, which now looks no more than an insignificant
spit of land far below us. As I begin the attack, the whole
peninsula disappears under the nose of the aircraft. I continue
the line of attack, the green circle in the HUD winding down
all the time. With five seconds to go, I throttle the engines to
idle and sweep the wings to forty-five degrees. At two seconds,
I roll the aircraft inverted. Suddenly the land is above my head.
I pull sharply down to point the nose of our aircraft at the
target and then roll back the right way up. We are forty-five
degrees, nose down, in a 'screaming Jesus' Stuka dive, thirty
tons of metal descending earthwards at 500 miles an hour.

My right hand twitches the stick, to position the bomb-fall
line through the target, while my left hand presses a button
twice to change the computer mode of attack. This is very
much 'rub the stomach and pat the head' stuff. I adjust the
mark on the target, as the nav calls out our heights, without a
break: 'Twelve thousand', 'Eleven', 'Ten', 'Nine'. . .each thousand
feet dropping away as quickly as he can say the words. Calling
to the nav to lock the radar on to the target, I get a height
update, make the switches live and uncover the 'pickle' button,
all the while dropping like a stone towards the earth. A shout

from the back: 'Filming', my eyes flicker once more to the parameters and then I call 'Committing' and release the bomb. In split seconds we have dropped to 7,000 feet. I pull the stick abruptly back, a four-G pull, cranking the aircraft back out of its breakneck descent.

It takes a further 2,000 feet of free fall before it recovers from the dive, and with full power on again, we climb back to height for a second pass. After five more different bombing events, we switch to firing our guns, the old-fashioned, air-to-ground weapon, two Mauser cannons with two rates of fire; slow rate at 1,000 rounds per minute, or fast rate at 1,700. The armour-piercing and high-explosive rounds wreak havoc when strafing convoys.

Already the next formation has called the Frasca Range Controller, they are six minutes out and closing. We have time enough for one, maybe two strafe passes, before we have to clear the range. The strafe targets are large white sheets, hung up like washing. Scoring is done acoustically, by microphones picking up the noise as the shots hit home. From 1,500 feet, I rolled the aircraft into a ten-degree nose dive, nothing like the rate of descent of the dive-bombing run we had just done, but at this low altitude, it still felt steep. I put the green dot in the HUD on the target. This 'death dot', as we call it, is gyro-stabilized, with the computer calculating the point of impact. Wherever you put the dot, the bullets will hit, but you still have to 'fly the dot' onto a very small target and low-level turbulence can make this difficult.

The range wound down and I squeezed the trigger. The whole airframe reverberated as the guns grunted and coughed out the rounds. A quick blip on the trigger and I once again recovered the aircraft to climb to altitude, the smell of cordite permeating the cockpit. Sweating heavily, I made the switches safe and checked fuel. That was the last pass. We joined up the formation and departed the range, as the lead aircraft of the next formation called: 'Finals hot' and began his approach.

On return to Deci, we held a 'hot debrief' while our films were rapidly processed and the formation then converged on the gloom of the cine room where, like vultures, we picked over the bones, critically assessing each other's bomb scores. There was no hiding place. Everyone fastened on to even the slightest mistake, a few knots too fast or a few feet too high, not a difficult error to make flying at 500 miles an hour and 150 feet. The banter flew as pilots and navs defended themselves.

Huddled around the black and white images in the semi-darkness, everyone was hawkishly looking for 'Pigz' – penalty points. Every mistake costs Pigz Points, which are recorded on a Pigz Board and translated into fines in time to fund a squadron party at the end of the detachment. The more mistakes you make, the more you pay towards the party.

The rules of the game are laid out in a table of 'Pigz Rools', with the Pigz Points varying, according to the more or less serious nature of the offence:

PIGZ ROOLS
Forgetting to film – 1
Bombing wrong target – 4
Dropping or attempting to drop wrong weapon type – 2
Arguing with the Qualified Weapons Instructors – 1
Deliberately cheating (and getting caught) – 2
Generally screwing up – up to 10
Sulking – 1
Imitating Italian accent on the Radio – 1
Not confessing to crimes in the hot debrief and hoping the
    Weapons Instructor won't notice in the cine room – 2
Any other cock-up not covered here, but spotted on an individual
    basis by the Qualified Weapons Instructors (yes that does
    mean that we'll make up the Rools to suit ourselves) – up to 10

At the end of the detachment we have a precision bombing competition, with all of us, like thoroughbred horses, paraded before the ground crew, who place bets on the likely winners. Of course it is all just for fun and no air crew is really concerned about where he stands in the betting . . . not!

We have a separate detachment at Deci for air-combat

training, which is far less complex than the ones that John's fighter squadron fly there, since our job is to avoid getting involved in dogfights whenever possible. Unlike John, who also has the 'Fox One' radar missile ability, our only missile is the 'Fox Two', the Sidewinder, heat-seeking missile. We fight in a bracket from base height of 10,000 feet, right up to 30,000 feet, which is a very large piece of sky. People think a dogfight takes place in a small area, but at the speed they travel, aircraft like Tornados, which are non-agile bombers without a tight turning circle, need miles of air space. Base height is not to be transgressed under any circumstances, because in real combat, base height would be zero feet – the ground, the hard and lumpy stuff that has a kill factor of 100 per cent – 'bong' the base height and you are dead.

We do not fly combat for the sake of it, but to learn to win and kill the opponent, or at the least, to know when to run away to fight another day. The pilot and navigator work together. If the nav sees the other guy before you, he talks you round on to him with sharp commands: 'Roll left. Stop. Pull stop. Left ten o'clock, low. Roll left . . .' until you have 'tally' – sight of an enemy. Once you are in the turning fight, although the navs are still meant to be able to control it, ultimately it is the pilot's 'seat of the pants' flying arena. Dogfighting is very reactive and one slight error will yield all the advantage. You would be too slow if you relied solely on the nav, so most of the navs just yell helpful encouragement like: 'Kill him, kill him, shoot him, shoot him, kill him, kill him, come on, get him'.

Once you are visual in the fight, you have your opponent in your sights all of the time, but under G, which can be three or four times the force of gravity as you turn, dive or climb, you are constantly pushing, grunting and straining to get your head around far enough to keep your eyes on him. That is why you are so vulnerable to another attack.

A two-seat aircraft like the Tornado scores in a 'two v one' or a 'multi-bogie' environment, because he who sees kills, and with two sets of eyes and someone working the radar, I can engage one guy while my nav searches for the other. If he says:

'Bug out, bug out, right', I know that while I may be winning that particular fight, there is some other guy in my six o'clock. I have to listen to my nav, because he is looking back and the guy that shoots you is the one the pilot never sees. That is why fighters come in twos or fours. Working together, one threatens the foe, making my flight path predictable, while the other positions himself to take the shot. I could be straining to escape one threat, while the unseen wingman picks his moment to kill me at his leisure.

9

A lifestyle as well as a job

LIFE ON BASE

John Peters: The RAF is very much a lifestyle as well as a job, but this is even more evident and all-consuming in Germany than in Britain, where most people live off base in their own villages or towns. They enjoy the social life that is part of the Air Force, but they also have their own local pub, and their lives centre much more around their families and civilian friends. In Germany, work and social life are never quite separate, with everything revolving around your squadron, the Officers' Mess and your Air Force friends, while UK friendships tend to be put on hold.

During the Cold War, Germany was the front line and was where careers were made, but even now a spell in Germany is still one of the most eagerly sought postings. Almost everyone lives behind 'the wire' – the base perimeter fence – and wives find themselves without jobs as the price for following their husband's career. Many resume work on returning to Britain, but in Germany much of their energy is directed into the hectic social life, in between the numerous squadron detachments.

Living on base in Germany is a bit like living in student digs. It may be your own house, but if you are having a barbecue, once the noise of the stereo and the aroma of smoked meat begins to drift on the breeze, people just pile up there and climb over the back fence, bringing a few drinks or a bit of food with them. You can start the day with a barbecue for four

95

and finish up with ten times that number. The cheapness of the booze helps the social life along enormously. A litre of gin costs about £2.50 and a crate of large bottles of Becks beer is only £6.00, so people bring far more booze than they are going to drink and just dump a crate and say 'Hi'.

We do miss two things about the UK social life: brown beer and curry – a pint of brown English beer instead of a stein of pale German lager and a red-hot curry. Germany does not have curry houses at all, and although there are some in Holland, they are not the tandooris we know and love, complete with red flock wallpaper, taped sitar music, a few drunken customers, poppadums, pints of lager and a curry hot enough to strip paint off the walls.

At one time the whole of the Air Force was one big community, wherever you were serving; you lived together, worked together, played together. Now, more and more people live outside 'the wire' and the wives are far more likely to have jobs. As a result, the old-style Air Force community has largely disappeared from the UK, but Germany still retains much of it. When I first arrived in Germany, I got lost in the atmosphere; the first couple of months just shot past. It was so exciting, being part of a squadron, flying around the world and having a tremendous time. That is the advantage of living on base. The lifestyle is compulsive and unreal in our own little world, but you can only work and play at such a pace for so long; one or two three-year tours is the maximum, otherwise you would burn out. I certainly would not want to do it for a lifetime, but for a short while the introspective lifestyle is tremendous. People who do not serve on squadrons in Germany miss out immensely.

Helen Peters: Squadron life can be rather less wonderful for the wives and families. Even in civilian life, when people from an office are in the pub and a married man is setting off home, there is always this macho man reaction of: 'Don't be such a poof, get another pint in'. In the RAF, the reaction is like that, only more so. Friday is beer-call night and the men all go straight to the Mess, getting home at anything from seven to midnight. 'Ladies' are actually not allowed in the Mess during Friday Happy Hour, between five and six – not only requested not to attend, but actually not allowed in – and if you did anything as heinous as phone the bar to find out if your husband was on his way home, he would have to buy a round for everyone in the bar. There are quite a lot of those rules and regulations.

Unlike other families, we never, ever eat with the children as a family, because there is no way that I can guarantee that John will be in at six, or six-thirty, or any specific time. It will be seven o'clock on a good day, so the likelihood of John being home in time to do anything like bath the children, feed them, eat with them, or put them to bed is vanishingly small. In Britain, a wife can have a career and a circle of friends outside the Air Force, but based on squadron in Germany, we have little choice but to play the role of devoted forces wives.

Even in the recent past, the Air Force did not appear to spend much, if any, time worrying about the welfare of the men's wives and families. The prevailing attitudes are summed up in telling little ways. An attempt to allocate thirty marks from the Brüggen Mess funds to subsidize a crèche for the children, for example, was vetoed by the Mess Committee, who felt it was a waste of money. The next item on the agenda was a request for 200 marks to pay someone to coach the Sergeants' Mess football team. That was passed without demur.

The US forces have tended to treat their men's dependants much better, going to considerable lengths to keep the forces wives happy. It made good sense for them to do so, from every point of view, for a pilot who is getting his ear bent every time he goes home because his wife is unhappy, is not likely to have his heart and mind fully on his work. The British forces at last appear to have taken that notion on board, but American concepts like 'spouse satisfaction' still seem to be regarded as little more than a joke.

*

John Nichol: The operational side of a British base like Leeming is not that different from one in Germany, but the social life is a world apart. Forces personnel always seem to have the reputation of being 'men about town', wherever they are stationed. For the single men, the reputation is possibly justified, but there is perhaps less temptation for a married bloke to be 'one of the lads' than outsiders might think, particularly when stationed on a base in Britain. We go away as a squadron so often anyway – at least once a month for anything from a week to four weeks, or even three months in the case of Bosnia – so everyone can get out and party then. Most of the wives understand and accept that the guys are going to be away a lot, it is part of the Air Force life, but when we come home, most people want to leave it all behind and relax a little with their families.

In days gone by, we would all regularly go into the bar and get absolutely 'hoovered', but things are different now. There are always parties and dinner parties at weekends, but during the week, people tend to chill out a little. A lot of guys do not drink at all during the week and most of the others just go into the bar after work, have a pint and then wander off home. I tend not to go into the bar very much, because I am not the type to sit around sipping a mineral water and I will not drink if I am driving home. My social life revolves much more around my friends down in Ripon, some of them service, some not. Quite a few of the squadron guys live there; it is the only town of any size within an easy twenty-minute drive of Leeming. It has a few good pubs and restaurants, and enough people live there to make for a decent social life.

There are about three formal dining-in nights a year when the whole squadron dines together, either in the Mess or at a restaurant, to say farewell to people who are leaving and welcome those who have just arrived. In addition to the dining-in nights, there are three big social events of the Air Force year: the station Summer Ball, the Christmas Draw and the Battle of Britain cocktail party.

On the bases in Germany, the Battle of Britain cocktail party is called a 'Spring Reception', for obvious reasons of tact, and is even held on a different weekend. The officers host local dignitaries, and after everyone has had a few drinks, the RAF Germany band marches up and down for a while and the day ends with a formal ceremony. There is a drum roll, followed by the national anthem, and then the Last Post is sounded as the flag is lowered, with all the guys standing to attention. As the final note fades away, a formation flies overhead – all very stirring stuff.

An interesting variation on this theme was introduced at Laarbruch one year, when our Station Commander, Group Captain Neil Buckland, stood rigidly to attention and solemnly began his salute, only for the drum roll to segue straight into a jaunty rendition of 'Copa, Copacabana' as the rest of us stood, shoulders shaking, trying desperately not to catch his eye. I think he saw the funny side of it ... eventually. When XV Squadron was disbanded a couple of months later, there was only one tune we could use to introduce the Station Commander's farewell speech.

We also have 'all-ranks parties' a few times a year, when we get together with the airmen. It happened much more regularly in Germany, because everybody was together on base there anyway, but at Leeming the social life is not all that heavy, as a lot of the guys live off camp. We only have the odd social together, but even so, there is still a lot of: 'Oh bloody hell, why do we have to go to the airmen's bar?' or 'Why do we have to go to the officers' bar?'

I enjoy the all-ranks parties, although I know a lot of people do not, and I think it is also important that the ground crew realize how much they are appreciated. A lot of air crew might just walk in and say: 'Right, the aircraft's broken, fix it' and forget that those guys are working hard, probably harder than we do a lot of the time.

We could land at six o'clock, after flying a really rewarding sortie, say: 'Sorry we've knackered your jet' and walk out. It might take ten hours to fix it and we will then wander back in after a good night's sleep and go off and fly it again. You always have to remember that there is a huge organization behind the one aircraft that you are flying. There are probably three and a half thousand people working to keep forty aircraft and one hundred air crew flying, but a lot of the guys tend to forget about those support staff. It is vital that everyone, including the most junior member of the ground crew, feels that he is part of the team. After all, multi-million pound aircraft can be rendered useless if the guy checking the oil does not do his job.

10

The most exciting flying

DISTANT FRONTIER, ALASKA

John Peters: Checking the oil is particularly important on the NATO exercises held in the wilds of Alaska and northern Canada, which are incredibly hard work, providing us with a fantastic chance to practise our wartime skills flat out. We experience the most demanding and exciting peacetime flying of all as day-to-day speed and height restrictions, in force throughout Europe, are relaxed to allow us to push both the jets and ourselves to the legal limit.

Distant Frontier is a joint RAF/USAF exercise held in August at the huge Eielson United States Air Force base in the middle of Alaska, just 200 kilometres south of the Arctic Circle. The base is in the Yukon military operating area where we can go supersonic, operating to war speeds. To the south of the area, there are huge mountains, ranging up to the highest in America, Mount McKinley. To the north lies the valley of the Yukon river, desolate tundra spattered with a myriad of lakes and ponds.

An F3 squadron, 43, was there as well, supporting us in practice combat against American F-15s and F-16s. They fly so fast and the operational area is so great – 7,000 square miles – that they can be in two fights at once, separated by as much as fifty miles, pumping out of one scrap at top speed to blast into another one a couple of minutes later.

Even in that vast area, the risk of a collision was very real, particularly flying in the narrow, twisting valleys south of the tundra. I was an impotent bystander when another pilot found that his number was up. An American fighter, an F-16, dogfighting with one of our Tornado F3s, flew into a hillside, killing the pilot instantly. A group of our Tornado bombers, escorted by the F3s, had been engaged by the F-16s. The bombers ran for it, leaving the fighters to battle it out. They could see the mix-up going on above their heads; they were down among the weeds, trying to hide, while high in the sky up above, all hell was breaking loose. One of the F-16 pilots tried to roll his aircraft but fatally misjudged his height. The crash site was only seventy feet across; the plane just 'tent pegged' – smashed straight into the ground.

The Boss, Wing Commander Ian Hall, came into the planning room where I and my navigator, 'Torbs', and the rest of our formation were planning for the afternoon wave. To pre-empt any rumours, he quietly called the boys together and broke the news that the F-16 pilot had been killed, prompting a spate of questions: 'How, where, what happened?' 'Has he got a wife and kids?' 'Why do they always have young children?'

The F3 crews returned from their sortie looking drained. They had been fighting the F-16s, trying to achieve a simulated 'kill' with their missiles when the real death occurred. Very subdued, they changed and were whisked away into debriefing. Morbid curiosity made me want to question them about what they had seen, but this was not the time for gossip. Seeing an aircraft crash and the pall of smoke rising into the air leaves an emptiness inside you and a feeling of desolation that makes idle chatter the last thing on your mind.

All the F-16s were grounded until it was established that the crash had not been caused by an aircraft failure. The accident system took over as the evidence for an inquiry was collected, seeking the unadorned facts, before the distorting mirror of individual memory took over. The F-16 squadron became automated and in limbo as officialdom, not uncaring or insensitive, but relentlessly professional, tried to get to the root of the accident, so that the necessary lessons could be learned to prevent the tragedy occurring again. It is the Air Force attitude: learn from your own mistakes; even better, learn from someone else's, however unfortunate.

The accident was a severe shock to all of us, but it was quite transient, quickly fading as we resumed our work. The F-16 squadron did not take part in the rest of the week-long exercise, but as they would have expected, we continued to fly, indeed we flew again the same afternoon. To outsiders it might have seemed callous or indifferent to return to the air so soon, but there was another time and place to give emotions free rein.

On the Friday the F-16 guys invited us into the bar for 'goodbye drinks', as a wake for the dead pilot. In Royal Air Force tradition, the deceased man's bar book is left open for one night and everyone drinks at his expense. The following morning, the bill is written off. His squadron had already set up a fund to put his children through school, to which we contributed, and now they wanted to toast their departed friend. It was held in the Officers' Club bar, its wood-panelled walls lined with hunting trophies – moose heads and bear skins. The jukebox played softly but was drowned in the noise as each man drank a toast to lost friends and celebrated his own survival. Some sang rowdy bar songs, the Brits in their bright green flying suits competing in volume with the Americans in darker green 'olive drab'. Other people sat in quieter groups, having deeper conversations.

This was the release for us all, and we had all been through the grief of losing a friend and comrade at some time. I drank a lot of beer and got pissed. Never having met the dead pilot, I had no personal grief to express, but I listened to anybody who wanted to talk about him; they knew we would understand, because we fly fast jets too.

Even over flat land, we fly so low that our camouflaged shapes meld with the ground. It is a double-edged sword; if we are glad that we are hard for enemies to spot, there are times when we wish we were a little more visible to each other. Even in normal tactical formation, two miles abeam, it is often a case of 'now you see him, now you don't'. Torbs, my back-seater, constantly gives me updates on my wingman's position as we twist and turn through the terrain. The moment we are 'tapped' – looked at – by fighters, we split and widen, scattering out of visual range of each other to make ourselves more difficult targets. We have to crosstalk to update each other on the threat and to avoid the risk of collision as we converge on the next timing point. We have to hold a mental air picture of the whereabouts of the rest of our aircraft, even split by ten or fifteen miles, crosschecking our distance from the next reference point and our heading towards it. If we lose track of any of the components of the air picture, we could end up dead. The theory is fine, of course, but when the weather is poor, there are twelve aircraft in the sky, the adrenalin is pumping and we are being attacked, it is not quite so easy coolly to assess where everyone else might be.

In Alaska, with all the hills around, as soon as we disap-peared into the valleys, our radios were blanked and we flew 'blind' with only a mental air picture of where the other aircraft could be. One day we were in a straight fight, with four of us facing six F3s. We were 'tapped' and immediately split out of visual range. My number two went right into one valley, I went into the next on a different course, about twenty-five miles from our next navigational point. I got a trace on my radar warner – an indication that a fighter was looking at me with its radar – and easing it onto the nine o'clock, I plugged the burners in to get maximum speed – fighting speed – but steadily the trace travelled round, through the eight and seven o'clocks. The speed of rotation told me that I was the chosen one, the fighter's victim for the day. The adrenalin began to pump. My number two confirmed my fears, calling 'F3 in your stern'.

I rammed the aircraft down into the deck of the valley, snug against the left-hand wall of broken rock, trying to hide from the fighter's radar. As yet the fighter would not have seen me, it was closing on the information from his radar. My only hope was to lose him before he could get visual with me. Ahead there was a ridge about 2,000 feet high, a cliff face closing off the end of the valley. I had no choice, nowhere else to go but over it into the next valley, even though the fighter would see me as I popped up over the ridge.

Reluctant to expose ourselves, but faced with the inevitable, I yanked the stick back and raced to the summit of the ridge. Before reaching the craggy top, I slammed on bank and rolled inverted to limit our exposure time above the line of the ridge. I yanked the nose down to hug the ridge line, flying upside down, 100 feet from the jagged rocks, at 600 miles an hour. As soon as we dropped below the ridge, I plugged the burners back in, to regain the speed lost in the climb and sent the aircraft plummeting downwards, towards the valley floor, rolling the jet back the right way up as we dropped.

I glanced left and right and caught a glint of light from the reflective strips on the back of Torbs' helmet – my navigator – as he pushed against the casing of his computer screens, twisting his head and shoulders around hard against his straps to catch sight of the fighter. Torbs shouted: 'The F3 is closing', and the trace on my RHWR – Radar Homing and Warning Receiver – grew larger. I hugged the ground. Now it was a trailchase; the fighter was six miles in trail and gaining, even though I was flying at 600 knots. A dogleg in the valley loomed up, around a column of rock. I smacked the Tornado into a hard turn around the rock as the fighter strobed us for the first time, the radar warning that the fighter had locked us up on its radar, the prelude to firing a missile. I lost fifty knots making the turn, but broke the lock, and again kicked in the burners to push me back up to the maximum 600 knots – over 700 miles per hour.

The ground blurred beneath us. For all the threat from the fighter's missiles, they only achieve a probability kill ratio of about seventy per cent; the ground remains the greatest threat, with a probability kill of 100 per cent. Suddenly the fighter was right in my drawers and I was running scared, caught in the middle of a valley with nowhere to hide. At that range, without a place for the bomber to hide, the fighter always wins.

I had already been through the target and did not even have a bomb left to try and throw in his face. The strobing started – sirens clamoured in my ears, warning of the missile lock. I was jamming, chaffing, breaking left and right, but he would not give up. I was desperate, caught like an animal in a trap, hearing the footsteps of the poacher approaching. Torbs was screaming: 'His range is coming down, do something – anything!', but suddenly the sirens died away as the F3 pulled off up to height in a lazy left-hand turn. I eased back out of combat power and called back to Torbs: 'Maybe we were lucky and he ran out of fuel before he could get the shot off', but we both knew that it was nonsense. He had fired off all his missiles and, had we been at war, we would have been shot to pieces. In the debrief afterwards, I discovered that the F3 had been doing 750 knots, almost 900 miles an hour at low level – no wonder he had gained on us.

We dropped back down to 450 knots, flashing over a moonscape of rock and water towards the Yukon river and our next rendezvous, Point Foxtrot. I called up the other members of the four-ship, preparing to regroup the formation and head for home. I saw nothing out of the ordinary as we formed up and climbed to height for the homeward run, but during the debrief after the mission, we discovered that the back pair of the formation had both entered a valley on convergent headings, resulting in a hair-raising near miss. One pilot told me that he did not even have time to flinch as a shadow momentarily darkened his cockpit. It was cast by the other aircraft flashing over the canopy of his jet, travelling at 700 miles an hour. In 7,000 square miles of area and 40,000 feet of operating height, he had escaped certain death by a distance of ten feet. When we landed he was still ashen-faced, thinking about his narrow escape.

Operating close to the limits always has its dangers but coming to terms with this dangerously alien terrain was a huge learning curve for us all. This incident was so serious that it required more than just the normal post-mission debrief by the formation. Our Boss, Ian Hall, called the whole squadron together to talk through every aspect of the incident and establish procedures to ensure that it could never happen again.

Off duty at Eielson, we stayed in a four-storey accommodation block, nicknamed 'Alcatraz', its exterior and surroundings a sea of bare grey concrete, pierced only by rows of tiny windows. The rooms were anything but prison-like, however, and quite unlike those in a British Mess, which still seem to be marooned in the 1950s. A room in a British Mess contains a bed, a wardrobe, a sink and nothing much else. The American quarters have a television, video, refrigerator, microwave, coffee machine, iron, ironing board and full en suite facilities. The same disparity was evident in the medical facilities at the start of the Gulf War. The American ones were out of this world, so good, in fact, that a hasty improvement was ordered in the British medical facilities. What had been regarded as good enough to deal with the casualties of Armageddon – an all-out nuclear war against the Soviet hordes – was suddenly not good enough for a limited war against Iraq. The comparison between the 'belt and braces' British facilities and the top-of-the-range American ones was just too glaring; new equipment was rapidly shipped in.

The imbalance goes all the way down the line. If the Brits have to open an airfield, we seem content to put in the airstrip first and if we run out of money, everyone will live in tents until we can afford to build accommodation. The Americans do not seem to go ahead until they can equip the base with everything – the swimming pool, the cinema, the McDonald's – because that is the way they operate. Eielson was typical. The base itself is huge. We have an 8,000 feet runway at Brüggen, but the runway at Eielson is twice as long, with literally miles of aircraft pans and concrete hard standing. There were superbly-equipped gymnasia to get us fit and superbly-equipped fast-food emporia to reverse the process as quickly as possible.

Fairbanks, the nearest town of any size to Eielson, is forty kilometres away. On our first day there, Jack, Lunty, Shoppo, Neil Johnson and I drove down to have a look. On the way we passed through the tiny town of North Pole, where we called in at the Father Christmas centre, alleged home of Santa Claus. You can buy a piece of the North Pole from there, if you really feel you must. An Alaskan souvenir shop nearby had 'swizzles' on sale, which turned out to be dried moose droppings on the end of a stick. They were the same shape as rabbit turds, but about an inch and a half long by half an inch wide. Inspired by this discovery, Lunty spent the next few hours screeching to a halt whenever he saw a pile of droppings in the road and scooping them up. Being frozen solid and completely dry and hard, they were not too unpleasant to handle, or so he assured us.

The purpose of his unusual collection became apparent when I got up the next morning. I took the top off my shaving foam and out dropped a moose turd. I got into my flying suit and found moose shit in the pocket. There were moose turds in my shoes, my clothes, my bags, my bedside table, even my books; there was moose shit absolutely everywhere. A burst of swearing from Jack Calder's room suggested that Lunty had also been busy in there. In revenge for this indignity, I sneaked into Lunty's room while he was out, covered the blades of his ceiling fan with about two pounds of talcum powder and sat back happily to await his return. Unfortunately a cleaning lady got there first, switched on the fan and emerged a few moments later, white as a ghost and emitting banshee wails of distress, while a fine white mist covered every object and surface in Lunty's room.

Out in the wilds, three hours from North Pole, Fairbanks, or anywhere else, we passed an even more bizarre sight than 'swizzles', a shop open twenty-four hours a day, stuck in the middle of nowhere, selling nothing but fireworks. As we drove into Fairbanks we passed churches of every denonimation under the sun, about one church per head of population, and almost as many gun shops; I am not sure which was more frightening. All the houses are raised on poles three feet above the ground to insulate them from the permafrost, for just below the surface the temperature never rises above freezing. Outside every house and all along the sidewalks are banks of electric sockets, where you can plug in your car to stop the radiator from freezing solid while you do your shopping or have a drink.

Flying around the world we get used to heading into seedy bars, which are invariably the most lively places in town. I have been in an awful lot of them, but on a seediness scale from one to ten, the 'Mecca Bar', an 'ethnic' bar in downtown Fairbanks, would rate at least nine and a half – peeling lino, paper hanging off the walls and half the mirrors behind the bar broken. The bar was full of dropouts and drunks and we were highly thankful that there were seven of us. It was like a scene from *Deliverance*. I was almost sure I could hear the twang of a banjo playing, and at any moment I expected someone to lurch towards us, saying: 'Squeeel like a pig, boy'.

Instead, a 'friendly' local about thirty years old came over to say hello, unhampered by not having a single tooth in his mouth. All had been recently extracted, possibly by force, judging from the state of his gums. He told us he was a Vietnam 'vet', which was highly unlikely as he was much too young, but I bet he says that to all the British tourists. He was a fur trapper, who lived 300 miles further north of Fairbanks with his wife and five kids, right inside the Arctic Circle. He came down to town to sell his furs and have what passes for a big night out in Fairbanks. For half the year, he was completely cut off from even the 'civilization' of Fairbanks, living on what he could find, catch and kill, like a hunter-gatherer from prehistoric times. It would take him a week to make the return journey to his crude cabin in the wilds, we would go back to the high-tech Eielson base and could be flying over the top of his home inside fifty minutes. I could not imagine what he did with his time, nor, I am sure, could he understand how we spent ours. Our lives were so far removed from each other that there was almost no point of contact at all.

On our way out of another bar we noticed a sign, like a small ad in a corner shop, with a photo of a young couple standing in front of a light aircraft. The caption read: 'Have you seen this aircraft? Last took off from Fairbanks en route to Anchorage. Never arrived.' Alaska may be beautiful, but it is still a harsh and unforgiving place where a person – or a plane – can disappear, never to be found. We were lucky to see it in its two-month summer 'window'; for the rest of the year, it is wall-to-wall snow and ice, though the base continues to operate, with the planes landing and taking off from runways covered in frozen, compacted snow.

After seeing that advertisement, we paid more than usual attention to our survival briefing the next morning. The information on what to do, should we be unfortunate enough to have to 'bang out' – eject – in the flying area was succinct; start praying. There are no airfields, no towns and no roads; with the exception of the trans-Alaska oil pipeline, there is nothing at all out there except forest, mountain, lake and tundra.

A picture of a grizzly bear was flashed on the screen. 'Welcome to the Alaskan food-chain' quipped the instructor – standard Air Force practice, start with the worst case scenario of having to eject into this frighteningly inhospitable terrain. 'If a twelve-foot, 400 lb grizzly shows some interest in you' continued the instructor, 'do not run, they can outrun you. If you had been flying in a two-seater, then you could consider running for it, but only if you were carrying a fat navigator and were confident of out-pacing him ... Seriously, if you get too close to a grizzly, your best tactic is to roll up into a ball. The bear may play with you and he might even give you a little nip, but with luck, he will lose interest and pass on.' Playing football with a 400 lb grizzly sounded no fun at all, especially if you were the football, and with its steel-trap jaws, the 'little nip' so blithely dismissed by the instructor, sounded pretty terminal to me. His advice was about as useful as a chocolate teapot. I cast a sideways glance at Torbs, to see if he would justify the description of 'fat navigator' if the worst came to the worst. Unfortunately for me, Torbs was a swift fullback with the Brüggen rugby team, rather than an overweight prop-forward.

Like all his ilk, the survival instructor went on to list every conceivable food source available in the wild – plants, shrubs, birds, animals, invertebrates and insects. As Crocodile Dundee once remarked: 'It keeps you alive, but it tastes like shit.'

We were also lectured on survival techniques in deep snow and temperatures well below zero, but we found that our arctic clothing was not needed, as a freak spell of warm weather, with temperatures up to 18 Celsius, exceptional even for August, removed any threat of us freezing to death. Unfortunately the conditions also proved ideal for mosquito breeding. The mosquitoes looked like black aircraft carriers and swarmed in their millions. Grown men have been reduced to tears by their persistent swarming and stinging bites, while their inescapable, endless, undulating buzzing can shred a man's nerves. A couple of days in the 'bondoo' – the back of beyond – would drive anyone completely insane. I would not have starved to death, I would have shot myself or gone and found a grizzly to play football with first, just to get away from the mosquitoes.

Having turned and burned, flown 'blind' through the mountains and skimmed the tundra of north Alaska, I was given another new experience at the end of the exercise, the chance to fly nonstop right across the whole of the North American continent, from Eielson to a base on the east coast of Canada. At those latitudes, it is a journey about one third of the way around the globe. The flight involved four midair refuelling slots and took seven-and-a-half hours, a long time to be strapped into an ejector seat. The flight brought home the almost unimaginable scale of the region. I had never flown over Hudson Bay before, nor realized how enormous it is; we were flying over it for two hours. Looking down I could see the ice, rippled and broken with cracks as the summer thaw took hold. The surface snow was brown, filthy from pollution.

We grew increasingly uncomfortable on the everlasting flight, cramped in the cockpit. Flying a fast jet is an incredibly bum-numbing experience at the best of times, but sitting in one for over seven hours is torture. The seat is a rock-hard fibreglass block and you cannot have a cushion on it, because if you are forced to eject, the gap between you and the seat created by the cushion means that the seat will be forced up against you so hard it will break your legs.

Our one concession to in-flight luxury is a 'hi-fi system'. Our mission plans are recorded as dots and beeps on audio tape and loaded into the aircraft's computers. By making a few switch and button changes, the system can also be persuaded to play your favourite audio tape as well. It would not be good policy to be humming along to Dire Straits in wartime, or while on exercise, but it helps to pass the miles on a long-haul, routine flight.

Our packed lunch came in a little white cardboard box, including juice in squashy containers, like you give to small children. There were no proper sandwiches, which are a real pain to eat in a cockpit, invariably ending up with a stray prawn jamming up your controls. Instead we were given more baby food – bread 'soldiers'. After drinking a couple of cartons of juice, I started looking around for my 'pee bag', a thick, rubbery plastic bag, with a sponge inside it and a neck which fortunately incorporates a non-return valve. On a long flight, you end up with a collection of used bags, tucked behind your ejection seat.

If you need a pee – and inevitably you do on a long flight – you have to make sure that the pins are in your seat, so the seat does not go off while you are relieving yourself. This actually happened to an American F-16 pilot over Bosnia; one minute he was relieving himself into his plastic bag, the next he was dangling from a parachute, still with his pee bag firmly attached to the relevant portion of his anatomy, while £20 million worth of American military hardware plummeted nose-first into the ground. Spending a penny is one thing, but spending £20 million seems a little excessive.

Relieving yourself into the bag is a very delicate operation, even if the seat does not go off underneath you while you are doing so. You unstrap yourself and then have what seems like twenty layers of kit to undo. Your G-suit covers your pelvic bone, so you have to push that up, undo the buttons of your cold weather kit, unzip your flying suit, get through your long johns and your underpants and finally – Eureka – you are ready to use the pee bag. Having done all that, you have to be able to relax enough to be able to urinate. One Tornado pilot was temperamentally incapable of taking a pee while sitting down. Luckily he was a little guy, so he used to lower his seat all the way down to the bottom, turn around and kneel on the seat clutching his pee bag in one hand, while hanging on to the back of the seat with the other. Not an easy task at 500 miles an hour, 20,000 feet above the ground. While peeing, you are praying all the while that the autopilot does not jump out, which can sometimes happen, sending the aircraft off abruptly in some entirely inappropriate direction.

Other personal emergencies can be less easy to deal with than a full bladder. RAF legend tells of the pilot suffering from a stomach bug, who was so desperate for a crap that he had to take one in his aircraft, struggling out of his immersion suit, which normally takes ten minutes to do, even in the relative comfort of the changing room, and being forced to use the only receptacle available; his flying glove. In the tight confines of a Tornado cockpit, the remainder of the journey cannot have been pleasant for either the pilot or the navigator.

John Nichol: The other unpleasant personal problem that can affect air crew is airsickness. Navigators are particularly prone to it, just as car passengers are more likely to be carsick than the driver. The navs are entirely in someone else's hands, having to read maps, use their stopwatches and check their computer screens, without any control over their 'attitude', as they are thrown into turns and rolled upside down, with little or no warning. There are guys who have been in the Air Force for ten years, but who are still sick every single time they fly. It must be a horrible way to go to work every day, knowing that in a couple of hours' time, you will have your head in a NATO standard-issue sick bag, bringing up your breakfast.

A good mate of mine used to be sick every time he went flying. Knowing this, I helpfully cut the bottom out of his sick bag one day, and restored it, neatly folded, to its place, before he took to the air. Twenty minutes into his sortie, he groaned and reached for the bag, only discovering too late that he was puking into a hollow tube. My merry prank was definitely not appreciated at the time, but he forgave me in the end; I was best man at his wedding.

The RAF has an anti-sickness course that the chronically airsick can attend, but it is definitely kill or cure. They take you out of the system for three months, put you in a simulator and spin you around, turn you upside down and inside out. They make you so sick that from then on, the most extreme motions of a fast jet will never bother you again, but some navs prefer to go on reaching for the blue paper bag every mission, rather than face the misery of the three month anti-sickness course.

11

A razor's edge
EMERGENCY LANDINGS

John Nichol: 'State Two. State Two. Buccaneer inbound with
a landing gear problem.'

The announcement came over the Leeming tannoy at ten
o'clock on a September morning. There are three 'states' for
the airfield emergency service. 'State Three' means get ready,
something is happening. 'State Two' is the instruction for the
emergency crews to man their vehicles and get out to the
runway and 'State One' means that an accident has already
happened somewhere on the airfield.

The fire and ambulance crews piled out to their vehicles
while the rest of us swapped rumours about what was going
on. The word was that the Buccaneer's landing gear had
suddenly come down during flight, which is a pretty unpleasant,
not to say dangerous, experience. On a good day it is catastrophic,
on a bad day it is fatal. Having 'flimsy' wheels coming down at 500
miles an hour is a sure recipe for disaster, which is more or less
exactly what happened. The 'gear limiting speed' is normally
about 250 miles an hour, which means that if you are travelling any
faster than that, you do not want to have your landing gear down,
because it will inevitably be damaged.

The Buccaneer had been on exercise off the Irish coast,
flying at a hundred feet over the sea, doing a practice attack on
a naval ship, and had pulled into a turn at 480 knots – 550
miles an hour – when the landing gear spontaneously dropped

down. They had flown 800 miles to reach Leeming, with hydraulic fluid leaking out of the system because the pipes had been ripped off when the gear dropped down. There was also a fuel leak, forcing them into a midair refuelling from a tanker.

With all the landing gear damaged, the emergency procedure, detailed on the aircraft's emergency cards, was to make a normal landing approach, get the plane down on the runway and take the approach-end cable to come to a halt. Since the landing gear had been torn apart and the brakes were attached to the landing gear, the cable was the only thing that could stop the aircraft anyway. They had had no alternative but to fly all the way from the Irish coast to Leeming, passing one airfield after another, because all the others either did not have good weather or had no runway cable.

We did not know all of this at the time, but because the Buccaneer was coming in on a 'Mayday' call – a dire emergency taking precedence over all other air traffic – we knew that it was going to be a pretty serious emergency, so everyone, myself included, started to gather outside the hangars, watching the runway. A few even brought their cameras in case there was a chance to get some pictures of a Buccaneer crashing. This was not morbid, it was just morbid curiosity. A search and rescue helicopter, which had been scrambled in case the aircraft came down before it reached Leeming, also appeared and hovered over the airfield.

The Buccaneer eventually emerged out of the mist about three miles away, came in, touched down and took the cable. There was a puff of smoke from the landing gear as it did so and nothing else for a couple of seconds. Then suddenly the left landing gear collapsed completely, the wing hitting the runway in a torrent of sparks and bursting into flames. The pilot managed to get the wing back off the ground, wrestling the stick the other way, but almost immediately the aircraft slewed off the runway and onto the grass, with flames still belching out of the left wing. Luckily for the crew, the cable held. Although the Buccaneer carved out a huge furrow of grass and earth like a giant ploughshare, the aircraft remained upright and the cable dragged it to a halt within one hundred yards. The emergency vehicles were round the aircraft in seconds, throwing ladders against the sides to rescue the crew.

The crew had probably got through a year's supply of adrenalin in the two-and-a-half hour flight back to Leeming; they were shaken, but luckily unstirred. Our first-rate medical team can never get enough chances to practise their valuable skills, however, and before the crew's feet had even touched the ground, they were being whisked away to the medical centre, where the team were testing their eyes and blood pressure and checking whether they needed their wisdom teeth removed.

After an hour or so of this, we decided the poor Buccaneer crew had suffered enough for one day and rescued them from the medical centre, administering further remedial treatment in the shape of a few medicinal beers in the crew room instead. The crew admitted that they had been pretty scared by the whole experience and were very glad to be alive. Apart from that, they were remarkably calm, considering that they had been just a hair's breadth from disaster.

It was a dining-in night for XI Squadron and normally the guys would have been eager to get off home to change into their finery, but the abrupt arrival of a crashed Buccaneer changed all that. Everyone wanted to stick around in the crew room, chew the cud and learn from the Buccaneer crew's experience – how did it happen, why, where and when – all of us wanting to know every detail, because it might help us survive a similar problem in the future. In fast-jet terms, the difference between life and death can often be as narrow as a razor's edge, and this time at least, they had finished on the right side of that narrow line.

The very next day, I had extremely good cause to empathize with the crew of the Buccaneer, as my pilot, 'Guido', and I were returning from a routine training sortie. All the pilots regularly have to do a number of basic manoeuvres with the aircraft, and Guido decided that he would practise one of his 'roller' landings – putting the wheels down, but then overshooting the runway to go round again.

We broke into the circuit in the way that dates from the 1940s, when radios were rather less sophisticated. We announced our arrival on the airfield by blasting in at 400 knots, keeping up our speed in case we were 'bounced' by enemy aircraft, and then bleeding off our speed by 'breaking' into the circuit, 'pulling a max rate turn' – the hardest possible turn – which immediately washes off all the speed. We then flew down the side of the runway, came round on our approach and Guido plonked our wheels down. We rolled down the runway, put the power back up and took off again. We went through our routine checks, put the landing gear up at 235 knots, and went back round to the downwind position, parallel to the runway, ready to go in and land again. Guido called: 'Gear coming down' and lowered the landing gear.

Three red warning lights on the control panel show that the gear and the doors are unlocked, three green lights means the gear is down and locked, the safe configuration. The gear came down, but as well as three green lights, we also had a red warning light on the nose-wheel gear. Normally it is either red or green alone; the gear is either safe or unsafe; being told that it was simultaneously safe and unsafe was confusing and worrying. I did not immediately start thinking: 'Oh my God, I'm going to die', but it was certainly not a simple fault like losing one of the inertial navigation systems or part of the computer. A problem with the landing gear immediately gets you thinking hard.

I grabbed the flight reference cards, covering every possible emergency, and flicked through to the heading 'Landing Emergencies'. There is no room for individual action or differences of interpretation in the cards, which tell you exactly what you must do, and you follow those instructions to the letter. If you do not and are lucky enough to survive, you could face a court martial.

The first instruction was: 'If any red light remains on, the emergency must be actioned as though the gear is unsafe, even if it appears to be safe'. Step two was to recycle the gear once. Guido brought the landing gear up and all the lights went out –

the gear was stowed and safe. As soon as he put it down again, we got the same three green lights and one red one.

Before we did anything else, we flew past the tower and asked them to look at the landing gear as we went past, because if the gear had been half-cocked – not fully extended – we would have known we had a real problem. The guy in the tower told us that the gear looked down and safe, but it is very difficult for a man with a pair of binoculars in the tower to track you and see that the locking strut is down, when you are flying past him at 200 miles an hour.

I went back to the cards. The next step was: 'If the gear still appears to be unsafe, use the emergency undercarriage lowering'. Normally the gear is lowered on a set of hydraulic systems, but in an emergency we can pull a big black and yellow lever which shoots nitrogen into the system to jettison the gear down and lock it. Once that has happened, the gear cannot be retracted again. I did not really feel like doing this, because playing with black and yellow handles in the cockpit always means that you are starting to get a real emergency, but we had no choice.

Guido pulled on the handle. Nothing happened. We still had three green lights and one red one and we now really did have an emergency, because apart from the landing gear problem, we had also dropped below our minimum landing fuel – the fuel that we had to hold to allow a diversion to another airfield if something put Leeming out of action. In circling around, wrestling with our landing gear, we had used up so much fuel that we no longer had enough to divert to anywhere, even Teesside twenty miles up the road. We had no other choice but to stay at Leeming and land there.

Things were starting to get a little bit more tense. The blood was beginning to pump a bit faster and the breathing was getting heavier. We have a phrase 'a warm and fuzzy feeling', which is the way you should always be feeling in your aircraft – cosy, warm and contented. We were not feeling warm and fuzzy at all. We flew past the tower again and the guy with the binoculars again told us that the gear looked down and straight, but he could not tell whether it was safely locked. I read through the rest of the emergency card, which told me that we had to go into the procedure for landing with the undercarriage unsafe. There were a number of different configurations, covering every possible combination of failures on the three wheels.

I worked my way down the card, skimming thankfully past illustrations of aircraft with no wheels at all, but pausing, despite myself, on the one showing no nose wheel and only one other wheel. The instructions for dealing with that one are admirably concise. No matter how serviceable the rest of the aircraft might be, you have to fly out over the sea and eject. Having already done that in the Gulf, I was not anxious to repeat the experience and I was relieved to see that the instructions for two main wheels but no nose wheel were rather less daunting.

The card spelled it out in terms which allowed for no misunderstanding: 'Prepare for a forced landing. Do a flat approach to land beyond the arrester cable'; if we landed before the cable and the nose collapsed, it would go underneath the cable, which would come across the top of the aircraft and rip off the canopy, doing unpleasant things to any bits of pilot or navigator it happened to encounter on its way. If we were trying to eject because we were out of control or had caught fire, banging out into the cable would be like pushing pork sausages into a chainsaw.

'Do an aerodynamic landing.' Normally we put the nose wheel down and then use the thrust-reverse buckets and the brakes, as you would on a commercial jet aircraft. In an aerodynamic landing, you keep the nose wheel off, so that you go down the runway at forty-five degrees to the ground. At the last moment, you put the nose wheel down, say at 100 miles an hour, which is more or less the last moment for an aircraft. If you put it down at 170 miles an hour and it collapses, you are not in a pleasant situation at all, whereas at 100 miles an hour, even if it does collapse, there is a fair chance that you may just carry on straight down the runway until you grind to a halt.

All the time I had been studying the cards, the fuel had been getting lower. Guido put out what we call a 'PAN' call and a fuel-priority call, warning everyone else: 'We are in an emergency, no one else is allowed to use the airfield – we cannot go anywhere else'. Anyone coming in to Leeming would have to divert, we took priority over absolutely everything except a 'Mayday' – a dire emergency, like the engines on fire or a total hydraulics failure. The tower alerted all the emergency services on a 'State Two', the second in twenty-four hours. As we were circling, we saw the firemen jumping into their vehicles and heading out to the edge of the runway with their blue lights flashing, followed by the ambulances, and that sight did give us a warm and fuzzy feeling . . . or at least it would have, had we not also been able to see the vivid black scar carved in the earth by the Buccaneer slewing its way off the runway the previous day.

As well as worrying about the landing gear, we had to prepare ourselves for a possible ejection. If the nose collapsed and the fuselage broke, we would have no choice but to eject. I pulled out the relevant emergency cards and, following the instructions, we prepared for a premeditated ejection. We are always ready to eject if something suddenly goes wrong with the aircraft. If both engines catch fire, we can be out of there in half a second, but we had some advance warning this time and in those circumstances there is a sequence of about twenty steps we could take to prepare ourselves. It was not a good feeling to be studying that particular set of cards and going through the pre-ejection checks.

I made sure my helmet was seated properly, tightened my lap and shoulder straps, checked my arm and leg restraints and locked the seat belts, which are similar to the inertia-reel system used in a family car. I put both visors down and laid a cloth which we use to keep the visors scratch-free over the top of them. If the canopy explodes, which it can do if it fails to jettison as it is supposed to do prior to ejection, shards of a 300-kilogram piece of perspex backed by an explosive charge – commonly known as 'a bomb' – can be flying in all directions. When you pull the ejection handle, the straps tighten, pulling you down into the seat, and the restraints drag your arms down to your sides. As the seat begins to move up the guiding rail, the canopy is blown off and you are hurled up out of the cockpit by the rocket motors. If for any reason the explosive charges fail to jettison the canopy, a bomb goes off directly over your head, shattering the perspex so that you can eject through it.

The point at which you decide you have to eject from an aircraft is not something that can be tidily laid out in a set of emergency cards. When John and I ejected in the Gulf, the aircraft was on fire and we knew that we had reached the point where had to bang out of there, but there were pilots in the Gulf who did not even know that they had ejected. It is such an instinctive reaction that one minute you are flying along at 600 miles an hour, the next there is a flash and the next thing you know, you are floating down on your parachute. One of the guys saw a point of light coming towards him which turned out to be a Roland Surface-to-Air Missile. By the time he had realized what it was, the missile had exploded. He lost consciousness and came to sitting on the floor of the desert with his parachute draped around him.

In some ways the instant, gut-reaction, ejection is easier to handle than the premeditated one, because you have no time to think about the consequences. I remember being told about a Lightning pilot who had a total gear failure and had no option but to take his plane out over the sea and eject. He called up on the radio to say: 'Scramble the search and rescue helicopter, I am about to eject'.

'Roger, helicopter on its way,' came the reply.

'Roger, ejecting.'

There was a pause, followed by: 'You're sure the helicopter is on its way?'

'Yes, search and rescue on its way.'

'OK. Definitely ejecting this time.'

'OK.'

There was another pause, followed by: 'It looks bloody cold down there, you're sure the helicopter is on its way?'

'YES.'

'OK. Ejecting.'

He finally did bang out, but not before thinking about it for some considerable time.

Almost inevitably, you do some damage to yourself when you eject. You have the equivalent of a dozen shotgun cartridges along your back and a massive rocket pack strong enough to throw you 300 feet into the air under your backside, so there is always some danger. You can damage your back if you are not sitting in the correct position, but if you eject in peacetime, you are immediately taken to hospital and laid flat on your back for two weeks while they check your spine for signs of cracks or crushed vertebrae.

There is another danger, because our parachutes are not like the military ones used by the Paras, who will only jump in a maximum of 15 knots of wind and with a large 'chute that can slow their descent. Nor are our parachutes like the ones used by display teams, who have steerable 'chutes and can land and walk away, as if they had just jumped off a small box. The parachutes we use when ejecting are quite small, resulting in the same kind of impact speed on landing as if we had jumped off a twelve-foot box without wearing a parachute at all. We also fly in up to forty knots – fifty miles an hour of wind, so in addition to jumping off the twelve-foot box, which already makes it quite likely that we will damage ourselves when we hit the ground, we are also doing the wind speed; the twelve-foot box could be travelling at fifty miles an hour.

For those reasons, it is not uncommon for people to break legs and ankles or damage their backs after ejecting. It is not something you do lightly, but just the same, there is considerably less danger in ejecting than in sitting strapped in a burning aircraft, heading for the ground at 500 miles an hour. Ten years ago, with the old generation of ejector seats which were almost literally like sitting on top of a stick of dynamite, the rule was that after three ejections you had to pack it in, you could not fly fast jets any more. Since the introduction of more modern seats, there are guys who have already ejected three times and who are still flying around.

We knew that if the nose wheel collapsed we might have to bang out, because if you go off the runway with the nose down, it is quite easy for it to dig in, toppling the whole aircraft over. Guido and I talked it through, front seat to back.

'Right, let's make sure we know exactly what we're going to do' said Guido. 'We're prepared to bang out if we have to. I'll put the nose wheel down, if it collapses and we continue to travel straight down the runway, we'll stay with it, but if we start to go off the runway to either side, we'll eject.' While Guido was telling me this, I could hear his breath coming harder and faster over the headset.

'Do you know you are actually breathing very quickly, Guido?' I asked innocently.

'No I'm not' lied Guido, 'I'm fine, I'm fine. I work better under pressure.'

I had read the emergency cards from start to finish and we both knew exactly what we had to do, but we still flew one more circuit, partly to use up a little bit more fuel, leaving less in the tanks if anything nasty did happen on landing, but to be honest, probably more to delay the moment when we had to come in and put the nose wheel on the runway and find out if it was going to collapse. At last we could delay it no longer. We came round to make our final approach, came in flat and Guido put the main wheels down beyond the cable. We rolled along with the nose wheel still off the ground, until we reached the point where he had to put it down. We both took a deep breath and I took a firm grip on the sides of the aircraft. Guido dropped the nose wheel and . . . nothing happened. The landing gear was down and locked and we rolled to a safe halt – another emergency survived.

Even on the ground, emergencies remain a regular feature of our lives. In a twenty minute period one morning at Leeming, a lumbering Hercules, taxiing out to the runway past a row of Tornados parked 'on the line' outside the hangar, was within six inches of slicing off the tail of our aircraft, when a frantically signalling ground crewman managed to bring it to a juddering halt. Scarcely had we got over that fright, when the pilot of the F3 alongside us pushed the wrong switch as he was winding up his engines to taxi out, an easy mistake to make when you have around 500 switches, toggles, buttons, triggers and levers to choose from in the cockpit. As a result, he blew a torrent of fuel from his under-wing tanks onto the tarmac, within feet of his red-hot exhaust.

Our landing gear problem had been just another of those heart-stopping situations in an aircraft, where a warning light is telling you that something is wrong, but you do not know what is going to happen. It is a bit like driving down the M1 with your oil light flashing and your heart in your mouth. Until you pull off and get it looked at, you do not know if you need a new big-end or a new bulb in your oil warning light. The only difference between that and an emergency in an aircraft is that in a car, even a worn-out big-end will probably not cost you your life.

John Peters: A worn-out big-end is not normally a problem you tend to associate with a Tornado, but despite its state-of-the-art technology and the sophistication of its electronics and weaponry, the Tornado's routine maintenance is well within the grasp of the owner of the average family saloon car.

When we go to air shows, people touch the Tornados with such reverence, as if they are afraid that they might break them, while we clamber all over them, sit on the spine and walk on the wings. People also ask if they can look in the cockpit, but this is rarely allowed, although one or two lucky people do sometimes have the opportunity. We normally have proper steps, but can just chuck a couple of ladders up against the side of the aircraft. The lucky person gingerly steps up, not too sure what they can touch and afraid that they might break the aircraft simply by looking at it. We just jump up and go clomping around everywhere with our size tens. Three or four of us could stand on the wings having a chat, without anything falling off and on a big aircraft like a Hercules, you could have forty or fifty people standing on the wing.

Tornados are fragile in some ways, but they are also thirty tons of war machine – kick the tyres and light the fires – lumps of metal that go at 600 knots. When you start flight training, you never open a panel at all because you are afraid you might damage the aircraft, but eventually you begin to realize that it is just like a car, you have to open the bonnet and check your oil, although a Tornado is serviced rather more frequently than a car, being serviced every time it has been flown.

We get used to returning in torrential rain, the air bleed from the engine blasting the water off the canopy like a windscreen wiper in a car. Peering through the cascades of water, we can see the drenched ground crew marshalling us back into the sanctuary of the Hardened Aircraft Shelter. They service the aircraft for the next sortie in the freezing cold, while we jump straight from the warmth of the aircraft to a van that whisks us away to our crew room.

When you land at a foreign base, you often have to carry out your own servicing. There are never any ladders, so you have to lumber along the side of the cockpit in your rubber suit, like Mr Marshmallow Man, until you get to the Sidewinder rail and drop off. You put the pins in the undercarriage, so it will not collapse if there is a pressure failure, and then wander round checking for loose panels. When you have done that, just like a car, you think: 'Well, better check the oil'. There is an eight-inch-square door underneath the engines which you flick open, give a screw a quarter turn and down drops a dipstick. The engine gearboxes also need oil, but this is a job pilots always try to give to the navigator; while we do the paperwork, they get all the dirty jobs. The gearbox cap is in the engine, which is scorchingly hot, and to reach it you have to thread your hand through a maze of equally hot pipes. You always use a glove but still burn your wrist, first on the gearbox cap, and then on every other piece of hot metal in there as you try to pull your hand out in a hurry. The oil has to be de-pressurized through some pan pipes, and you quickly learn to check the wind direction first. If you do not, you are liable to get a faceful of hot oil.

Any luggage is always carried in the 'spent links bay' where the spent shell casings collect when we fire the guns. It is also the store for spare cans of oil and so all luggage is always double-wrapped in polythene to protect it from oil residue. The space is not very large, especially for a two-man crew. To jam our bags into the space, one of us lies on his back, legs in the air, and pushes the panel closed with his feet, while the other one snaps shut the locking brackets. You can always spot the Tornado crew stuck away from their home base, they are the ones with creased everything, smelling strongly of the aftershave that broke in the bag and with shampoo and conditioner stains all over their new brown suede shoes.

Foreign bases are sometimes not too sure about how to refuel the plane, or what kind of aviation fuel it takes, so we may have to do that too, which is just like stopping at a motorway service station. You take the nozzle from the fuel bowser, stick it in the tank and fill it up. We even get issued with a credit card to pay the bill, though not all 'service stations' accept it. On one occasion, returning from a squadron detachment in Oman, Steve Randles and 'Shed' Mitchell had an engine problem. They were forced to make an emergency landing at a base in Saudi Arabia, a strip in the middle of nowhere, without any air traffic control or anything. We were on the second tanker thirty minutes behind them, and flew overhead. We could see them from 20,000 feet, just stuck there deep in the desert. We chortled happily to ourselves as we flew on, finding their predicament hugely amusing. They spent the night in a container truck on the base and the ground crew turned up the next day to change the engine. The Saudis filled the plane up with thousands of gallons of fuel, but when Shed offered the British government credit card, the Saudi guy refused to accept it. Luckily Shed also had his own personal American Express card on him. He showed it to the Saudi guy, who said the Arabic equivalent of: 'That'll do nicely' and charged it to that instead. Since that incident, all navs are now issued with what amounts to an American Express RAF corporate card.

12

Sheer seat-of-the-pants flying

GOOSE BAY, CANADA

John Peters: You could probably use a credit card in Goose Bay too, but only if there was anyone there to take it, and that is far from certain. Goose Bay is in Labrador, northern Canada, in the middle of nowhere. There is a twenty-six-mile-long road, a town and that is it, with nothing for some 500 miles around it. We normally have another airfield to which we can fly if something goes wrong, just as civilian jets divert to Manchester if there is fog at Heathrow. At Goose Bay the diversion tends to be Goose Bay, because there is really no other option.

It is quite beautiful, a place where rich Americans and Canadians take their fishing holidays. A little Beaver aircraft flies them to an isolated log cabin and leaves them alone for a fortnight in millions of acres of forest with just a river, a few bears and an occasional half-wild mountain man for company. As there are no people around, apart from the sparse Inuit population who, perhaps understandably, are becoming increasingly vociferous in their opposition to low-flying aircraft, we can operate our jets to VNE limits – Velocity-Never-Exceed – our war limits. We also practise our work using Terrain-Following Radar in cloud – eight jets flying in formation in cloud at 500 feet in a twenty-mile-square box, not visual with each other or the ground – which again, we cannot do in Europe because of restrictions on low flying.

The first thing you notice about Goose Bay is that the air is crystal clear. There is no pollution, no smoke haze, and when it is not pouring with rain, the sky is incredibly blue; you can see for what seems like a hundred miles. You get a Met briefing with 80 kilometre views, which is unheard of.

The flying itself is also great. With all the restrictions under which we operate in Europe, it is not easy to do OLF training – Operational Low Flying – and it is getting more difficult. On a two hour sortie to the UK from our base at Brüggen, we will spend less than thirty minutes at 250 feet, whereas at Goose, like Alaska, we can spend the whole of a sortie at low level, a hundred feet above the ground. It is something we only get the chance to do once or twice a year, it is incredibly demanding and very exciting.

Unlike everywhere else, where we have to climb to avoid populated areas, we just take off, stay at 250 feet and, once we are outside the zone of Goose Bay itself, we go down to a hundred feet and spend the whole sortie at that height. We have two areas in which we can fly, the north and south areas, which are both about the size of Wales. The south area is pine forest, stretching away as far as the eye can see. The north area is tundra. As we go out we pass trees, but they get smaller and smaller and fewer and fewer until we are out over the tundra itself. With crystal-clear visibility, all we can see is water, rock, moss and lichen – moon territory. The decreasing size of the trees is potentially very dangerous for us. When I am flying at low level, I have a mental picture of what the world should look like. As the trees imperceptibly begin to decrease in height, however, there is a real danger of believing that I am now flying too high and adjusting the position of the aircraft in the sky to restore that familiar picture. If I am not careful, I can find myself being drawn closer and closer to the ground, as the trees, which are normally around 50 feet tall, shrink to as little as ten feet high. It is a well-known optical illusion of low flying and everyone is made very aware of the danger in our pre-exercise briefings, so that a fatal mistake is not made.

The flying is as testing and exhilarating as any we encounter in the world. We fly down huge valleys and there are 'mirror' lakes everywhere; Harp Lake is ten miles long and about a quarter of a mile wide, in the bottom of a steep-sided valley with the cliffs rising 300 feet sheer on either side. We drop down into that and get a real sense of speed from the walls of rock flashing past. A wise man does not push it too low there, because the water is so still it is really hard to distinguish between water and sky. That may sound ridiculous, but the surface of the lake is a perfect mirror image of the sky above and pilots have been killed there after confusing the two; if you guess wrong, flying at a hundred feet and 600 miles an hour, there is precious little time to correct it.

One valley is nicknamed 'Star Wars Valley', after the canyon on the Death Star, where Luke Skywalker uses 'the Force' against the enemy. It is fifteen miles long and quite wide at the start of the valley, but it rapidly narrows and twists, bending from side to side, just like the canyon they fly through in the film. The further down the valley you fly, the more it twists and narrows. I have to roll the Tornado onto its side and pull hard, sweep the wings forward to increase manoeuvrability and squeeze the aircraft around the sheer walls of rock. Finally I have to say; 'No, no further', yank the stick back and pull out; it is sheer seat-of-the-pants flying.

We also practise our night flying at Goose Bay, using our Terrain-Following Radar, which is quite surreal, because the night there is completely black. It is not like doing night flying in the UK, where you do have a sensation of the ground and an idea of which way is up and which is down, because you pass a city with a mass of orange and white lights and you think: 'Right, that's the ground and that's the sky'. In Goose Bay, there is nothing to help you, no one lives there. I took off on a dark September night with cloud cover hiding the stars and was in total darkness, black cotton wool, as if someone had thrown a blackout curtain over the cockpit. I could not see the ground, or any indication that I was over hills, lakes, mountains or anything. I was completely reliant on my instruments to tell me whether I was flying upside down or right side up.

Bad weather in daytime, with poor visibility, can be equally dangerous. Like the sea, it can be unexpected and totally unforgiving. Flying a mission out of Goose one morning, I saw a bank of cloud and nudged our formation down a valley to avoid it. It turned out to be the wrong choice. The cloud began to mould itself surreptitiously around the hills. Imperceptibly at first, the visibility decreased, shading in the ground around us. Ahead the sky was smudged with shades of grey. Everyday familiarity immunizes us to the speeds at which we fly, but suddenly I was rudely reacquainted with them as events began to avalanche and the cloud-covered granite hills accelerated towards us at frightening speed. My wingman moved up and formated on me in 'arrow' formation, twenty yards away, and we began to weave through the weather together, eyes straining to find the best route through the threatening hills. The weather dictated our decisions and it was dangerously easy to forget that the ground was only as far away as a squeeze on the stick.

The stress of flying in those conditions for even a short time can leave us exhausted, but the most challenging flying we ever encounter in a Tornado is when we blend flying on Terrain-Following Radar with a spell of visual tactical flying – evading fighters who have us in their sights – and then return to base at low level, landing on instruments through cloud. The transition from the precise and methodical 'blind' flying using the vast sophistication of the Tornado's instruments to the aggressive, physical, white-knuckle challenge of operational low flying, is the most difficult, but also the most satisfying flying there is.

The weather at Goose Bay itself may be absolutely appalling, while the area to the north is clear, and what we are able to do at Goose, which we cannot do in Europe because of the neighbours, is to pass through the bad weather at low level, using the Terrain-Following Radar to reach the good weather area. We have to be very exact. The first pair of aircraft from the four-ship takes off with a twenty second trail, putting us about two miles apart, and at a pre-determined range, we each turn ninety degrees, instantly manoeuvring into a parallel track – from line astern into a square. The second pair takes off forty seconds after us, again with a twenty second split, producing the rectangular 'box' formation which we maintain unseen, flying through the cloud and rain. Flying in grim cloud can be unnerving. I cannot see ahead because of the cloud, but at Goose Bay I always seem to be able to see the ground beneath me, and watching the horrible ground flashing by and a rock rearing up at me is worse than not seeing anything at all and just flying on the kit.

With the computer autopilot flying the plane, I sit with my left hand resting on the throttle, and my right lying uselessly in my lap, twitching towards the stick every time I see a rock looming up from the ground below. I stare intently at the 'E-scope', a tiny display screen that shows me an image of the ground ahead, as the TFR in the nose sweeps the terrain ahead of our flight path. The jet soars over a ridge, prompted by the TFR, and then plunges down into an unseen valley, our anti-collision lights reflecting back from a solid wall of thick, grey cloud. The nav hunched in the back has only my running commentary to brace himself for the next lurch as the plane twists, soars and swoops, following the terrain as if glued to it.

For twenty minutes we fly like that, on track and on time, but not talking to anyone except each other, and then suddenly we pop straight out of the wall of cloud into bright sunshine. I paddle the TFR – we have a paddle bar on the stick, which cuts out the autopilot – reset the radalt bug, the height warning system that sounds off like a police siren if you drop below a specified height, and push down to a hundred feet. As I look left, my mate is exactly abeam. I look back and there are the other two guys, just popping out of the cloud. We are there in a complete four-ship box, exactly where we should be, with everyone pressing down to a hundred feet together.

One minute we are in a remote, detached world, flying a little green screen in thick cloud, in the clinical, intellectual environment of the electronic jet and its computers, the next we are suddenly out into manual, aggressive flying – and it is very aggressive flying at one hundred feet. You have to force yourself to stay there, at a good height to hug the ground. We went from the surreal to the very real, because suddenly somebody shouts: 'BUSTER!' and the 'bounce' – the fighter attack – is on us, a very physical threat, right on us, trying to shoot us.

We dodge the fighters for twenty minutes and then disengage and head south once more, approaching the bank of cloud still hanging like a curtain across the tundra. I call: 'Right. India. India. Go!' – IMC, the acronym meaning instrument flying in cloud. We pop up to 500 feet, reset the TFR and disappear back into the cloud again. The system can fly at 200 feet, but in peacetime we are restricted to 500 feet for safety reasons.

After recovering from the 'bounce', we fly back to Goose Bay, stepping down through the speeds at exact points, determined in our pre-flight briefing. 'At point F you will put your airbrakes out and you will set eighty per cent on the engines. When the speed goes below 280 knots, you will set your flaps. At 250 knots you will put your airbrakes in. At 235 you will put your gear down and fly 215 knots up to point G. After G, follow a planned track to an approach path to the runway. You will call on the radio to check in, but without any help from any outside agency, such as ground radar or Air Traffic, you will maintain your final approach speed and land.'

To do that successfully is probably the biggest buzz we get out of flying as a Tornado crew. We had taken off, flown 'blind' through cloud, gone down to low level, with the 'bounce' from the fighters, and then come back in cloud – four aircraft in a close piece of sky, within a couple of miles of each other. We had flown for an hour and a half, on time and on speed, four invisible jets flying to an invisible base over an invisible land.

While we normally do our approach to land visually, in bad weather we can do it virtually on instruments alone. The nav identifies the runway on his radar, fixes on a landmark like a tower, a pylon or a peninsula just before the runway, and talks me around to do a full approach.

'1,500 feet, coming around.'

'Right, you're coming on to the centre line now, turn left, OK.'

I cannot see the runway, because we are still in cloud, but the nav puts a cross on the runway on his radar screen and counts down the range to it.

'Seven miles. Stand by to lose height.' I get the jet exactly on the centre line.

'Six miles, descend now.' I push down, because the nav has a cross showing the end of the runway on his radar. The cross is transferred onto my HUD – Head-Up Display – but all I have is a mark on a piece of cloud. If the cross is motionless, it means that the nav has a good fix on the runway, if it is moving around, the nav is probably not sure exactly where the runway is. You need to have a bit of trust in your nav, because if he gets it wrong, when he says 'Descend', he could be dropping you onto the main road into Goose Bay, instead of the runway.

The green aircraft symbol on the screen actually shows the flight path, so if you put the flight path indicator on the cross and fly down it, you are flying a perfect approach down to the runway, although it would be rare to fly right down to the limits, as the weather has got to be really bad for that. The limits we fly to are 200 feet cloud base and 600 metres RVR – Runway Visual Range – which is seriously poor weather.

Instrument flying is very precise, a measured pressure on the stick for gentle corrections to track or height, nudging the aircraft down the slope towards the invisible runway.

'Left two degrees. Three miles.' We are on a two-and-a-half degree glide path, travelling forwards at three miles a minute and dropping at 700 feet a minute.

'160 knots' – approach speed.

'Countdown.'

'400 ... 350 ... 300 feet.' I am staring ahead, straining my eyes for a glimpse of the runway. Sometimes I only see a couple of bars of the runway lights and I really am struggling, but I am safe as long as I can get enough of a visual clue to have time to make the decision – 'Yes, I can make it' – to set myself up to land. If I cannot see any lights, it is time to put the power back on, climb back to height and start praying, because if the weather does not improve before I run out of fuel, I will be ejecting into the sea.

This landing is tight, but just within the limits. A bar of lights appears through the cloud, then another and another. 'We're going to live', I called to my navigator, who does not always appreciate my sense of humour. 'I've got the lights'. Our four aircraft land in perfect formation. You could do that as a single aircraft and feel good, but if you turned a bit late or overshot the runway heading, it would make no difference, you could still come back onto track and correct because there is no one behind you to worry about. To do it as a four-ship is the most outrageous buzz you will ever get as a team. Every navigator has managed the navigation kit and radar precisely and every pilot has flown his parameters perfectly.

Goose Bay's other attractions are rather more elusive. We stay in bare concrete blockhouses, set in rows, and have to use connecting tunnels in winter, in case we get lost in a whiteout in the snow. In summer the main problem is black fly, which is as bad as the Alaskan mosquitoes. It is slightly better these days, because the area of the camp is sprayed, but if you go outside the base you are in a wilderness and will get eaten alive by the black fly . . . if the bears do not get you first.

There is very little to do off duty, so we create our own entertainment. The first priority is to fill the fridge with beer, the second is to organize a video man. The communal room is known as 'the brain death room', because we spend hours in there staring at videos – there is absolutely nothing else to do, except for 'detachment sports'. A bridge four is invariably in operation within minutes of the aircraft wheels touching the ground and the more physically active push weights, play squash or swim. One or two old-timers still hark back nostalgically to a time when things were different. Passing through a deserted bar at five o'clock in the afternoon one day, I encountered 'Geggy', a nav in his mid-forties, perched at the bar and puffing on a cigarette – known as an 'oxygen thief' and a rarity in the Air Force these days. 'It's time to leave the squadron' said Geggy. 'In my day everyone finished flying and hit the bar for the night, nowadays everyone works out or surfs or plays golf. It's a waste of good drinking time.' I left him to his solitary pint and went off to play squash, confirming his complaint.

Some traditions are still upheld, however. We always have a curry night, in which the squadron's 'chefs' concoct abominably hot curries. The evening is treated with proper reverence and no detail is overlooked, down to the naan bread, onion bhajis and poppadums. We also hit the town, what there is of it, from time to time. The Goose Bay nightlife could not be described as sophisticated. There are a couple of bars on the main street, in real *Deliverance* style. Everyone wears big boots, checked shirts and wool jackets, and acts surly towards strangers. There is a shop in town called Northern Lights, which is a must on every tourist's itinerary. Upstairs there is a supermarket. Downstairs there is another one, but with a difference – a gun supermarket. There is a wall about forty feet long, smothered in crossbows, handguns, high-velocity hunting rifles, pump-action shotguns, assault rifles and machine guns – an arsenal of weaponry – any and all of which which you can just buy across the counter.

There are two more traditional nights on every trip, a pilots' cocktail party and a navs' benefit dinner. The first one is always the Pilots' Cocktail Party. On this trip, the pilots all decided to wear *Top Gun* stuff – T-shirts, jeans and shades – to emphasize our social superiority over the humble navs. The first cocktail of the evening was tabasco sauce and vodka. We all drank the same cocktails, but since we were in control of things, the pilots got a dash of tabasco and the navs got it mixed half-and-half with vodka. Silly Mess games then began, with rules heavily biased towards pilot superiority, after which, to soothe their injured pride, each pilot was supplied with two bandages to 'help' his nav. Some navs had their legs bandaged together and had to pogo everywhere for the rest of the evening, others had one hand bandaged to their head.

In this state, we set off around town in a big yellow bus, like the school buses you see in American films. We called at every bar in town and had a cocktail in each. To avoid being thrown out before we had even got in the door, one of us would go in first, acting as sober as was possible in the circumstances, and get thirty-five Harvey Wallbangers lined up. The rest of our motley crew would then come staggering or pogoing into the bar, smothered in bandages. The Canadian bar offered 'shooters', shots of incongruous mixtures of drinks like cherry brandy and rum, served in a test tube to be gulped down in one . . . a sad and lonely pastime. We ended up in the Goose Bay 'night club', which was fairly laughable, because we were the only people in there. Perhaps it is busier when the moose are mating.

In revenge for the indignities they suffer at our hands, the navigators hold a Navs' Benefit Dinner later in the week. On this particular occasion, the pilots' invitations were all stuck to something and whatever they were attached to we had to bring with us to the dinner. One guy's invitation was stuck to a motorbike, which he had to bring along – not altogether easy, since the motorbike did not belong to him – and another guy had to unscrew his door and bring that with him. My invitation was dangling from a trophy moose head hanging on the wall. With the aid of a borrowed set of socket wrenches I managed to prise it loose from the wall and staggered triumphantly in to dinner, accompanied by a moose head complete with six-foot antlers.

The navs then gave us nasty cocktails and the King Nav at the dinner, the chief navigator John Scholtens, set the rules for the evening. Naturally the pilots were not informed of the rules; instead we had to try and guess them as we went along. If we did not do the right thing at the right time, we had to drink a penalty, a raw egg, or our squadron drink a 'green and yellow' – an advocaat floating in a sea of crème de menthe. For a major trangression, we had to 'do the tube' – a three-foot plastic tube with a funnel at the top and a pilot at the bottom. While you put the tube into your mouth, a helpful nav pours the contents of a 'tinny' down the funnel, three feet above your head. You open your mouth and have a can's worth of beer inside you before you can blink. It is all rather childish, and not exactly recommended practice by the Alcohol Advisory Council, but it is good fun just the same, especially if you are not the one at the bottom of the tube.

13

Firing . . . Firing . . . NOW!

MISSILE PRACTICE CAMP, ANGLESEY

John Nichol: Even mating moose would not have distracted
me from one of the big events of our year, missile practice in
Wales, involving the firing off of £2 million worth of radar-
guided Skyflash missiles and heat-seeking Sidewinders. It gives
us a rare chance to use the jet for its real purpose – firing
missiles – which, for obvious reasons, we very rarely get a
chance to do; the missiles are just so expensive.

Missile Practice Camp – MPC – takes place at RAF Valley
in Anglesey, which seems to have been deliberately designed to
be one of the most God-awful places on the face of the planet.
It is perpetually windy, cold, wet and miserable, with a 360
degree vista of streaming bogs, sodden hillsides and bedrag-
gled sheep. If it is bad through the week, it is worse at weekends
– even the sheep die of boredom during a weekend at Valley. Our
whole aim is to get down there, fire our missiles and get the hell
out of there as quickly as possible. We also have to make sure
we get it right, however. A Skyflash missile, our radar missile,
costs somewhere in the region of £300,000; a heat-seeking
Sidewinder is around £75,000, and every report that comes out
from MPC goes right up to the highest echelons of the Air
Force . . . so if you messed up in some way, everyone is going
to get to hear about it.

Even before we set off for Missile Practice Camp, we had
practised each missile 'profile' countless times out over the

139

North Sea, going round and round in circles, making all the calls, pressing all the buttons and pulling all the triggers. The only difference was that we were not actually firing the missiles, which is quite a big difference.

The engineers go down to Valley by road, but we fly our jets down there, which was where the first problem occurred. We came into work on an October morning, all psyched up and ready to go, but the wind was so strong that the aircraft were almost being blown off the line outside the hangar. After a few hours of sitting around, we managed to get airborne, holding enough fuel to go somewhere else if we could not get in at Valley. The base has a very short runway and we were just on the limits of it. As we dropped out of the cloud cover, coming in to the runway, our aircraft was canted off thirty degrees away from it, blown off course by the wind. At times like that, the Tornado's impressive technology is not a great deal of help. 'Podge', my pilot, was tacking in towards the runway as if he was sailing a dinghy into the wind. If you are in something big like a jumbo, you can offset your steering to handle the wind, but you can't do that in an F3 Tornado; you have to tack in and kick it off as you get on the runway, before the wind blows you halfway across the Irish Sea.

We managed to get all the aircraft down safely and then sat around twiddling our thumbs in our wet Welsh mountain eyrie as we lost day after day on the firing range to the weather. The nightmare came true; we had to stay at Valley for the weekend. The crew room at Valley is a standard NATO model, entered through a pair of double doors from the room where the flying clothing is kept, with its usual battery of drab grey lockers, the same throughout the Air Force.

Lining the crew room walls are the traditional photographs and mementoes you would find in any crew room, some of the mementoes even dating from the First World War. The crew room at Coningsby, for example, has the uniform of Albert Ball, a captain in the Flying Corps who was a Victoria Cross holder. The photographs at Valley are different from those at other bases in one important respect. In addition to the usual pictures of aircraft dropping bombs and firing missiles, they also have a photograph of every single Missile Practice Camp that has ever been held there. There are literally thousands of them.

The collection started with the usual 'school photograph' type of pictures, with a dozen or so guys standing in front of an aircraft, but it gradually evolved as the years went by. From people standing at attention and looking serious, it moved to a considerably more relaxed style of picture, with people grinning, pulling faces, sitting on the wings and adopting a series of increasingly ridiculous poses and disguises. Competition is intense for each squadron to produce a yet more ludicrous team photograph to commemorate their Missile Practice Camp and cap the massive collection of absurd pictures on the walls. There are pictures of crews standing with their backs to the camera, crews in every fancy dress you can conceive, and people all standing on their heads so that it looks as if their aircraft is upside down.

I knew that something out of the ordinary was being planned for our own commemorative photograph, but I did not know what. My old drinking buddy, John Conway, inevitably nicknamed 'JC', had decided it would be splendid entertainment to use Flight Lieutenant A.J. Nichol's torture by the Iraqis as the theme of our photograph. He finally let me in on the secret as well: 'I've got this really good idea for a photograph, John, but I don't know how much you'll like it.'

'Tell me about it.'

JC's plan involved me being tied to a chair, as if held in an Iraqi gaol, and then tortured with a missile, which would be firmly inserted into any available orifice. Since the missiles have fins about ten inches long, this was not a part of the photo opportunity that I was particularly looking forward to. They all thought I would say: 'No, I'm not going to do this', but it seemed like a good idea at the time, so we all got ready while the official photographer came over to record the golden moment. In an attempt to look as Arab as possible, all the rest of the guys had decided that they would remove their bedspreads from their beds in the Mess and tie them around their heads with bandages. To watch a dozen highly paid fighter pilots trying to disguise themselves as Arabs, using only the standard issue, multi-coloured NATO bedspreads in hues of orange, green and blue, was hilarious. I could not move or even speak for about ten minutes because I was lying on the floor, laughing my socks off at the sight of my pathetic 'captors'.

Eventually they got themselves organized. The Boss was poised over me with a pair of scissors, ready to cut off any convenient appendages, while the missile was held ready for insertion; but the shot looked more like a nativity play – Joseph and Mary and some sheep. It was so embarrassing and ludicrous that the 'Arabs' resorted to covering their faces with the bedspreads to try and conceal their identities.

The photo opportunity at an end, there was nothing else to do but drink and get bored, and we did both all weekend. One consolation was meeting up with similarly doomed people from other squadrons that I had not seen for years, and in the Air Force those years mean nothing. You do not keep in touch because you get to know so many people that you would end up writing letters twenty-four hours a day, but we know that when we do bump into each other we are going to catch up on what everybody has been doing, have a great evening together and then all go our separate ways for another five years.

A lively evening was developing in the bar when the Boss, who was in charge of the whole show, said: 'Right, that's it, everybody out. Shit, shower, shave, get changed and then all back to the bar, ready for dinner.' If it is a 'combat shower' – a quick spray with a deodorant – you have to be back down in ten minutes, but we had about half an hour to get out of our sweaty green flying suits, or 'stinking green growbags', as the ground crew affectionately term them, and clean ourselves up.

Further drink was then taken and during dinner we went through our entire repertoire of stupid Air Force games, like not eating with your knife and fork. We also invented a new game, called 'Guess the Chocolate'. I went round the table with a box of Milk Tray, and a chosen victim had to guess which chocolate I had in my hand. If he guessed wrong, the chocolate went in his ear and the guy on his right then had to eat it out of his ear. In the cold light of day, it probably sounds like a pretty stupid game, but after a drink or two it is actually very funny – we really think the BBC should take it up.

The rest of the weekend passed in similarly cultural vein and on Monday morning we began missile practice again. In between the wind, rain, hail and snow, most of the other guys managed to get their missiles off, but Podge and I seemed to be doomed. Every time we had a slot on the range, either the weather turned foul or our jet was faulty and someone else took our place. Friday was our last chance, because not even the most sadistic senior officer in the RAF would condemn anyone to two consecutive weekends in Valley. While Podge and I were preparing for our big moment, everybody else was waiting to get home, because although the others had all completed their slots, squadron etiquette dictates that nobody leaves until all the missiles have been fired.

For no logical reason whatsoever, we had already decided that having had so much bad luck and so many engineering problems during the fortnight, it was all going to work for us on the Friday. So we had all gone out on Thursday night and had a huge party in the Mess, determined that, come what may, we were going to get the missile off and get home in the morning.

While the rest of the guys carried on far into the night, Podge and I were subject to the 'twelve hour, bottle to throttle' rule that we impose before we go flying – no alcohol within twelve hours of a flight. I was a model of brisk efficiency when I fell out of bed the next morning, but God knows what the guys who weren't flying felt like.

Before you can fire your missile, there are hundreds of factors that have to be right. There is the Jindivick, a pilotless aircraft that tows the target. There is a Hawk aircraft, that flies alongside you to take still photographs of your missile coming off, and an F3 that videos the missile firing. There is a secondary firer, in case you have a problem as you go in towards the target, and a tertiary firer, in case of a problem on the ground. So you have four F3 crews, a Hawk crew and all of the missile spies and ties down at the place from where the Jindivick takes off, all working to get this one missile off.

Podge and I, as primary firers, and the secondary and tertiary guys all got into our aircraft and began the mountain of checks. In addition to the normal ones, we had the highly temperamental telemetry to worry about – the electronics linking the missile to the ground stations, enabling the scientists to study the missile in flight and track it homing in on the target right up to the moment of impact. We all wound our aircraft up, turned the radars on, got all the systems up and working and then started the telemetry checks. Of course Sod's Law is that somebody's telemetry missile is not working. When that happens, everybody normally shifts up the scale. The secondary firer becomes the primary, the tertiary becomes the secondary, and the primary is back in the crew room having a coffee and thinking 'Why me?'

Inevitably, Sod's Law was fully operative. Our missile telemetry would not link down to the ground station and Podge's anguished scream into my headphones of: 'I don't believe this – not again', added further tension to the sortie. As soon as we let the controllers know about our little problem, they immediately wanted to replace us with the secondary firer, but we were not going to miss our last chance to get a missile off for anyone. Podge radioed back: 'No, hang on, we're going to hack it'. We got the engineers out, who put on a new missile. We did our telemetry checks again and this time everything was working. Meanwhile, all the rest of the non-flyers, complete with their prodigious hangovers, crowded into the crew room, where we have a direct radio link so that everybody can hear what is going on.

There was then another delay, not because of any further problem with our aircraft, but because the wind was too strong to launch the Jindivick. We sat and waited some more. Eventually the wind dropped a little, we got our ground checks completed and took off along with the secondary firer and the Hawk aircraft that was to film the firing. We went through what we call the 'missile gate', to get on to the range. We were now over Cardigan Bay, and there were fishing boats and oil tankers coming in and out. If those ships are not in a safe position on the missile trace – the area where the missile could possibly go if things go wrong – then you are forced to abort, which happens on countless occasions. For once, instead of hearing: 'Abort. Abort. Ship in the missile trace', we were all clear, out on the range with the telemetry checks and the down-links all right.

The next hurdle was to get the Jindivick airborne, and trying to get this remotely-piloted thing with two wings into the air is an amazing feat in itself. There are three guys on the ground; one is responsible for roll control, another, with a different stick, is responsible for pitch control and another somewhere else has overall control. The three of them actually try to fly this robot around the sky, when just getting it airborne at all is a pretty interesting trick.

We had another thirty-five minute delay. The scientists could not get the target into the correct space of sky, and we had two passes with it before we could actually do anything. By now, I was sweating buckets as the pressure began to mount.

At last they gave us the green light, and we turned inbound for the target. There is a set sequence of checks and radio calls that we have to go through as we approach the target, and it is all laid down in minuscule detail. Base called at five minutes – five minutes to missile release – and we went through the series of checks: radar on, missile cooled – the head is chilled with liquid nitrogen, helping it to detect heat sources – missile arming systems checked, no ships in the missile trace.

'Four minutes.' We went through the same checks again, plus another series of checks: making sure we had our video camera on, and that we and the target were both at the correct height and speed. While we were going through the sequence of checks, the guys back in the crew room were getting ready to go home. The first four had already gone out to their aircraft, started them up, put in their bags and were sitting at the end of the runway with their engines running, listening to what was happening over the radio.

We came in, through the three minute and two minute calls. By now I had already read the checks through for Podge about six times, who was saying 'Yes, I've done it. Yes, I've done it' to each one. I was also searching on the radar, trying to locate the target. It was a very short pick-up, I should have been able to spot the target at thirty, even thirty-five miles. I could not, there was nothing on the screen. Calls were coming in over the radio: 'Target's on your nose thirty miles ... Target's on your nose twenty-five miles' and there was nothing.

'Target's on your nose twenty miles' again nothing.

'Where the hell is it?' I screamed, when at last that welcome little blip showed up on the screen. I called 'Contact' over the radio, to tell the control room that I had the target. 'Radar locked.' When they heard that call from us, all the guys in the crew room and waiting in their aircraft were saying: 'Yes, that's it.'

We were closing fast on the target and at ten miles we turned in to it – until then, we were four miles displaced, simulating a typical attack pattern.

'One minute.' Yet another series of checks.

'Fifty seconds.' The checks were coming thick and fast. I was trying to make sure that we did not get any of them wrong or out of sequence. We had four guys in the air, two guys in the chase aircraft, three guys flying a Jindivick, thirty people sitting in a crew room and God knows how many scientists in their little bunker listening in, and I was desperate to ensure that we were not the ones that were going to screw up.

At that point Podge called: 'Smoke on' and the guys on the ground put smoke out of the target to help us pick it up, because it is not a big thing to be looking for; it is only the size of a small sofa in a very big sky. Enemy aircraft in wartime would not be so obliging, but the point of the exercise was actually to fire the missile, not spend two hours hunting round

Cardigan Bay for an invisible target, before giving up and going home.

We were closing fast. I called to Podge: 'Target's seven miles, ten right of the nose'.

'I can't see anything.'

'Five miles.'

'I can't see anything.'

This was all happening in seconds, but I was getting a sinking feeling, surely we were not going to blow this?

'Four miles, on your nose.'

Suddenly Podge called 'Yes, visual' and I felt the plane lurch as he pulled the nose on to the target.

After the fifty seconds call, there were further calls at thirty seconds and twenty seconds. Then, as we got down to the vinegar strokes, the three big calls that we had to make were: 'Firing' – pause – 'Firing' – pause – and 'Now'.

When you call 'Firing', you do not fire the missile and you have to release the transmit button so that the safety people can call: 'Stop. Stop. Stop' at any point right up to the death. If there is silence after your first call of 'Firing', you repeat it a second time, 'Firing', and again you release the transmit button, so that they can call 'Stop. Stop. Stop.' Finally you call: 'Now' and then you pull the trigger, which you have to do with a different hand. It is not unknown for people to pull the missile trigger instead of pressing the transmit button, so that the call becomes: 'Firing . . . Oh hell', but that did not happen this time.

We were perfectly calm, everything was working. Podge called: 'Firing', paused, and nothing came over the radio. 'Firing', he paused again, and again nothing came over the radio. Everybody in the air, back in the crew room and down in the bunker held their breath . . . 'Firing' . . . 'Firing' . . . 'NOW!'

There was the loudest WHOOSH! I have ever heard, as £75,000 worth of firework came off the side of the aircraft past my left ear. I saw it flashing forward and as I watched it, I made the exultant call of: 'STORE AWAAAAAAAAAY', which unlike 'Misfire', means that the missile is off the aircraft. I am really not sure why we call it a 'store', it is a missile, not a supermarket, but such are the mysteries of life in the RAF. We could almost hear the cheer as the rest of the guys wound up their engines and taxied off, heading for home. Whatever happened from now on was down to the missile, not us.

I watched the missile streaking across the sky in front of us. It is called a Sidewinder because of the way it moves – just like a snake, weaving from side to side as it homes in on the target. I could see it whacking backwards and forwards until suddenly BOOOM! There was a blinding flash as it hit head-on with the target, and that was it. Two weeks of Welsh woe and £75,000 of high technology obliterated in a split second, just like that.

14

The deadly game of cat and mouse

EXERCISE NORTHERN BANNER

John Peters: Clanggggg! The steel locking bars on the doors were thrown back with a sound that reverberated inside the shelter like a cathedral bell. It died away into a silence broken only by the steady whine of the jet's electronics. There was a low rumble as the massive steel doors slid open, leaking grey, pre-dawn light into the shelter. With it came a faint scent of resin on the breeze from the pine woods, an alien fragrance in the shelter, intruding on the familiar cocktail of metal, aviation fuel and hydraulic fluid.

My navigator, Jack Calder, and I had entered the gloom of the Hardened Aircraft Shelter half an hour before takeoff, shivering in the cold of a November morning. He climbed the ladder, strapped into the back seat and began to programme the inertial navigation kit and feed the routeing of our mission into the main computer, using the audio-cassette tape he had prepared during planning.

I checked the aircraft externally then looked over the 'Form 700', the little black book of the aircraft giving its history, limitations and servicing record, and signed for the jet. The ground crew helped me to strap into the front seat. I took a deep breath and then began the pre-flight checks with Jack, an endless litany of challenge and response, with over 200 checks to be made even before starting the engines.

Checks complete, I called up the ground crew clustered

around the jet, 'Clear start APU' – the Auxiliary Power Unit that fires up the Tornado's two engines, two monsters developing 30,000 pounds of thrust and burning 600 kilos of fuel a minute at maximum power.

'Clear to start APU, Sir' came the response over the headset.

'Clear. Starting APU.' The Auxiliary Power Unit rumbled into life as Jack began cursing and swearing in the back seat. The cassette tape had failed to load, forcing him to type all the mission data for the entire route into the keyboard of the computer. For once, I had no problems in the front seat and I smiled smugly to myself.

'Clear for engine start.' I pushed the switch to start the right engine. There was a whine, which grew to a rumble and then became a roar. The temperature gauges on the turbines leapt from the ambient temperature of six degrees Celsius up to 420 degrees. There were now twelve minutes to takeoff, four minutes to check-in time with the other members of our formation. I pushed the switch to start the left engine, which burst into life, the sound rattling like thunder around the concrete shelter. Even with my helmet on, the noise was deafening and my body was shaken by the roar and the vibrations.

Giving a warning: 'Closing canopy' to the ground crew on the intercom, Jack and I lowered our visors and closed our eyes as the ground crew scattered for cover, ducking under the wings or behind the generators until the canopy was safely shut. There have been cases where a canopy has exploded as it came down, blasting fist-sized shards of perspex out in all directions. I checked the canopy and then activated the lever to close it. As I did so the warning siren began to sound, audible even above the roar of the engines. The canopy snapped shut and the siren died away. Inside the cockpit, the engine noise had dropped to a muffled growl. The ground crew reappeared from their refuges as the radio crackled into life.

'Voodoo – check in.'

'Two.'

'Three.'

13. An 11 Squadron Tornado F3 goes vertical over the North Sea.

14. John Nichol's mates on 11 Squadron think it will be good therapy for him to relive his Gulf War ordeal. Some squadrons will try anything to produce a memorable photograph of their Missile Practice Camp!

15. 'Podge' and John Nichol fire off the Sidewinder missile that signals the end of two weeks of delay due to bad weather at Missile Practice Camp, Anglesey.

6. A Tornado GR1 demonstrates its missile capability against a possible fighter threat. A Sidewinder missile streaks from the rail.

7. A 31 Squadron GR1 'mud-mover' flies through the fighter threat at low level to penetrate UK airspace over the Northumbrian coast on Exercise Northern Banner.

18. John Peters strapped in the front seat at the pilot's controls. In front of him is the Head-Up Display. The bulk and complexity of the ejection seat can be appreciated in this photograph.

19. John Nichol straps himself into the navigator's seat, facing the computer screens. The white helmet with dark visor is essential for fighter crew, who fly at high level in bright sun; bomber crew wear dark green helmet to blend in with the terrain at low level.

20. John Peters at home with Helen and children Guy, six, and Toni, four.

21. An 11 Squadron F3 about to deploy to the Bosnian air defence region, armed with four Skyflash and two Sidewinder missiles. Fuel tanks are attached to the wing pylons, and under the wing tips are chaff and flare dispensers. Just back from the nose of the aircraft is the cannon. Twelve hours after this photograph was taken at RAF Leeming, this aircraft was on patrol over Bosnia.

22. John Nichol shares a beer with some NATO friends at the Fairford International Air Tattoo. The top of their aircraft makes an ideal viewing platform; the inside makes an ideal 'party wagon'!

24. Previously enemies, British and Hungarian air crew now meet on friendly terms. John Peters exchanges mementoes with the crews of the Mig-21s he escorted to and from Fairford. Speaking on the telephone in the background is Tony Shopland.

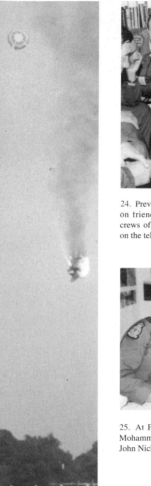

25. At Fairford, John Nichol and Si Stevens get together with Mohammed Mubarak, the Kuwaiti pilot held in the same gaol as John Nichol and John Peters in Iraq.

23. A Russian Mig-29 Fulcrum plummets to the ground in flames following a midair collision at the Fairford International Air Tattoo. The pilot floats down on his parachute, having ejected only seconds before a certain death.

26. Flying high over the German–Czech border, John Peters and Ian Hall, the Squadron Commander, formate with Hungarian Mig-21 'Fishbeds' before escorting them to the Fairford International Air Tattoo.

'Four,' came the rapid-fire replies, as all four aircraft checked in, bang on time, in what sounded like a single transmission.

The other members of our four-ship, deep in their concrete and steel Hardened Aircraft Shelters, were preparing, like us, to emerge; war machines sliding out of their dark caves into the light like fire-belching dragons emerging from their lairs. I signalled to the ground crew and, brakes off, slowly nudged the Tornado out of the HAS, gingerly inching forward as two of the crew gave thumbs-up signs for clearance at the wing tips. There is only five feet to spare at either side.

The formation linked up and taxied out together in two pairs, pilots and navigators carrying out the interminable routine of check and counter-check as we rolled out along the taxiway towards the end of the runway.

I gave Jack the 'abort brief' – the standard litany of what we would do in the event of emergencies on the takeoff run: 'Light wind from the left. Dry runway. With the wheels still on the runway, for a major loss of thrust or major caption (a warning on the emergency panel), I will abort, engaging thrust reverse. I'll brake if I need to and use the hook (snagging the arrester cable across the runway). If you think I need the hook, call it and call the abort. 'If we have a problem from "Rotate" (takeoff speed), I will select combat power and climb straight ahead and deal with the problem at height. If I can't maintain the climb, I'll call: "Jettison". You take off the under-wing tanks (the instant reduction in weight and drag drastically increasing the chance of getting airborne). If it all goes "tits up", I'll call: "Eject". Any questions?'

There were none. We paused as the lead pair of our four-ship, led by Steve Randles and 'Shed' Mitchell, with wingman Rich Fewtrell and 'Shoppo' Shopland, drew up alongside each other on the runway, then my wingman and I nudged our way in behind them, inching forward and lining up, all four aircraft squeezed onto the end of the runway together. We take off in pairs to get our aircraft airborne in the shortest possible time, minimizing our vulnerability to attack while we are helpless on the ground, but it requires considerable precision. The two aircraft go down the runway at 180 miles an hour, two thirty-ton lumps of metal, with only a two metre gap between their wing tips.

As the lead pair wound up the power, their jets strained against the brakes, and tongues of blue-amber flame flashed thirty feet back from the engines, lighting up the dawn still further. My aircraft rattled and shook in the turbulence, the blazing engine plumes from the aircraft in front of me reaching to within inches of my wing tips. Then they were gone, accelerating faster and faster, still in perfect alignment as they rocketed down the runway and lifted off into the mist.

Before they were airborne, we were already requesting departure from Air Traffic Control and being cleared for takeoff. We both went swiftly through our final engine checks and then I, in the lead aircraft of our pair, gave the wind-up signal to my number two, Chris Lunt and his navigator Humpo. Holding the aircraft on the brakes, we both wound up our engines through maximum dry power and on up to fifty per cent on the reheat – the afterburner. The fuel burn leapt from sixty kilograms a minute to 600. The jets were shuddering between the hammer and anvil of engines and brakes. Chris gave me a thumbs up, we were ready. I looked across at him and abruptly nodded, and as I did so, we both came off the brakes. I slowly pushed up the power to full, and then back to eighty per cent on the reheat, moving the throttles smoothly, so that the number two could stay in position as we accelerated down the runway.

The familiar surge of power slammed me back in my seat. As we sped down the tarmac, Jack and I kept up a constant crosstalk.

'Engine's good, caption's clear.'

'100 knots, RHAG.' This as we flashed across the safety cable wire.

'130 knots. EMBS.' Emergency Braking Speed – the last chance to brake the plane to a halt. At that speed, the plane would come to a stop with two red-hot, worn tyres and the braking systems smoking and worn down to the limit, but it would stop. Any faster and we would run out of runway first.

'165 knots. Rotate.' We were past the point of no return. Whatever happened now we were committed to takeoff, we were going too fast to abort. I glanced at my instruments, called: 'Engines good, captions clear, rotating', and eased the stick back. As we lifted off, I glanced to my left to see Lunty's aircraft, still exactly abeam, rising into the air with us.

'Gear travelling . . . and the flaps.'

'250 knots. Out of reheat.' I eased the throttles back out of reheat power as we tore on up through the grey banks of cloud. We held the acceleration up to 325 knots, the normal climb speed for departure and levelled off as we punched through the cloud at 12,000 feet into clear skies, with the dawn reddening in the east. Lunty was still on my wing tip and I waved him out to 'fighting wing' position, swept back sixty degrees from the leader and 200 metres behind. If we are going to fly through thick cloud, the wingman – the second plane – flies in close formation on the leader, separated by no more than twenty feet. The leader flies normally, but as smoothly as possible while the wingman does nothing except watch the leader and mimic him exactly, playing a literal game of 'follow my leader'. It requires absolute trust from both parties; if it goes wrong, the consequences can be terrible.

Air display teams like the Red Arrows fly the same way, with the lead aircraft acting as the eyes for all of them. A foreign air display team lost all seven of its aircraft and their pilots a few years back, when the leader misjudged his height and flew into the ground. The other six members of the team, with eyes only for the wing tip of the plane ahead of them, followed him into the ground, one after another.

We levelled at 20,000 feet, following two specks, our lead pair, trailing streams of white vapour behind them. I set the autopilot and checked the cockpit. We crossed the Dutch coast, heading north-west, and out over the North Sea. I swept back my wings and set my radalt bug. We descended to low level, 250 feet, accelerating to 420 knots, 500 miles an hour, our normal cruising speed. In combat, when we are really burning, we fly at 600 knots and as low as we dare. We flew over the superstructure of a tanker and flashed on over the grey waves, marching to the horizon.

As we descended into low level, Chris pushed out into 'battle' formation – abeam with me, about four kilometres out to the side. I could just make out the cockpit of his aircraft, a black, one-inch silhouette against the sky. The other pair of our four-ship flew six kilometres ahead of us, completing the 'card' formation of two battle pairs, aligned one behind the other. Somewhere out in front of us, a Combat Air Patrol (CAP) of hostile fighters was lying in wait – Exercise Northern Banner was about to begin.

We were part of a huge NATO force on a raid against targets in the north of England, while the UK Air Defence squadrons – including John Nichol's – were trying to defend them. In the Gulf, John and I had been together in the same Tornado bomber, but he was now on the other side of the fence, flying a fighter, and there is no love lost between bomber crew and fighter crew.

We flew at high speed and low level, using the 'battle' formation to give cross-cover. At four kilometres apart, each partner in the pair can see a good seven or eight kilometres behind the other. Since a standard heat-seeking missile shot for a fighter is about two to two-and-a-half 'Ks' – kilometres – from the stern, it allows time to give your mate a warning if you see a fighter drop in. If we are quick enough and see the fighters early enough, we 'buster' – hit maximum power and get the hell out of there, quickly enough to prevent him from ever closing the gap.

The formation protects us against both radar and visual attack, but the first threat we would encounter would come from Beyond Visual Range (BVR), a radar missile threat – a 'Fox One' – from fighters out of sight to our eyes, but not our radar warning equipment. On the right-hand side of my cockpit was a tiny green screen, a Radar Homing and Warning Receiver (RHWR), guarding us against attack. As soon as a fighter used his radar to target us, the RHWR would sound a warning. The fighters use their radar like a blind man uses a white stick, probing out in front of them. Whenever the 'stick' touches us, we turn away from it, forcing them to start probing for us again. We react and manoeuvre our aircraft and formation purely in reaction to warnings from the RHWR. If someone looks at us with their radar, we get an indication of that – a trace – on the RHWR, which is also clever enough to indicate what sort of aircraft it thinks is the source. If someone locks us up on their radar, the prelude to launching a radar-guided missile, the RHWR flashes a strobe – a line across the screen – and sounds a warning.

We crossed the FLOT – the Forward Line of our Own Troops – the line on the battlefield separating the two sides. If they were not already aware that an attack was under way, any fighters waiting for us would soon have irrefutable evidence on their radar screens. As we hit the FLOT, we immediately threw in a turn through sixty degrees. At the least, that would force any fighters already looking at us to manoeuvre and re-evaluate their attack plan. By the time they had done that, we would already be going faster and faster, much lower and 'jamming' them with electronic countermeasures.

Our screen was still blank, but the lead pair, six kilometres in front of us, had picked up the first signs of danger. 'Voodoo two, trace right, two o'clock.' The fighters had found us. They were sitting up at 20,000 feet and had swept the formation with their radar. If we took no evasive action, they would swiftly hunt us down.

'Kick left twenty degrees.'

The curt order came over the radio; the cruel, deadly game of cat and mouse was on.

John Nichol: In some future war, I may be 'riding shotgun' on JP's bomber, protecting him as he flies a mission against the enemy, but during Northern Banner we were on opposite sides, using every skill we had learned and every ounce of power that could be squeezed from our jets in a duel that, in wartime, would end in death.

I was flying on Combat Air Patrol, cruising at 20,000 feet, a hundred miles out in the North Sea, searching for all the packages of four, six or eight bombers haring over the border, heading for the target for today, the Otterburn Ranges in Northumberland. Air defence is a complete, one hundred per cent, contrast from bombing. It is as different as carpentry from bricklaying, with no real connections between the two, except that you are still flying around in a sophisticated aircraft. I now sit in a grey jet instead of a green and brown one, flying at 20,000 feet instead of hedge-hopping and mud-moving, coming down out of the sun straight into the middle of the bombers. I imagine them all down below, just like I used to be, saying: 'I can't see any fighters, they must all have stayed at home.'

There is plenty of rancour between fighter and bomber crews, which is partly in joke and partly serious. Bombers are 'mud-movers' in the view of fighter crews, scuffling in the dirt, while we command the skies. Bomber crews concentrate on staring forward, because flying at a hundred feet, they have not got the luxury of unrestricted lookout, they are far too busy trying to avoid flying into the ground. The fighter crews look down on them in more ways than one. Fighter pilots are the glamour boys, up at 20,000 feet, monarchs of all they survey. Flying fighters for real is nothing like the *Top Gun* image; films like that are always far too perfect. Nothing ever goes wrong, nobody is overweight, nobody ever has an accident, nobody ever dies and nobody screws up; it is completely different from a real air force.

We prefer to be called air defenders rather than fighters; we defend our airspace against attackers – bombers – trying to penetrate that space. Our job on Combat Air Patrol is to plug the gaps between our missile zones, creating a solid wall of defence. The basis of an air defence formation, the air defenders' bible, is a 'four-ship CAP', with four fighters flying a 'racetrack' in the sky, out over the North Sea, where the Soviet threat would have come from and where the mud-movers still simulate their threat. They come over at high level and then drop down forty or fifty miles from the coast to try and get underneath us.

We normally sit at between 15,000 and 20,000 feet in two synchronous pairs, two guys in battle formation on opposite sides of the racetrack. At any one time, there will always be two guys 'facing up threat' as we call it – facing towards the enemy, searching the sky with radar, an electronic extension to our own sight, allowing us to see bombers many miles away.

We have various Standard Operating Procedures within that four-ship CAP and all these SOPs are written down, so that in theory a Combat Air Patrol could be manned by fighters from four completely different squadrons, all meeting at the same point in the sky. A CAP would form itself, because everything is set out exactly: how it is going to be flown, including what times on the hour you get to the beginning of the racetrack, and so on. A four-ship CAP will have a box of sky to look after. We sit at the back of the box, but our desired engagement zone – our kill zone – is normally at the front, so that, if we do miss any 'muds', we can turn and re-engage them before they reach the back of the box.

As we come round, we turn 'hot' on CAP and we face up threat; our radars are on and we are searching. Within each pair, the leader looks low with his radar and the number two, the 'wingman' – the subordinate element – looks high. We co-ordinate the contacts that are coming in over the radar between the two aircraft to build up an 'air picture' – a mental picture of our piece of sky with the relative positions of the aircraft flying in it. When the radars start to pick up contacts, we put them into the 'kit' and end up with a God's eye view down onto the earth on our radar screens. Each contact is given an allocator – A, B, C and so on. Each has a velocity vector, showing if it is fast or slow, and we can call up its speed, height and heading on the computer display. The lead aircraft has to co-ordinate all the facts coming in from four, or even eight different aircraft if it is an eight-ship CAP, including his own.

We had just turned 'hot' when I picked up the first contacts on my radar. My former comrades-in-arms were dots on the screen in front of me. Only a few months before, one of those dots would have been me; now I was getting ready to destroy them. They were forty miles away and coming in fast at low level. I called in to the CAP leader: 'I've got two contacts, thirty left at forty miles, low level, heading in to us on zero nine zero, high speed.'

The words 'High speed, low level' immediately set our mental alarm bells ringing. It could be a real threat. It was now up to the leader to decide what he was going to allocate to each target. He could either despatch two aircraft to go and 'tap' – intercept – the targets that were coming in, or send all four, with everyone turning hot into them.

It takes a short time before we can distinguish the individual targets on our radar, during which, at a closing speed getting on for ten miles a minute, the threat has moved much closer. Between thirty and twenty miles we can pick out the formation, and at about that point the mud-movers' radars pick us up. Once they know there is a fighter looking at them, they kick off, and the cat and mouse game is set in motion.

John Peters: 'Kick left twenty degrees.' A left turn would instantly begin putting space between ourselves and the waiting fighters, making their job more difficult.

'Screen clear.' I had nothing on my screen to indicate the presence of the fighters, but they would soon look at us again, see us manoeuvring and try to follow.

'Track twelve.' We resumed the heading in towards our target. Then they looked at us again. They were not stupid, they did not keep on prodding us all the time, warning us that they were there, but they were probing us, watching our reactions, trying to plot an intercept. In return, we were manoeuvring, changing direction, trying to disrupt their calculations.

We kicked left again and then further left, but again they picked us up. Then there was another trace out to the left;

there was another Combat Air Patrol there, so we kicked right, back in, and held that course. The two CAPs were now co-ordinating in a classic pincer movement, a 200-year-old tactic, but using aircraft instead of cavalry regiments. We had to hold the changes of course long enough for the position of the aircraft to have moved on their radar screens. If we just wiggled, our mean line of advance would stay the same and they would rapidly intercept and destroy us.

'Notch left.' Things were hotting up. We notched – put the aircraft into a hard G-turn as a pair, at ninety degrees to the previous heading – away from the threat, trying to put it on the beam. At the same time, we punched out clouds of chaff – aluminium foil, the very same stuff used in the Second World War – to confuse the fighters' radar. First came the action call: 'Notch', followed by the information call: 'Strobe, two o'clock, F3.' A Tornado fighter had locked one of us up on his radar and was about to fire.

The modern pulse doppler radar is a big improvement on the old type, but it still does have a blind spot. It detects you by your speed towards it, and if your forward velocity disappears, so do you. If you put your aircraft on the beam – at right angles to the fighter – your speed towards the radar drops below its threshold, and you just disappear off the screen. You hold that course for twenty seconds or so, which puts you two or three miles away from your original position, and then resume your track. The fighters have to find you again, replan their intercept and re-lock their radar onto you, using precious time, which they can rarely spare.

As soon as we resumed our original heading, we were again picked up by the radar, but we had to make progress towards the target. Fighters do not have to shoot us down to succeed, they only have to stop us bombing the target. If they can make us dump our bombs or make us run out of fuel, the only thing left for us is to go home – they have achieved their aim, because we cannot go and bomb the target. If they can shoot us down, or make us fly into the ground, so much the better, but they can also just get into our formation and hassle us to such an extent that we start thinking 'I've got a fighter in my drawers – in my six o'clock – unless I do something, I'm going to die. I'm dumping my bombs and getting the hell out of here.' Their aim is to minimize damage sustained by their own forces and facilities and inflict maximum attrition on the enemy. Today the enemy was us.

John Nichol: 'Four-ship, low level, card formation' – they were in two battle pairs, aligned one behind the other, coming straight at us. 'Nitro three and four. Turn hot. Let's tap them.'

Our first task is to assess whether the targets are bombers or fighters. If we are not picking up any hostile radars on our warning equipment and the targets are flying at low level, the odds are that they are bombers. If they start to turn away from us and run away, that is again looking like bombers, but if we start to get hostile radars looking at us and our targets are turning in towards us, then they are either fighters spoiling for a scrap, or bombers with a death wish. We also have to keep searching for a fighter escort with the bombers. It is very easy for everybody to point their radars down at the bombers, going: 'Great, which one can I kill?' but while we are all looking down at low level, there may be a package of fighters 10,000 feet above us, doing exactly the same to us.

Our radars looking up were clear. The mud-movers were dodging and weaving, but we were closing on them.

'Fifteen miles.'

'Ten miles.'

The radios were alive with crosstalk as we began the 'sort'. Four fighters on CAP and four mud-movers coming in, and every fighter has to sort and fire at a different target. Everyone has to be sure of whom they are fighting, and that everybody has the same picture in their minds.

Our basic tactic is to fly 180 degrees out from the bombers, offset by three to five miles to one side. Between ten and six miles, we then turn in towards them, so that we come in to them at an angle which is easier for us to pick them up and best for the missiles. We do not want to come in straight down their throats, because they tend to be looking straight ahead, concentrating on their flying. We want to come out of the side and also high; coming out of the sun, classic First World War fighter tactics, still valid eighty years on.

Inside ten miles, the 'sort' – the targeting priority – was declared by the leader, each fighter being assigned a specific target. Every time the muds kicked, we re-sorted and reacquired them. The range was still closing.

Once we get inside a certain range, even if the muds do a hard break on to their beam, it will be difficult if not impossible for them to avoid our missiles, which will still track them and still guide home – or at least, that is what the manufacturers say. Whether it is going to work in real life is another question. Very often the muds put on their electronic countermeasures and start dumping chaff out of the back, and manoeuvre into the radar's blind spot. We may lose the lock and our missile, which is already in the air, will just fly off.

We try to lock our radar on at a similar range, because as soon as we do, the mud-movers get alarms sounding in their headsets and they immediately try to break our lock. We were in the missile launch success zone. The calls came over the headset from each fighter: 'Sorted.' 'Locked.'

I called 'Fox One, Fox One' and my pilot Podge pulled the trigger. A First World War 'ace' in his canvas and wood fighter used the same kind of trigger, but instead of bullets, we were firing a missile the size of a telegraph pole which goes blasting off the underside of the aircraft at three times the speed of sound.

The call: 'Fox One' came from all four aircraft in rapid succession – the missiles were in the air.

John Peters: We came back on to our initial heading, and by now we were very low and flying at 700 miles an hour. Another strobe; we just kept on manoeuvring, trying to disappear off their screens, chaffing and jamming. Each time we moved, they had a lot of aircraft to re-sort and reacquire before they could take that shot.

Flying as pairs, we keep watch on each other. If a missile is fired, we will see it in the air and give a warning: 'Missile in the air. Break left.' Even though the missiles are excellent, if you pull six G in a turn – six times the force of gravity – at the speed it is travelling, it has to pull about twenty-five G, just to get around the corner. If you are lucky, it may miss you. You would have to be extremely lucky, but it could happen. The missiles do not actually hit you, they have proximity fuses which detonate when their sensors tell them they are close to the target, sending thousands of titanium cubes exploding outwards, a circle of white-hot metal obliterating anything in its path. The proximity fuses do give us another avenue of escape; we fly as close to the ground as we can in the hope that the proximity fuse will detonate off the ground instead of our aircraft. Again, you have to be lucky, but in war you would do that perilous, last-ditch manoeuvre because it might save your life.

We had battled through the radar missile threat and no one had blown up on us, the danger now was of a Fox Two shot – a heat-seeking missile in a visual fight – and in that kind of combat, fighter threats appear without warning.

Suddenly a voice shouted in my headset: 'BUSTER!'

When you hear that word, you do not take time to think, you ram the throttles forward as far as they will go and force the aircraft down so low that it is practically scraping the ground.

Crew room stories from old, bold pilots profess that the Buccaneers could allegedly go down to sixty feet and 'surf' on the pressure wave from the ground. Even if the pilot releases the controls, the plane will go no lower; it sticks to the pressure wave as if chained to it ... or so legend has it – you would have to be very brave or very foolish to see if it was true. The Tornado definitely does not behave like that; take your hands off the stick when flying at sixty feet and you could be dead before you can even say: 'I wish I hadn't listened to that story'.

The formation spread like birds before a sparrow hawk.

Lunty and I widened, splitting to about seven kilometres abeam.

'Fighters coming down, five o'clock, five miles.'

'Where the hell are they?'

'Look back, look back, look high.'

I was looking forward and flying low, concentrating on not flying into the sea, while Jack was straining, pushing against the TV tabs – the computer screens – and with all the kit on he was really straining, trying to pull his neck round to see where the fighters were. 'Blast, still haven't seen them.'

Then Rich Fewtrell called: 'Bogie (enemy fighter), two o'clock high, descending on Voodoo One – on you, turn right, zero three zero.' The initial threat reaction and then the exchange of information to get everyone's eyes locked on to the threat. 'Bogie left, ten o'clock high, descending on number two' – the classic pincer move.

In a fight there are sudden staccato bursts of activity or information, then a tense pause, then another burst.

'Buster. Widen' – spreading the formation to make things harder for the fighters.

'He's coming in right, four o'clock. He's on you, number two.'

'Tally' – which means you have sighted the bogie. 'Tally' means you can see hostiles, 'Visual' means you can see friendly aircraft.

'Tally.'

The navs give us the information that we all need: who has got the fight. The pilots concentrate on looking forward and avoiding the ground, while the navs effectively fly the aircraft by voice commands.

'Bogie, seven Ks on Voodoo Three, closing.'

'6 Ks, on you, closing.'

'In your six o'clock.' Ice knotted my stomach. In combat, a fighter in your six o'clock for more than a few seconds means a heat-seeking Sidewinder missile will shortly be flying up your exhaust pipe at twice the speed of sound, packing twenty-five pounds of blast/fragmentation warhead. Your only hope is to draw the missile off with a flare, which burns hotter than a Tornado engine and can fool a heat-seeking missile into detonating on it rather than the aircraft.

'Turning left, zero-three-zero.' I threw the aircraft into a turn. It wallowed round, weighed down by fuel and a full bomb load, a St Bernard hounded by a whippet. The fighter flashed past, the first time I had even glimpsed it, hunting down my number two.

'Bogie on me, going over the top of me now.'

'Off you, on to us.'

If there is a threat warning, the pilot will react without even talking to the nav, but normally the process is a conversation between front and back seats. You do not tend to argue. The nav may sometimes say: 'Turn left, turn left', and the pilot may say: 'No, I'm going right'. He may be correct, but if the nav really believes he is wrong, he will shout: 'NO, GO LEFT NOW!' and the pilot will tend to do as he is told, because the nav is the man with his eyes on the threat.

Fighters pick one target and go for it. They are bullies who do not attack in ones, but pairs, fours and everything. At the same time, they have to be careful. They cannot just drop in willy-nilly and go 'Yahoo, this is a chicken shoot'; they first have to make sure that the bombers coming up behind are not going to be able to take a pot shot at them.

John Nichol: On CAP we fly at 420 knots, over seven miles a minute, though we go much, much faster in combat; our top speed is 800 knots – 900 miles per hour. The mud-movers will be doing at least seven miles a minute, producing a closing speed of fifteen miles a minute. At a radar pickup range of forty miles, that gives us a total of two-and-a-half minutes, which is not actually all that long.

We had fired our Skyflash – our radar-guided missiles at close range. By the time we got into visual range, we only had another three miles. Travelling by now at a speed of ten miles a minute, that gave me from ten to twenty seconds between getting the missile into the air and getting my pilot's eyes first on to our 'sorted' target, and then on to the whole formation. We were converting from the radar fight, where the guy in the back seat – the nav – does all of the co-ordination of the fight from a radar, like playing a computer game, to a visual fight, where the nav's job is to get his pilot's eyes on to the target.

Our main target was still the same, because we were still locked with it, but once I had my pilot focused on that one, it was imperative to get his eyes on to all three other aircraft as well. If you cannot do that, then you just 'blow through' – run away and regroup before continuing the fight – because you have lost what we call 'situational awareness' on the fight.

The be-all and end-all of flying is knowing what is going on around you. If you lose the air picture and do not know where all the other air defenders and bombers should be, then you are a danger to yourself and everyone else. In wartime it could mean soaking up a missile, in peacetime it could mean flying headlong into someone else. It is all very well going in for a visual missile kill on one of the mud-movers, that is brilliant, but there are three other bombers out there as well. You cannot go into a fight and 'tally' with just one man or even two, when there are another two planes a couple of miles behind them. That is the last thing in the world you want to do and would probably be the last thing you ever did do.

I already knew where the target was, because our radar was locked on and we were pointing at it. As we came in, I was lining Podge up with each target in turn.

'Five miles . . . Four miles . . . Two degrees down, thirty degrees right, first man.'

'Yeah, I've got it.'

'Right. Look another forty degrees right, second guy.'

'OK.'

'Two miles further, you have a battle pair behind them.'

'Tally.'

The mud-movers do not want to get into a visual fight because they are not agile enough, especially when they are tooled up with full fuel tanks and bombs, so their tactics are to duck, weave and get away from the fight as soon as they can, using their flares, electronic jamming and chaff to deny us any shots.

Over the sea our job is not too difficult, because the muds have nowhere to hide. They can only kick off – turn away – and go off as fast as they can, running away in their usual fashion, avoiding a punch-up at all costs. Over land, it is different. They dive off down the bottom of the deepest valley they can find and go as fast and low as they can. The best radar in the world cannot see through a mountain, so that is when you start to lose them. If you are over the hills of Northumberland, once they break your lock and disappear down a valley, that is it, you are never going to see them again, so it is important to get visual with them straight away.

There would be no escape for our target this time. Podge barrelled in behind him, dropping into his six o'clock as the 'mud' frantically threw his aircraft left. The growl of the missile aiming system changed to a high-pitched tone as it locked on to the heat source, the intruder's engines. Podge made the call: 'Fox Two, Fox Two' – heat-seeking missile – and pulled the trigger.

If we had been at war, there would have been one very dead bomber in front of us.

15

That extra intuition

THE DEBRIEF

John Peters: Contrary to popular myth, neither bomber crew nor fighter crew are solely interested in proving who are the better pilots. A bomber pilot just wants to avoid trouble, fly along the planned black line on his map, drop his bombs on an undefended target and get home. Fighter pilots would far rather take a missile shot from beyond visual range, kill the target and return home for 'tea and medals' than prove their virility by 'turning and burning' – dogfighting. Unfortunately for both, life is rarely that simple.

By the time you are dogfighting, you are pushing your luck, because while you are fighting one guy, another unseen one will take a shot on you. Fighters co-ordinate their attacks in just such a way, to set you up for a sucker punch. Air defence is not a gentlemanly 'Steady on Carruthers. Take that you rotter' one-on-one combat, with the better pilot automatically coming out the winner. That is fine for the movies, but no one gives a damn about that in real life. It is all measured on results; if you are the one left alive when the shooting stops, that is a good result. If there is only one of you and ten of them, so much the better for them; their only reaction will be: 'Great. Who's going to kill him?'

Air defenders actively want to avoid the enemy fighter threat and convert their attacks to the bombers. There is a fundamental difference in attitude of mind between fighter pilots and bomber crew; they are the hunters, we the hunted.

As a 'mud', you never operate over friendly territory. Until your bombs are coming off your aircraft, you are the prey, being hunted down in a hostile land. Only as the ejector rams spit your bomb load off the rails do you become the aggressor, raining down havoc and destruction from the sky. Muds know that at the target itself, we are going to have to grit our teeth and fly directly into the line of the Triple-A – the flak – to drop our bombs. Whereas we know that we are going to come under fire, air defenders – who almost invariably operate within their own sovereign air space – are wimps, turning tail and fleeing at the first sign of hostile fire.

Fighters have to shoot other aircraft down, but they aim to do so without exposing themselves to danger. Despite their wimpishness, however, fighters often have to get into a visual fight with us, and we are still not an easy 'kill'. Although they usually have 'overtake' – they can go faster than us – we go as fast and as low as we can. Over land our camouflage works very well and in bad weather in wartime we would fly into cloud, using our Terrain-Following Radar, losing the fighter instantly.

If the fighter put a missile in the air, we would break into a hard turn, putting out decoy flares to fool the heat-seeking element into detonating on the flare rather than our engines. With luck we might even make the fighter fly into the ground as he was trying to achieve his missile lock. If the fighter got right in my six o'clock, I would hope to get information from another member of the formation, although if I was targeted, it would be my job to divert the fighter away from the rest of the formation, either escaping or 'dying like a man'. We are even briefed to do this, it is just another of our countermeasures, leading the fighter away so that the other muds have a better chance of getting through. My mates would probably have 'exited stage left' by then anyway, to avoid becoming the next targets, although one of them could take a shot at the fighter if he was in a good position, doing a quick pop-up of a couple of hundred feet, locking the missile, firing and hitting the deck again.

It is a tough decision to make, because fighters never come in ones and it would highlight you to the rest of the pack of wolves; a flaming telegraph pole coming off the side of your aircraft marks you out in a fairly obvious way. Firing your missile to shoot down one fighter would be like swatting one wasp in a swarm. Until that point, they might not have seen you, but the moment you fire a missile, everyone sees you. You would probably only succeed in making them really angry and they would come straight for you.

Even in a straight tail-chase, we can remain a spiky prey for a fighter, for if we have retard – delayed action – bombs loaded, we have what we call a 'BIF' option – Bomb In Face. Bombers always put a time split between aircraft over a target, long enough to avoid 'fragging' each other with our own weapons, because the fragmentation envelope – the shrapnel – from the bombs we drop is about three-and-a-half thousand feet in all directions. If you mistime your Time On Target, you are likely to be flying through an airborne scrap metal yard, which is not a good place for an aircraft to be. That is exactly what we can arrange for a pursuing fighter.

We could throw one 1,000 pounder at the fighter and still have four out of five bombs left to do our job and hit the target. The fighter would be in our six o'clock and coming down towards his firing solution, which is about two-and-a-half kilometres behind us, but before he got there, we would do a slight pop in the front and pickle off a bomb. I hit the button, the bomb comes off and its parachute deploys, slowing the bomb and putting separation between us and its fragmentation envelope. The fighter will probably be pulling up by then, because he will have seen something coming off us, but if he does not – BOOOOOM! So either the fighter hops to a height of several thousand feet, or turns off, which gives us some separation and some hope of escape, or, best of all for us, he does not see the bomb or is such an idiot that he keeps coming in anyway, going: 'Yes, I can see him. Locked-on. Stand by . . .' but instead of firing his missile, he has a 1,000 lb, high-explosive bomb in his face.

The Combat Air Patrol does not hassle us all the way to the target. If we get through their engagement zone, they will pass information to other fighters and missile bases. The CAP is only one part of the defences which we must deceive or fight our way through before we can reach our goal.

'Screen clear. Resume track twelve.' We pulled back out of combat power, conserving our fuel. We were clear of the CAP and heading in towards our target, a redundant tank parked in a field on the Otterburn Ranges. The Range Controller records scores and times for all the bombs dropped and from those we can assess the performance of the individual aircraft, the four-ships and the squadron as a whole. Of course, if we have already been shot down by the Combat Air Patrol on the way in, our bomb scores become rather irrelevant.

John Nichol: In addition to the four fighters manning the CAP in our own piece of sky – our Fighter Area Of Responsibility – there might be eight in the next box to the north and six in the one to the south as well. Nothing enters those boxes without permission; if it does, it dies.

After an engagement, we report our fuel and weapons 'states' to the Operations Centre. Our fuel usage increases five or tenfold when we go supersonic, so below a certain fuel level we can only carry out a subsonic intercept. Once that happens, we either get sent to the tanker to refuel or are sent home. If heading home, we call our own squadron's Operations Centre and tell them what fuel, missiles and ammunition we have left and as soon as we land, even before the engines wind down, the engineers are swarming over the aircraft like ants. Fuel goes in, oils are checked and the missiles come out of the sheds and are loaded on, so that we can declare 'on state' again – able to scramble and be airborne within ten minutes. It is like a pit-stop in a Grand Prix, with the ground crew working as fast and as accurately as the Williams team mechanics.

The actual 'on state' time varies, dependent on the level of alert currently operating; these can range from enough time to finish your coffee, to sitting in your jet, next to the runway, awaiting instructions.

Throughout the Cold War we had crews sitting in their jets in the Q sheds at a very high state of readiness, twenty-four hours a day, 365 days a year, able to get their wheels off the ground inside a few minutes. Life is a little easier since the Wall came down, but only a little; these days the guys are still sitting there but the readiness state is now slightly more relaxed. Looked at that way, the end of the Cold War has not had a massive impact, we are just a few minutes further away from going to war.

Once the engagement has finished, we go back up, reset the CAP and wait for the next set of 'trade' – unsuspecting bombers – to come through. Whether we pursue bombers beyond the area of our own 'box' depends on the Air Defence Control Centre. If we were allowed to, we might chase a bomber down for forty miles over the North York moors, but that would be unusual. We are just one strand in the air defence system and the bombers that escape the CAP still have to contend with air defence missiles, Rapier sites and the gun sites over the target.

The air defence system works by attrition. The long-range missiles will take out some of the bombers before they reach the CAP. Our radar-guided missiles will remove a few more, and our heat-seeking missiles and guns will claim others. Some will escape, but the UK air defence missiles will eliminate some more, as will the airfield defence missiles – the Rapiers – and the guns on the airfield itself. It is a layered system and every layer overlaps.

When we are training, everything is exactly as it would be in warfare, except there is no big flash and no missiles come off the aircraft. As fighters we register kills a lot of the time. Whether the mud-movers would agree is less certain . . . In the real case there are always problems which reduce the effectiveness of the air defenders; power systems do not fire, arming systems do not arm, radar systems do not see, missiles fly into the ground, and so on. We have a video system on the F3 that tapes all the major components of the weapons attack system. When we play back the tape, which is like watching a very sophisticated computer game, it is easy to see if a missile simulated in the air is successful or defeated.

On landing back at Leeming following Northern Banner, we held the film debrief, assessing the success of all the shots that we took, and noting the time and place that they occurred. That mission report was forwarded to the Exercise HQ, who compared it with the information received from the mud-movers, and then sent a signal back, listing all the raids that took place within our Fighter Area Of Responsibility and our success in stopping them, allowing us to assess our individual and collective performance. The Exercise HQ collated information from all the raids during Northern Banner, a mammoth task for a week-long Exercise, with raids going in continuously from 8 a.m. to 5 p.m. every day. From the welter of individual statistics, they were able to build towards an overall picture of how the UK air defence system would perform in a real conflict and how successful our own bombers might be at penetrating an enemy air defence system.

When I was a mud-mover myself, we used to think that fighter pilots were all lying swine, especially when they told us that they had shot us all down, but that is exactly what they do.

John Peters: To mud-movers, fighter pilots are all silk scarves and wild claims. All the fighter squadrons seem to have bold silk scarves in ridiculous patterns – black and white checks or black with gold embossing – and they all seem to assume that if they have seen a mud, they must have shot him down. When we are at war and fighting for real, there is no room for doubt about the winners and losers of air combat. The winners are doing victory rolls in the air, or stroking the barrels of their Triple-A guns, while the losers plummet to earth in flames. In peacetime, the evidence is rather less conclusive.

A few years ago, it was virtually impossible to say with any certainty who had 'lived' or 'died' after an engagement. As a result, everyone would claim every available kill, no matter how implausible. A debrief was sometimes more like a bear garden, with puce-faced fighter and bomber crew shouting abuse and ridicule at each other's wild claims.

Even now, with all our technology, there are only certain large-scale Exercises where we can say with near-certainty who has survived and who has been shot down. On the giant NATO Exercise Red Flag, held in the Nevada desert tantalizingly close to the trillion-watt glow of Vegas neon lighting up the night sky, we all carry 'telemetry pods', which record every aspect of the fight and downlink to a computer the size of a banana republic and costing several times its national debt. We debrief after the mission in a huge cinema, while the computer replays the whole battle on the screen. The assembled multitudes whoop and holler their way through the conflict, each man acclaiming his triumphs but falling strangely silent at his failures.

Without that system, things are rather less clear. We know when a fighter has locked us up on his radar and we have a pretty fair idea of whether we would have escaped or been destroyed, but unlike the long-range radar missiles, our warning equipment does not detect when we have been locked up by a close range, heat-seeking missile. Just the same, if a fighter is in your six o'clock for more than a fraction of a second, it is a pretty safe bet that in wartime a Sidewinder would be flying up your exhaust pipe within seconds, turning your engines and your jet into metal confetti.

We rely on the honesty of each other not to claim missile 'kills' that were out of range or did not time out properly, but in truth the result of a training engagement is far less important than the experience gained from it by both winner and loser. Our training is an endless learning curve and being 'shot down' in an exercise is unimportant, providing the lessons are learned, so that it does not happen again in a real war situation.

As soon as we got back to Brüggen after each raid during

Northern Banner, we completed a mission report, stating whether we had reached the target within our Time On Target bracket. We also filled in a separate report giving details of the exact times and locations at which we were 'tapped' by fighters.

The information was collated by the Exercise HQ, together with the reports from the air defence squadrons, and signals then went out to all of us, telling us who had been shot down and who had survived. Our four-ship lost one aircraft shot down, and another went through the range 'dry' – unable to drop his bombs because he could not acquire the target. The other two got through and successfully bombed the target. That was about an average result, and considerably better than the four-ship immediately behind us, who were all shot to pieces by the fighters.

The aircraft shot down are precisely identified: 'GR1 in the Appleby Valley at 13.10, Tornado four-ship, left-hand man', but even without such meticulous debriefing of a mission, there are few, if any, arguments about 'kills' these days anyway. The F3 force do not seem to make wild and fraudulent claims. They really cannot do so, even if they wanted to, because a video system records everything that goes on. It must be hell for them, because if they screw up an intercept, there is no way that they can disguise the fact, it is there for everyone to see when we debrief.

The first time I was on the receiving end of this technology was as part of a four-ship flying over Goose Bay, in Canada. We were convinced that we had got rid of the fighters chasing us, but when we met up with the F3 crews afterwards, they told us: 'We got Fox Ones on all of you. You were flying a goose formation, weren't you? We got that one there, that one here', and so on. I just sat there thinking: 'How the hell do they know all this?' Then at the face-to-face debrief – still a rarity – they showed their video tapes. The plan delineated exactly where we had been flying, where we had manoeuvred, kicked and notched. The four blips had all been numbered and sorted and the missiles all timed out. It left us all pretty deflated. There we were working our nuts off, flying really low and fast, grunting and sweating, shooting down valleys and thinking we had disappeared, but those guys did not even have to see us. They just chased us down, cruising at height, almost on autopilot, until they had everything: speeds, times, headings, the lot. Had we been at war, all four of us would probably have been shot down.

Despite that, the odds are not as bad as they sound. The next day I led a pair through two Combat Air Patrols, each made up of four F3s, and they did not even get a sniff of us. There are so many variables that can affect the outcome each time we fly.

Missiles work on a PK – Probability Kill – the probability of success from acquiring the target, locking on and launching the missile, to the target being destroyed. A missile may have a PK of seventy per cent, making a kill seven times out of ten, but that is against non-manoeuvring targets in ideal conditions, without bad weather or electronic jamming. Air crew are paid to produce the best possible results with the least possible equipment, but that does not mean that they will maintain that seventy per cent PK in battlefield situations. That is why we send four or eight bombers against a target instead of just one or two – to guarantee its destruction. There is always a measure of overkill, to allow for operator error, a confused scenario, jamming, stress, night, sleeplessness and a host of other factors, which can all affect that PK.

A new generation of missiles will complicate the lives of bomber crew enormously. AMRAAMs – Advanced Medium Range Air-to-Air Missiles – are awful news for us, because they are 'fire and forget' missiles. At the moment a fighter firing a Fox One – a radar-guided missile – has to lock us up on the radar, fire the missile and keep us locked up until it hits home, before he can acquire another target. Meanwhile, we get a strobe on our radar warner and can take evasive action; break the chain and the missile will miss. With an AMRAAM, we may only get a momentary warning, a brief blip on the screen when the enemy aircraft acquires us. The blip will disappear from the screen again, and we may think that we are safe. The first warning that the missile is in the air might be when it blows us to pieces.

Given that combat between bombers and fighters is so heavily weighted in the fighters' favour, it might seem crazy that we 'muds' operate so frequently without any fighter cover, but the sad truth – from the bombers' point of view – is that we do not rate any higher on the scale of defence priorities. The fighters' first priority is air defence, protecting our own sovereign air space against attack. There are insufficient fighters to escort every bombing mission as well. Fighter cover will normally only be allocated as part of a 'gorilla' or large package of aircraft – which, like a 500 pound gorilla, can do any damn thing it likes – going against a high value target such as an enemy command centre. Fighters are far too valuable to be sent off with every Tom, Dick and four-ship bombing raid.

Fighter cover is there often enough to make enemy fighters think twice before moving in on us, but in the majority of cases, it is our wits, our skill and our airmanship, not forgetting a generous helping of luck, that keeps us alive, not a fighter escort.

Our tactics may change a little to combat the AMRAAM threat, but the basics will remain largely the same. Our aim is to complicate the fighters' task all the time, and keep providing them with more things to think about. For all the technology, it is actually like a game of chess. If you can bluff, or cheat, or outthink the other guy, you will still win. That is the exciting thing about flying. Although we do have all the computers, in the end it still comes down to using your head. It is the man in the cockpit, not the computer, that will win the fight.

The blip may go off the screen, but because you know how each other fights, you know where the other guy is going. For twenty seconds you might have lost the blip, or in a visual fight you may have lost sight of him, but you move your head in a certain direction, I cannot explain why, and suddenly you have reacquired him. There is a science of flying, but the art of flying is having that extra intuition or instinct, call it what you will, but it is the reason why some people always seem to get shot down and others do not. It is not just luck, it is all situational awareness; you know what the other guy is trying to achieve . . . especially if you used to share a cockpit with him.

16

The shocking reality of warfare
PREPARING FOR WAR AGAIN

John Peters: The prerequisite for excellence in flying fast-jet aircraft is a degree of danger in training with them. The only way to acquire the skills that will make you a successful bomber or air defence pilot in wartime is to push progressively closer to the limits while training in peacetime. Training restrictions are rigidly imposed, both to avoid waking up the civilian neighbours too often and because fast jets – and the men who fly them – are such expensive commodities that the Air Force does not want to write off either of them unnecessarily, but a completely risk-free training environment would be a complete waste of time. It is only at the edge, or close to the edge, that air crew learn their business.

In wartime, things change. In the build-up to the Gulf War, the training intensified and the risks increased, while the rule book was interpreted to the limit. We were expecting to go to war and it was our responsibility to know our own limits. Even when we were given carte blanche, we remained surprisingly circumspect. No one wanted to be a complete exhibitionist and get himself killed before we had even got to the Gulf.

Some aspects of Air Force training have remained virtually unaltered since the formation of the RAF, seventy-five years ago, but others change dramatically in response to new aircraft, new weaponry, new technology or new experiences in actual combat. Air power is technology: more powerful engines, bigger payloads, more agility, longer-range missiles and radars. As technology changes and our experience grows, tactics change as well. The lessons learned from the Gulf conflict have already been assimilated and our flying tactics modified, particularly in response to the effectiveness of Iraqi Triple-A – flak – against our low-level bombing missions.

Even our own ordeal at the hands of the Iraqis had its uses. All the PoWs were extensively debriefed and the information on how we reacted under deprivation and interrogation is now included in RAF interrogation training, which had previously been unchanged since the end of the Second World War. We have been excused the training ourselves – we have already had ample experience of the real thing – but colleagues who have undertaken the course assure me that it is both realistic and 'deeply unpleasant'.

No matter how dangerous and intense our training, it can never completely replicate the shocking reality of warfare itself. The Gulf War experience has become part of the fabric of RAF life, but it has also etched itself deeply into the lives of individual air crew. It was not necessary to have been captured and tortured for the experience of war to have left an indelible mark.

When the squadron was again involved in a build-up to genuine conflict in the Gulf, it set off a turmoil of conflicting emotions in me. I was staying with Helen's parents in Birmingham when one of 31's Flight Commanders phoned, recalling me from my weekend break as the crisis blew up. Punitive bombing strikes against targets in Iraq were being planned in retaliation for breaches of the Gulf War peace agreement. When I put the phone down, my pulse was racing. My first thought was: 'Here we go again', but I still desperately wanted to get out there. Part of the reason was that the one mission I had flown in the Gulf was a failure; we did not get our bombs away, were shot down and became prisoners of war. That could have happened whether or not we had dropped our bombs, of course, we were just in the wrong piece of sky at the wrong time, yet I still wanted to go back to the Gulf.

I do not desperately want to drop bombs and kill people, and I do not feel that I have to prove anything to anybody else, but I wanted to be out there for the sake of my own professional and personal pride. Having been a prisoner of war was a double-edged sword. I found a certain strength of character and have certainly suffered no long-term damage, but the stress we PoWs faced was different from the stress faced by the other guys. As they wonder whether they could have undergone my experience, I question whether I could have faced theirs, for I did not have to get back in my cockpit, having been shot at, and fly another mission, and another.

Apart from having survived, I have nothing to be proud of from my war, no sense of achievement at a job well done, and I would willingly swap our public accolades since the Gulf for the private satisfaction of knowing that I had produced the goods, doing what we are all paid to do. In my quieter moments, I do reflect on the fact that our 'loft' attack failed. Had our bombs come off, had we completed the attack successfully and then been shot down, I would not be so concerned, feeling that I had done my bit and that being shot down was just a piece of bad luck; but I will always harbour the disappointment that I failed to achieve 'the airborne result'. That is the fundamental difference, the thing that gnaws at my guts. I am somehow waiting for someone to turn round and tell me that I was not 'up to it' and that I screwed up. I already know my retort: 'You have your hair set on fire and your head beaten with a baseball bat, and then come and talk to me about it', but it has never occurred and I never really expect that it will.

I accept the disappointment as I accept what happened to us in Iraq; it is something I cannot change, it just happened. The difference is that none of the other Gulf veterans that I know would ever wish to return there, justifiably believing that there are others, unblooded in warfare, who are only too willing to go and prove themselves. They have already 'been there, seen it, done it'. Masochistically perhaps, I would still like to have returned there.

I was not chosen. The guys went off almost exactly a year

after the first time, some on 26 December and the rest on 30 December. Reading the newspaper reports back in Germany felt very strange. My only contribution was to take off as an airborne spare, ready if needed to take an aircraft down to the Gulf. Unfortunately, all the other aircraft worked perfectly and I had to turn back at Nice in the south of France.

Back at Brüggen, desperate for news, we lived on rumours from day to day – they were going in, they were not going in – then I woke up one morning to hear on the news that they had attacked during the night. Although the raids were very short and quick and the squadron was not away for long, sitting it out in Germany helped me to understand the frustrations of those who were left behind last time.

When the guys got back, the first comment, which I knew I was going to get, came from Platty, the nav who led the bombing wave. 'Well, at least I've done half a sortie more than you', he said with a wicked smile, because he had flown one, whereas I had only got half-way through my one and only sortie – cheeky git, but very good banter!

Helen Peters: In the days when it was Armageddon or nothing, I suppose the wives shared the sense of unreality, the belief that there would never be a time when the boys would do it for real and go to war. Once they went to the Gulf, as the deadline came closer and closer, I was pretty sure that they would be involved in some form of attack. When it finally happened, I was very surprised that it was our lads who were right in the forefront, given the numbers out there. The Americans had hundreds of thousands of people and the Brits had a couple of thousand, and yet the news reports made it seem as if it was our boys right in the front all the time. Whenever the news came up about air crew lost, killed or captured, it was somebody we knew and that definitely was not something that I had anticipated.

When rumours began to spread that the boys might have to go back to the Gulf, half of me felt: 'Oh God, here we go again', but the other half felt very much that John would want to go and prove himself. I suppose to a certain extent, that was because of people ribbing him about only flying half a sortie. I really felt for him, so I was almost as desperate for him to be able to go as he was. At the same time, I was thinking how ridiculous it was to be wishing him back out in the Gulf under fire, and his mother was on the phone saying: 'Oh my God, what are we going to do?' as well, so it was a bit of a mixture of emotions.

John Nichol: The call-up for Bosnia came out of the blue. I was on a training exercise in Sardinia with the squadron at the time, fighting against Dutch F-16s as part of my build-up to being combat-ready, I had only been flying the F3 for five months and it takes somewhere between six and ten months to become combat-ready.

No Air Force base is ever truly picturesque, there is too much concrete and barbed wire for that, but the Italian base on Sardinia at Decimomannu comes closer than most. Deci is a windswept, palm-fringed oasis in the desert, in the south of the island not far from Cagliari, though far enough to be in the middle of nowhere. The base is carved out of rock which is blindingly white in the glare of the Mediterranean sun, and set in a sandy basin surrounded on all sides by mountains, which concentrate the already intense heat even more.

The only shade is provided by the palm trees, from which the noise of the cicadas sometimes seems as loud as the roar of the jets. The only other visible fauna are the lizards, basking on every rock and so tame that they race up and down the legs of the tables outside the bar, the 'Pig and Tape', where we congregate after work every night. The bar is scarcely de luxe, just a concrete bunker, some fridges full of beer, and a patio-load of battered garden furniture outside. Perhaps because of the lizards, there are no flies at all – a welcome contrast to other hot spots like the Gulf, where there were squadrons of them on permanent alert, dive-bombing any glass of beer left unattended for even a second.

Although invariably hot, the weather can be very strange, with bizarre localized fogging. At six o'clock, when we go to work, it is usually bright sunshine, but by eight o'clock, there is often fog up and down the runway, even though it is completely clear fifty yards either side. Ten minutes later, the fog disappears again without a trace.

The beach is only a short drive away and a lot of our leisure time is spent down there, even in March, when we sprawl on the sand in our shorts while the Sardinians sit outside the beach cafés in their overcoats and mufflers, gazing in wonder at these white, lardy Brits trying desperately to get a suntan. We always have lunch at Enrico's, a small shack the size of a garden shed, out of which a chef miraculously produces fantastic Italian food. We eat sitting outside in the sunshine, surrounded by palm trees ... it is not easy being air crew sometimes, but someone has to do it.

Deci is jointly held as a training base by ourselves, the Dutch, Germans and, of course, the Italians, which can make an evening out a bit like an American's tour of Europe – into the Dutch bar for a couple of gins, the English bar for a few beers and the German Mess for a dinner of steak or sausage and sauerkraut, then on to the very stylish Italian club, all marble floors, walnut panelling and crystal chandeliers. Most evenings seem to end there, knocking back sambuccas and cappuccinos and crunching amaretti biscuits.

Deci is a great place to get a suntan, but one of the worst places on earth, Iraq always excepted, to spend your days encased in a flying suit. By the time we have walked out to our jet in the morning, we are already soaked with sweat and we continue to sweat buckets for the rest of the day, dreaming of the first cold beer of the evening.

One Wednesday night we had finished work and gone back to the bar. We were all sitting down, having a quiet beer and idly tossing stones at the 'French Embassy' – a boulder fifty yards away, given its name partly because people are always throwing rocks at it, and partly because of the incident when the Americans bombed the French Embassy by mistake during the attack on Libya. One of the weapons instructors suddenly appeared and told us that there was news of a deployment. Everybody had to stop drinking and get ready for a briefing. An hour later one of the Flight Commanders appeared and said: 'We're on stand-by to go back. It could be tomorrow morning. The squadron has been put on twenty-four hours' notice to go out to Bosnia.'

Hearing that gave me a very strange feeling. This was only my second squadron in the Air Force and here we were getting ready to go to war again. The second war in two years; it was becoming rather a tedious occurrence. I watched our jets set off for home at first light the next day. The few of us left behind were supposed to wait for transport home later on, but luckily there was a Hercules at Deci to collect equipment for Leeming, and by hook, crook and other means, we managed to stow away on it and were back only a few hours after the jets.

As usual with the Air Force, after the instant reaction, there was then a period of 'phoney war', in this case while NATO deliberated about whether to send in forces. The squadron used the time to develop the tactics it would need in Bosnia, intercepting helicopters from one of our other squadrons over Northumberland, because we had not trained against helicopters before. After a week of that, NATO, like the man from Del Monte, said 'Yes'. The Americans deployed their F-15s and the Dutch their F-16s, but, although the squadron was on twenty-four hours' notice to move, there was still no word of when it would be called into action.

The atmosphere during that time brought memories of the Gulf flooding back to me. Rumour and counter-rumour sped around the station. The tension grew as the guys filled in power of attorney forms and made out their wills, just in case.

A couple of weeks passed. On Friday afternoon, as normal, everybody went to the bar after work, but at half past five, just as Happy Hour was warming up, the Boss phoned, telling us not to move until he got there – never a difficult order to comply with when you are waiting in a bar. An hour later, he appeared, called us all outside and said: 'Right, we're going'. Forty-eight hours later, the F3s had flown out and thirty-two Hercules transport aircraft had taken off, loaded with equipment.

Although I was not yet combat-ready, I pulled every stroke in the book to try and get out there with the rest of the squadron, volunteering to be everything from intelligence officer to clerk, cook and driver. I was desperate not to be left behind, but it was all to no avail. The RAF has specialists for every job I was volunteering to do and after listening patiently to my incessant pleas, the Boss finally told me politely but firmly that my job was simply to get combat-ready as quickly as possible, in case more crews were needed out there. I hopped around, trying to help out where I could, but also trying not to be in the way as the guys got on with the business of preparing to go to war. I achieved combat-readiness while they were away, but it was agony to sit back at base as my mates on the squadron flew out, possibly into combat. I hated to watch them go.

Bosnia went exactly the same way as the Gulf, a mad rush to get out there, with teddies coming out of the cot and everything, followed by total boredom for six months and then a sudden escalation into talk of bombing missions. The Jaguars and Sea Harriers from the *Ark Royal* and our own F3s were all out there and it all looked as if it could have turned very, very pear-shaped quite quickly ... although it could just as easily drag on for another ten years.

It was a very frustrating time for the guys flying missions out there, who were virtually helpless, prevented by political constraints from stopping any of the hundreds of violations of the UN air exclusion zone. The Serb combat aircraft kept well out of the way of the Tornados, but their helicopters, which also kept well clear at the start, were soon flying around regardless of who was out there, operating almost as they pleased.

'We saw them, we tracked them, but whenever we asked

permission to shoot them down, we always got a negative', one of the squadron told me on his return from Bosnia. 'We would call them up and order them to land. Some would do so, others just ignored us. If we turned our nose towards them, they stopped, but as soon as we turned away, they carried on.'

Things got so bad that the guys suggested a new tongue-in-cheek call to be used when intercepting aircraft or helicopters. In place of the traditional: 'Stop. You are being intercepted by a United Nations patrol, land immediately or you will be engaged', a more appropriate warning would have been: 'Stop, or the United Nations will escort you to your final destination'.

The only 'action' I saw during the squadron's spell on the Bosnian Air Defence mission came when we flew out to southern Italy to deliver a replacement jet. We were meant to be coming home the same day, but bad weather forced us to stay overnight. Our hotel was an hour's drive further into the wilds of southern Italy. It had a sign proudly advertising its three stars and looked fine from the outside, but the interior did not quite match up. The rooms were clean, but as bare as Mother Hubbard's cupboard, and the bathroom had old sheets instead of towels. It appeared to be a peaceful little spot, but that proved to be as misleading as the three stars. By three in the morning, it sounded as if we were sleeping in the middle of a lorry park, with what seemed like every lorry in Italy parked under our window, revving its engine to near-destruction. There were shouts, bangs, crashes, slamming doors and grinding gearboxes – it proved to be a very sleepless night.

The next morning, we were back on base at ten o'clock ready for an eleven-thirty departure, but there was a fault on the aircraft and the flight plan had to be delayed. An hour later, when we finally got into the aircraft, the tower then told us: 'Your takeoff time is now 15.50 local time.' French Air Traffic Control, from whom we do not often get a warm and fuzzy feeling – the feeling we always like to have when sitting in a cockpit – had no slot for us until then. We had to stop it all, shut it all down, go back and sit around the crew room for another four hours and then go back out and try again, even though it meant we would not get back to Leeming until half past nine at night.

Back in the aircraft again, my pilot, 'Mork', tried to start the auxiliary power system – the small engine used to start the main engines. Click . . . nothing. Click . . . nothing. If it fails three times, we have to wait half an hour before trying again, and by then we would once more have lost our 'slot' from air traffic control. The third time it did fire, but as we went through all our checks, part of the fly-by-wire system failed. It was beginning to look like one of those days. The faulty part reset, however, and we got our clearance and routeing and were starting to taxi out when it failed again. Once more it reset satisfactorily, but as we got to the side of the tower, a different bit of the fly-by-wire failed. The only thing to do was stop and put the whole system through a full test, which takes about three minutes. While we were doing that, the tower came back on the radio, calling: 'Number two' – which was us – 'there is smoke coming from the rear of your aircraft.'

We whipped our heads around, trying to peer over the side of the aircraft, shouting for the tower to confirm, but we could not see anything amiss. The tower was emphatic, however. 'Number two, definite smoke from the rear of your aircraft, declaring an emergency.' Halfway through their sentence, I was already shouting at Mork: 'Shut down the engines, let's get out of here'. We had all the seats and canopy armed ready for takeoff, however, and if you are actually going to climb out rather than bang out – eject – you have to put all the pins back in, just like the cabin crew do in a jumbo jet when it lands.

There are also several drills we have to carry out to make sure that the aircraft is shutting down properly. Even though we have turned all the power off, it is possible for the Tornado's engines to be still running, like a diesel engine that keeps going even though the ignition is switched off. Without the electronic controls, the engines can get into a configuration where they just wind themselves up to self-destruction. That has actually happened on two occasions. The engines wound up and up, self-destructed and flew out of the back of the aircraft on their own, which was a pretty distressing experience for the crew involved.

When we got the canopy up we could smell burning, but before we could get out, we had to undo our lap straps, shoulder straps, leg restraints, arm restraints and the connector to our survival pack. A few years ago, when I had a fire in a hangar, I thought that I had unstrapped and disconnected everything and jumped over the side of the aircraft, only to find that I had forgotten to undo my arm restraints. I was left dangling from the side of a burning aircraft by my arm straps until rescued by the emergency crew. This time I got all my straps off in record time and while Mork was still shutting down the last systems, I was clambering over the top of his head, saying: 'Are you coming with me?'

By this time, the fire crews were racing down the runway towards us, but when we looked towards the back of the aircraft, there was no more smoke to be seen, so instead of jumping off and risking a broken ankle from the twenty foot drop, we stood on the wing until the rescue crew arrived. When the plane was examined, the engineers found that some of the coolant from the radar cooling system had spilled onto one of the hot fans in the equipment bay; smoke had been coming out of the aircraft, but we were not on fire.

That discovery came too late, for we had again lost our 'slot' with French Air Traffic Control. There was nothing for it but to stay another night. Rather than spending it in a lorry park again, I sifted through the Italian Yellow Pages and booked us into a hotel with some decent towels and no revving engines outside.

It was the third emergency I had faced inside six months and although this time it was not a serious one, each emergency makes the heart beat faster and sets the adrenalin pumping and the mind racing. Each time you wonder if this will be the one to bring an Air Force career to an inglorious end, dying not in some heroic rearguard action or impossible fight against overwhelming odds, but, like so many friends and colleagues, in a humdrum training accident; just one more of the boys who go out in the morning and do not come home at night.

After a two-month tour of duty over Bosnia, XI Squadron handed over to 23, another Leeming squadron. In a piece of very bad timing, the men of 23 Squadron discovered while they were still away on Bosnian duty that they were to be the latest RAF squadron to be disbanded. If cuts have to be made, something obviously has to go, but the timing of the announcement still cut deeply into the hearts of men who were risking their lives in a conflict that could have sucked them into all-out war at any moment.

All the Tornado F3 stations took turns on Bosnian duty, and just as our own spell ended, we were immediately faced with two other major commitments. We began our stint of sending crews to the Falklands, where we still hold a number of aircraft at combat-readiness in case the Argentinians ever decide to invade again. We also took a turn on Quick Reaction Alert, taking over from the Northern Air Defence base at Leuchars for a few days, giving us all long days and nights in the Q sheds, waiting for the nonexistent Soviet hordes to come piling over the horizon.

17

If our missile misses, we have a problem

MULTINATIONAL TACTICAL EXERCISES

John Nichol: Air combat has some parallels with racing Grand Prix cars. Some machines have a technical edge on the others; they may be faster, more agile, more reliable, better equipped, but just as in a Grand Prix car, the person in the cockpit can make a tremendous difference. Nigel Mansell in a second-hand Ford Cortina would still give Aunt Agatha in a Williams Renault a hell of a race, and similarly, a good pilot will mask the disadvantages of his aircraft and maximize the advantages, using his superior airmanship to outfly the enemy.

It is a consoling thought for Tornado crew, because on paper at least, the Tornado F3 is at a disadvantage against several other aircraft. Fighters have very different capabilities, but all have long or medium-range radar-guided missiles and short-range air-to-air missiles. Most fighters are also very agile aircraft – the American F-15s and F-16s and the Russian Mig-29 Fulcrums are incredibly agile – but the Tornado is not. In fact, the Tornado F3 is not really a fighter at all. It was originally designed as a low-level bomber – the GR1 – and has merely been fitted with bigger engines and air defence equipment. The Tornado is incredibly fast at low level, but it is not a good aircraft in which to be dogfighting or 'turning and burning' against other fighters. Take it above 5,000 feet and it is at a disadvantage because it is based on a low-level bomber, with engines optimized for performance in ground-hugging flight. To be fair, it was never intended to be fast and agile in dogfights, because its role was to act as a long-range interceptor, firing radar missile after radar missile at Soviet heavy bombers coming over from the Icelandic Gap.

The Tornado F3 does have advantages, however. Within the limits of the weapon system, you really cannot beat having two men in the aircraft because you have a division of labour, two minds thinking about the same problem. Not many fighters are two-seat, just the F3, the Tomcat and the new multi-role F-15E Strike Eagle. The F-15E is probably the most capable aircraft overall. It now has AMRAAMs – Advanced Medium-Range Air-to-Air Missiles – which far outstrip the ones that most aircraft carry, they are the true 'fire and forget' missiles. The Russians are supposed to be developing even longer-range missiles, while the Tomcat, the US Navy fighter, carries an extremely long-range missile, the Phoenix. You certainly do not want to get involved in a fight with that, because before you have even identified the aircraft on your radar, a missile could be coming at you over the horizon.

Fighter-to-fighter tactics are very different from those we use against bombers. Against a bomber we delay our shot as long as possible, to give him the least chance to avoid it. If we fire a long-range missile and the bomber turns away from us, the missile will never get there. If he beams us, our radar will lose him and we might never see him again.

Against a bomber, we would offset away from the target, to get some displacement, before turning back in. With a fighter we look to 'hot-nose' him straight away; point straight at him as fast we can, threaten and be aggressive, and we try to get our missile in the air as quickly as possible, before the other guy does.

We put a mental sphere around the enemy fighter equivalent to the range of his missiles, and we do not want to get into that sphere without having our own missiles in the air first. As soon as we get radar contact and assess that we are engaging a fighter, we first get our speed up as high as we can; we always want to enter the fight with speed, because speed is energy, and energy is life. The instant we get a firing solution, we start to launch missiles, even knowing that if he turns away from us the missile will be wasted, because at least we are getting something in the air and gaining the advantage by forcing him to be defensive.

As we close in, all sorts of thoughts race through my brain: 'Does he know that we're here? Is he pointing towards us, threatening us? When can we get our first missile off, and will it be before he fires his?' If we are locked-on by a radar before we have our missile in the air, we have to turn away to defeat a possible missile shot, holding that course for perhaps ten seconds and then turning back in. As we press back in, we are looking for our RHWR – our radar warning – to be clean while we try again to get our missiles in the air, but if we get in close and are locked-up before firing our missile, we do a 180 degree turn and get out of there as fast as we can – we run away. There is absolutely no point in pressing on into a fight like that, if he is firing missiles and we have none in the air, because we are just going to die before we even clap eyes on him.

That may not sound very dignified or courageous and it is certainly nothing like fighting a duel with pistols at dawn, or jousting at a medieval tournament in the golden age of chivalry, but it is the only way to fight and survive. We run back out to a reasonable range, fifteen, maybe even twenty miles and then face back up to him. Then it becomes what we call a rolling fight, like an aerial ballet, trading missile shots. Even if there is an enemy missile in the air, if we had launched our own ten seconds earlier it would defeat his missile shot, because if his aircraft disintegrates, his radar is no longer locked-on to us. Of course if our missile misses, then we do have a problem.

Tactical Fighter Meet is where we put all our air defence skills together, a NATO Exercise held at the Royal Danish Air Station at Karup in June, involving aircraft and crew from several different nations – British, Dutch, Norwegians,

Germans, Americans and Danish of course – about a hundred aircraft in all. It gives us a chance to work really closely together, as opposed to flying from bases in all our different countries and just coming together in the sky. It is still mud-movers versus air defenders, but the mud-movers also have fighter cover, making it a much more tricky exercise for the air defenders protecting the targets.

There is also communications and radar jamming. The Germans put up their jamming aircraft – huge generators with wings on – and some of that is very effective, too effective as it turned out. We flew one mission with four fighters going up to relieve another four who had been on CAP defending a naval group, but every time we tried to check in, a responsive jammer scanned the frequencies and jammed us. The leader would get as far as: 'Nitro check' and then the radio would go: 'BEEEEEP' or they recorded his voice and played it back, so that the attempt to check in became: 'Nitro Check. One . . . One . . . One . . . One' . . . into infinity. When we chopped to a prearranged alternative frequency, the jammers found us on that one and replayed another 'chop' to us. If you were not careful, you ended up following your own voice around the sky, just trying to find someone else to talk to. In the end we had all eight aircraft in different parts of the sky, all trying to do different things. Looking back, it was actually very funny, although we certainly did not think so at the time, because we could not make head nor tail of it. The flight leader was even threatening to get out of his cockpit and sort it out with his fists.

When jamming is as effective as that, we can just turn our radios down, because we have a number of Standard Operating Procedures to fall back on and we can go into a fight using them alone. It is not nearly as effective, and it can get quite difficult to keep a mental map on the battle, but we can do it. The alternative is to find the jamming aircraft and shoot it down, of course, and when we did locate it, the jammer soaked up about fifty missiles, with everyone venting their frustration, until the leader called us off, saying: 'I think we've probably wasted enough missiles on him now'.

Our F3s would alternate fighting the package with spells defending it and we normally found ourselves fighting against German Tornados, with Danish Dracon F-35s – quite old aircraft but quite effective – and American F-15s and F-16s. The F-16s did what we call 'Swing' – they are mud-movers but also have a good air-to-air capability, and can defend the rest of the package – while the F-15s are probably the most capable aircraft in the world.

On the last day, my pilot Guido and I were one of eight F3s and eight Dutch F-16s, fighting against a package of German GR1s, Norwegian F-16s, and American F-15s and F-16s, about forty or fifty aircraft in all. The Americans had AMRAAMs, which far out-range our own missiles, so from the start of the mission we were on the defensive, always having to assume that the Americans already had a longer-range shot in the air.

Our tactics consisted of trying to confuse the Americans' radar picture, so that they could not 'sort' us or decipher the way that we were flying. It involved quite a bit of planning from the air defence leader, because in confusing the Americans' radar picture, we were also doing a pretty good job of confusing our own. We were running in, turning back, descending, running back in, going up – getting all sixteen aircraft going forward and then turning back. It was a bit like the All Blacks taunting their opponents with the haka, or a strange sort of tribal dance, but we were hoping to get a few aircraft a bit further forward each time, until we were close enough to use our own missiles. Normally we try and fight as twos, fours or eights, but sometimes, especially in that kind of environment, we call 'Yo-Yo', which just means 'You're on Your own', although sixteen aircraft flying around a small piece of sky, all doing their own thing, can be interesting, to say the least.

A lot of people believe that we avoid collisions because Air Traffic Control tells us where everyone else is, but that does not happen. There is no such thing as Air Traffic Control in combat, whether you are at low level, flying around the countryside or high level, in a fight. The finest computer in the world could not distinguish sixty aircraft in a small piece of sky, all dogfighting, turning and burning at 600 to 900 miles an hour.

Instead, because you do not particularly want to be shot down, you are constantly looking around the sky, scanning to see what is going on. You rely on your air picture and your eyes to tell you that there is no one else around you and that when you barrel-roll into someone's six o'clock, you are not also going to barrel-roll into the top of someone else's canopy as you are doing it. You always have to look out and make sure that your path is clear before you manoeuvre.

We carried on doing our tribal dance over the sea, and on our third run in, Guido and I managed to slip around the outside without being targeted by anyone – our radar warning equipment was clear. We could hear a big mix-up going on in the middle of the area, a whole series of calls indicating a major mêlée:

'I'm engaged.'

'F-15 on your tail.'

'Break right.'

'Flares coming out.'

I could also see the action on my radar. Where normally there might have been one 'plot' with a heading and height, there were as many as thirty plots in one tiny group, far too many for our computer to cope with. We had to fall back on locating device Mark One – the human eye – and the most precise information I could give to Guido was: 'Fifteen miles, forty degrees right of your nose, there is a mix-up going on. Thirty right of your nose, twenty miles there is another one.'

I co-ordinated the information from our kit with the AWACs calls that were coming down from the great eye in the sky. As well as the intercom between pilot and nav, we have two radios, and when things begin to warm up there can be simultaneous conversations between me and my pilot on the intercom and myself and our wingman on one radio, while on the other system there can be three or four calls coming in from the AWACs, our battle commander, and our leader There may be as many as ten different voices, and we have to decipher them all to get the information that we need. As if all that was not enough, the jammer was still busy as well.

'Nitro check. BEEEEEP.'

Our fighters were busy engaging the hostile fighters, but if all you do is fight the fighters, while the bombers get through unscathed, you might as well not have bothered going up. Our job is to get into the bomber package and Guido and I were skirting around the mêlée to do just that, while still keeping an eye open for any opportunities to kill a couple of fighters along the way. We flew over the top of the first battle and could see F3s fighting American F-15s, while some Dutch F-16s circled around, waiting to pounce in at an opportune moment. There were flares going out all over the place and aircraft in a 'furball' – eight aircraft all in a one-mile-square piece of sky – trying to kill each other in one sense, but at the same time trying not to kill each other for real. It was classic Second World War stuff, with planes diving and swooping, pilots yelling and screaming and dogfights being won and lost. Guido, looking down, said: 'It looks like the Battle of Britain down there. This is definitely not a good place to be hanging around.'

As we flew over the top of the next mêlée at 20,000 feet, like a hawk waiting for its prey to break cover, we saw two F-15s disengage and break for home. Guido said: 'Those will do fine for us' and we barrel-rolled down into them, took a shot with a heat-seeking missile on the first one, and sprang back up to 20,000 feet, because while we were doing that, someone else could have been lining us up for exactly the same treatment.

We checked we were clear and then pounced back down on the second guy, who was still running for home, and took a shot on him, Guido yelling ecstatically: 'Fox Two, the F-15 at 10,000 feet'. It was an occasion to savour, because it is very rare for us to get in the drawers of an F-15, they are such fast and capable aircraft, but this time being in a two-seat aircraft really gave us an edge.

Once past the fighter defences, we could get into the bomber package. I quickly picked up a couple of contacts, fifteen miles on the nose. We dropped down beneath the cloud and, sure enough, there were the bombers. We took a few more opportunity shots on them, but we could not afford to stay in amongst them, because another one could have been coming up behind us and as an air-defender, the last thing you want to do is to be shot down by a mud-mover. So we flew down the line of bombers, turning in to take a shot and then turning out again.

Even though we all got together at the end of the mission to debrief thoroughly, as usual it was impossible to say accurately who got shot down and who got through, because there are just so many variables. Was the shot a good shot, was it within the missile's parameters? Would flares have decoyed it? Were you too low to take that particular shot? Would the missile have come off the rails? Would it have guided? Were you hit by a long-range missile before you could even take a shot? If you were shot twenty minutes before you even entered the fight, all the dogfighting and firing of missiles that you did after that is completely irrelevant; in the real case you would already have been dead.

Unless we are all carrying the equipment that down-links into a massive mission computer so that we can watch every shot and see if it guided home afterwards, we can never tell, but Tactical Fighter Meet gets air forces from different nations working together, thinking tactically and getting used to big packages of multinational aircraft. That is the way it is going to be from now on, just like it was in the Gulf.

John Peters: In order to fly aircraft as complex as modern fighters and bombers, air crew have to specialize. Very few aircraft can do both jobs and very rarely would a pilot fly bombers one week and fighters the next, because the aircraft and the tactics used in flying them are so completely different. Even when fighting as part of a multi-national, multi-force coalition, we operate in virtual isolation, focused solely on our own specific tasks.

A superb NATO course, the Tactical Leadership Programme, held in Florennes, Belgium, aimed to counter that narrow focus, developing the tactical skills of pair and four-ship leaders and teaching us how to work with other NATO forces in 'large packages' of aircraft. As well as combining aircraft and air crew from all NATO's member countries, TLP is also one of the very rare occasions that air defenders and mud-movers get together. We worked with Americans, Canadians, Dutch, Belgians, French, Germans – every NATO nationality.

Pronouncing the names was no problem, as everyone used nicknames rather than their real names – 'Jaybird', 'Sperm', 'JJ' and 'Fast Eddy' were just a few of those on offer, while the Americans all had ridiculously macho call-signs like 'Snake' and 'Mako', straight out of *Top Gun*. All of us were given a lecture to prepare on arrival, describing our aircraft's capabilities and deficiencies and the type of weaponry carried, because one of the ideas of the course is to learn to protect weak links, integrating all the aircraft into the most effective package possible. The Mirage V, for example, is an old, single-seat aircraft, which does not have good navigation kit, it is virtually stopwatch and compass. Other aircraft do not have a radar warner, which makes them effectively blind to radar-controlled missiles and early-warning systems – an almost impossible handicap on today's battlefield.

We started off with six aircraft and built bigger and bigger packages, culminating in a huge force of bombers, with a 'sweep and escort' of fighters. 'Escort' fighters are wolves in sheep's clothing, flying within the bombing package as if they were bombers, then suddenly emerging to engage enemies, 'Sweep' fighters fly about ten miles ahead of the package, sweeping and sanitizing the area of enemy fighters, so that the bombers can do their work.

The air defenders' job is not as simple as it seems. It is pretty cut and dried during UK air defence exercises, when anything coming across the North Sea is likely to be a threat. The rules are simple; if it is heading towards the coast, shoot it. In a real case like the Gulf, where you have raids going out from airfields and coming back over the border, it is much more difficult to sort out who is friendly and who is the enemy.

The Tactical Leadership Programme also presents both sides with problems about the rules of engagement, which they may not have previously encountered, such as different scenarios where we cannot use all our available weaponry, or are restricted by political considerations – problems constantly faced by air crew patrolling the exclusion zones over the Gulf and Bosnia. At what point on a border incursion, for example, do we decide that we are being attacked and shoot the aircraft down?

Am I actually allowed to make that decision as leader, or do I have to talk to the commander in the AWACs, or does the decision have to go even higher into the political realm? If so, remembering that the threat takes less than five minutes to cover forty miles, is that an inflexible command? Or if there is suddenly a big push of more than ten aircraft and I do not have time to go back along the chain of command, can I shoot anyway? It is far more complex than simply shooting each other down. If we 'muds' are unable to acquire our designated target, can we bomb any military target of opportunity, or would that present dangers to other friendly operations, or be politically unacceptable? In the Gulf we were limited to strictly specified targets, and some aircraft, unable to drop on target because of bad weather, had to bring their bombs home again.

One of our tasks on TLP was to mount an attack on an airfield, using F-111s, British and German Tornados, French and Belgian Mirages, with F-16 support. F-16s are capable of being both bombers and fighters, defending the package when necessary. Because TLP was primarily concerned with low-level tactics, we did not have the use of B-52s, the workhorses of every conflict since Vietnam, capable of carrying hundreds of bombs over thousands of miles. The first raids in the Gulf involved B-52s flying from bases in the UK, delivering their bombs within a five second 'window' and then flying on to Diego Garcia in the Indian Ocean, a round trip lasting twenty hours.

We had to allow for big, heavy F-111s, which have the largest bomb capacity and the longest range, but which have a high cruise speed. Other aircraft could not travel that fast, they were 'hurting for gas' – at the limits of their fuel – because of the distance to the target. We had to plan for them to do a track through on a different route to join us later, although they still had to be in the 'gorilla' – the package of twenty-five aircraft – before we met the enemy Combat Air Patrol, or they would have been easy prey. We needed 'compression' over the target, because we want to get as many aircraft through the target as quickly as possible, all coming from different directions, all bombing, chaffing and jamming. We want to saturate the area with explosive and confuse and panic the defenders, so that they are too confused and frightened to engage anybody accurately. 1,000 pound bombs going off around your ears can make targeting your Triple-A slightly more complicated than in a practice exercise; the temptation is to keep your head down, rather than raising it to look for targets.

The Allied bombing in the Gulf was so intense that some Iraqi gunners just jammed the triggers of their guns and waved them over their heads, keeping their gun muzzles up, but their heads down. If they hit anything at all, it could only have been by the purest chance.

Coming from different directions also gives us problems, however, because there is 'confliction' over the target. Planes are flying in from all different directions, making a spaghetti junction in the sky. The timing has to be absolutely precise or jets will not intersect, but crash into each other. We also have to make sure that the planes are delayed sufficiently to avoid the burst of the previous bomb load. If we are not a sufficient distance apart, our bombs will 'frag' the guy behind.

The Tactical Leadership Programme also got us 'muds' thinking laterally about problems that face us. A lock on a canal or a river, for example, is a very difficult target to destroy, but if the raid takes place while there is a ship in the lock, we only have to sink the ship to achieve our aim of making the lock unusable. If we want to stop a road over a bridge being used, we do not necessarily have to destroy the bridge; we might not even want to if it will be needed for a later push by our own side. Neutralizing it for eight hours might be enough for our military objectives. If there were troops around it, we could cluster-bomb it and leave a whole mess of corruption – dead people and dead tanks – all over the road, plus delayed-action mines, which make the task of clearing up even harder. They would not be able to use the bridge until they had cleared up, which would probably take eight hours.

After the mission, all the films and tapes from the aircraft are carefully scrutinized, so that our success in bombing the target and the 'kill' claims of the SAM, Triple-A and air defence crews can all be evaluated. The school rules are hard – no film, no kill. The muds and air defenders are debriefed separately and each individual aircraft's position, indications and actions during an engagement are plotted. With perhaps sixteen muds 'turning and burning' against multiple threats, the white perspex board rapidly comes to resemble a bowl of spaghetti Finally, mud and fighter crews come together in a briefing that covers every aspect of the mission. That is the point at which you finally discover whether you evaded the threats or were shot down.

Taxiing out for that mission at the head of a crocodile of twenty-four aircraft strung out along the taxiway behind me, all waiting to take off and fly to my plan, was one hell of a buzz for me, and also one hell of a responsibility; you stand or fall by the results. The course also gave us a great insight into the way that other sectors of air forces work. I have been in the RAF for twelve years, but the first time I felt I really understood air defence was on the TLP course.

18

That bond between us

GULF PRISONERS OF WAR REUNION

John Nichol: I know that JP still spends a lot of time thinking about the mission that we flew in the Gulf, but I do not see the point in wondering what went wrong, because harking back to it is not going to change anything. If we are called into action again, in Bosnia or anywhere else, I will want to go, but not because of anything that happened in the Gulf; I would want to go simply because I would want to be with my squadron.

Some of my contemporaries want to know exactly what happened to me in the Gulf, because it is something that they might well have to face themselves at some time in the future. They take the mickey out of me about the Gulf and the PoW bit, but only in the standard way that they take the mickey out of everyone. Even when people die, there are still jokes and 'witty' comments. It would not be the Air Force if people did not niggle at each other – it keeps you on your toes – but it has never been anything unpleasant.

I do not really like to think about our time in captivity in Iraq and I cannot bear to watch video tapes of the television coverage of the Gulf PoWs – it just upsets me too much. Even watching film of a captured American airman in Somalia was unpleasant, giving me the strongest sense of déjà vu. Somalia was a classic Vietnam syndrome for the US, sending more and more troops there in order to disengage. Just as in Beirut or Vietnam, they started off in a peace-keeping mission, welcomed with open arms, but ended up getting more Americans killed in a single engagement in Somalia than they lost in the whole of the Gulf war, when a million people were involved. I was transfixed by the horrific scenes on television after two Black-hawk helicopters had been shot down and eight Americans had been killed. It sent shivers down my spine, because it was just so similar to our own experiences in Iraq. I saw pictures of the Somalis dragging American bodies through the streets, and a surviving American pilot filmed under interrogation, against a stark white wall, his face battered and bruised.

It is only when I get that sort of jolt that I think about the Gulf War at all now. Although I remain convinced that I have not been affected by what happened to me in the Gulf, those television pictures certainly brought it all back to me. I was appalled to see that film of a bruised and bloodied pilot, speaking in a monotone.

Despite my aversion to film of captured and tortured air crew, I really do enjoy the reunions of the Gulf PoWs. It is something that we started on the first anniversary of the war, when Bob Ankerson invited us all, together with our wives and girlfriends, to his house in Marlow. We vowed to do it all again the next year and by six o'clock on the Saturday night we were all there except for one of the SAS guys, whose car had blown up on the M40 on his way there – a mechanical fault, not Iraqi sabotage.

We broke out the champagne and were offering up a toast to the guys who were not coming home again, when someone looking out of the window said: 'I don't believe this, an Arab has just turned up'. The Arab was Mohammed Mubarrak, the Kuwaiti pilot who was in gaol in Iraq with us. He had been on a course in London and had sent me a postcard, asking if we could meet for a drink. As a result, we were able to arrange Mohammed's surprise guest appearance at the reunion. No one had seen him in two years, since we had walked off the plane together in Saudi Arabia wearing our yellow PoW suits. He had lost around four stone in prison, but had put it all back on again and was in fine health.

There were so many stories told and so many things to catch up on, because all the guys are doing different things now. Some could hardly walk twelve months before because they had been shot in the leg or broken their legs. A lot of the guys had come out of the front line and gone back to instructing or desk jobs or, like me, had switched flying careers.

At about four o'clock in the morning someone got the videos out, about three hours of news coverage of all the hostages. Some of the guys seem to enjoy watching the videos, but I just could not stomach them, and there were a few of us out in the kitchen, keeping out of the way. I have never even sat through them properly because it just upsets me too much; I have to turn the television off. I have never watched the documentary either, I do not even know what it says. I have watched parts of it, but I fast-forward the faces on the TV or anything like that.

We reminisced till six or six-thirty in the morning, had a couple of hours' sleep and then everyone drifted off. The chances are that we will not meet for another year, but there will always be that bond between us, that knowledge that something extraordinary has happened to us. That will keep us meeting and getting drunk together, year after year.

John Peters: Although John cannot bear to watch the video tapes, hours of excerpts from the news coverage of the Gulf always seem to be played at the reunion for some macabre reason, while we all childishly point ourselves out on the screen. Watching the tapes really does not bother me at all. I am not proud of what happened, but I cannot change it and I do not sit there thinking: 'Oh my God, don't I look horrible?', I just think: 'Well, that was me, then'.

That was then, but this is now, and it is very different. John and I were abruptly propelled into the public eye by the Gulf War and for a short time we lived our lives in the glare of media attention. Some of it was great, I would recommend anyone to enjoy Andy Warhol's 'fifteen minutes of fame', but much longer and it can become intrusive and overpowering. Much of the attention faded as quickly as it came, but even after all this time, whenever I go to a function as 'John Peters, the Gulf prisoner of war', I still get a reaction. I also still receive stacks of mail, often quite intense letters, and the vast amount of mail is the most tangible result of our being paraded on television.

I get a lot of pleasure from the letters, particularly those from other servicemen, and especially old soldiers from the Second World War, with whom our story clearly struck a chord. In less enlightened times, when Post-Traumatic Stress Disorder was unheard of and the stiff upper lip was the only solution to problems, men and women had to struggle for years to exorcize the demons of their own war experiences and many empathized strongly with our own story. Former prisoners of war are particularly pleased that 'The PoW' had been recognized, as if they have at last received recognition for their own sufferings and privations. Many Second World War PoWs lost three, four, or five years of their lives, yet their sacrifice was rarely recognized. There were no medals for prisoners of war, even though they had made their own contribution to the war effort, not least in that tally of wasted years.

Astonishingly, out of the thousands of letters we have received, I do not think that we have had a single unpleasant or 'hate' letter. The only critical one I can remember came from someone who objected to me swearing on television. The majority are genuinely heart-warming and some are deeply moving and even humbling, such as the one I received from a woman, which I reproduce here, with her kind permission:

Thank you for telling your story in your own words. I don't know if you were aware of it when you recounted it, but your unflinching honesty is a beautiful gift to your readers. It certainly was for me. Your story has had the most profound impact on my life. Because I had been sexually and physically abused as a child, I immediately identified very deeply with your experience.

However strange it may seem at first glance (considering the differences in age, gender, temperament or external circumstances), I recognized many of the places you describe as ones where I have also been. Whether it be the helplessness and humiliation, the fear of what is inevitably coming, the sense that your body is theirs for them to do with as they please, or that you are threatened with extinction as a person with a place in the scheme of things, the shame and self-loathing at having been 'defeated' and having somehow let yourself down, or the determination to survive and to overcome, it all was, and is, painfully familiar.

Your story not only moved me, it served me as a bridge to recover my childhood experience of more than thirty-five years ago. I invariably found it a source of inspiration that gave me strength and hope and steadied me through the difficult times when I had to face my own memories. When I finally confronted my own father with what he had done to me as a child (he sodomized me over a period of five years), I thought about you. I had carried with me the terror of those rapes since the age of seven, and what I learned from your story is that telling the truth was the only way to free myself from both terror and shame, and to move on.

Your courage during your ordeal and your honesty and humour in sharing with strangers not simply the appalling details of your captivity, but the emotional impact it has had on you as a human being, have thus taught me lessons I will not forget. In this, I owe you a great debt of gratitude. I cannot tell you how happy I am that you did survive and overcome.

It is all behind now, but I wanted you to know that you helped one person (unwittingly for sure, but genuinely nonetheless), just by being who you are and sharing it so freely. I can only thank you again, and with all my heart, wish you and your loved ones understanding, peace and happiness.

Such a moving letter makes me feel very privileged, and puts my own modest sufferings into a truer perspective, but if that is an extreme case, our story has obviously affected many people. Some just want to pat us on the back or say: 'Well done', but others seem to have been affected in a much more intense and personal way. It is as if our story touches a chord that has nothing to do with being at war and everything to do with human suffering. Even three years down the track, people still come up and grab me by the hand or the arm and say: 'I want you to know that we care for you', giving me a really hard stare at the same time, as if to say: 'Look, I really mean this'. It is something much deeper than just saying: 'Well done, boys', it is as if we became symbols of people's husbands, brothers or sons.

Whenever people swap war stories on the squadron or start talking about the Gulf War – not that many people do now anyway – I tend to hold back, and I do not really go through: 'Do you remember when' with anybody, because there is no one around who does. At our annual Gulf PoW reunion, we are in a group of people that do remember. It is the only place where we can compare memories. Something gets mentioned and everybody is suddenly shouting at once: 'Oh God yes, do you remember that?' We all get thoroughly drunk, of course, but there really is something else there as well; I think even the roughie-toughie SAS guys notice that, an empathy based on shared experience. We all pitch up, from all over the world, and say: 'Well, here's to us; we're still here, and aren't we lucky?'

Helen Peters: When people mention PoWs, most are probably thinking of Colditz and Robert Wagner, or Vietnamese PoWs – people in groups, sharing group experiences. Yet our lads, most of the time, and John virtually all the time, were completely isolated, held in solitary confinement. As a result, all the men had totally different experiences and it is only when they are together in a group that they can start linking all these things together.

The wives of the PoWs have heard different things from their husbands and were also all in separate places, experiencing different things. We talk about whether our husbands have changed: are they more awkward, do they do the washing-up more often, have they kept up their brilliant promises to themselves that they were going to be so much better at looking after the children? The general consensus, to no one's very great surprise, is that the answer to most of these questions is: 'No'. Instead there were a lot of good intentions when they came back that lasted about a couple of weeks.

Of course you have to draw the line when a reunion becomes an empty ritual that nobody really gets anything out of but feels they cannot possibly be seen to stop, but as long as people genuinely want to do it, I would like to hope that the reunions would go on, year after year.

19

The social life is hectic

FAIRFORD INTERNATIONAL AIR TATTOO

John Nichol: After the sometimes grim realities of our day-to-day work, the chance to unwind at a relaxing Air Show is not to be passed up lightly. Air Shows are great for the public, because they get to see planes, meet air crew and get a bit of an insight into the world of fast jets, but they are just as much fun for us, because the social life is fabulous. We not only meet air crew from all over the world, we get to go to some very good parties too.

The International Air Tattoo, held at Fairford every July, is the cream of the crop; a huge display of aircraft, drawing in hundreds of thousands of visitors and raising enormous amounts of money for charity, mainly the RAF Benevolent Fund. It also provides air crew with a very lively weekend, culminating in a party on the Sunday night, an incredible sight, with 5,000 people packed into an aircraft hangar having a wild night. That party very nearly turned into a wake, for the Tattoo was marred by a crash that could have killed hundreds of people, were it not for flying display regulations that came into force after the Ramstein Air Show disaster.

I went down to Fairford on the Friday afternoon, with my pilot for the weekend, Si Stevens – inevitably nicknamed 'Shakey', after Shaking Stevens. Si looks nothing like him, but he plays a mean guitar . . . and he cannot sing either. We were held in a 'stack' while someone was doing a display over the airfield, and had just called Air Traffic Control to find out how long the delay would be, when someone called us up, saying: 'Totem One' – our call sign – 'Please come up the VC-10 tanker operations frequency.' It turned out to be a tanker pilot I had met at several other air shows. He had very welcome news: 'Hi John, it's Al here. We've got the party bus with us.' Things were shaping up nicely; our first party invitation and we had not yet even touched down.

The VC-10 makes an ideal party wagon, because it has a big space in the back. It is not quite as good as a Hercules or a Galaxy, but it is a damn sight roomier than holding a party in a Tornado and the VC-10 guys are always perfect hosts. They always make sure they have the necessary 'ingredients' for the favourite air crew cocktails – gin and tonic and Harvey Wall-banger, and their fridges, which normally hold the milk for passengers' coffee, can also hold a plentiful supply of beer. We promised to drop in on them later on, but we had other vitally important tasks to attend to as well. We intended to put ourselves about as much as possible and if that involved us in taking a drink here and there along the way, that was a price we were fully prepared to pay.

Most people parked their jets, had a spot of lunch and started heading for their hotels, but, having been to Fairford before, I knew that the hospitality tents on the other side of the airfield were always open on the Friday afternoon. We requisi-tioned some transport, one of the 'Follow Me' trucks that shepherd aircraft around the airfield, and followed it all the way to the first free drink of the day.

The hospitality tents always have guards on the doors who can often be quite insistent about technicalities like invitations, but we successfully harrumphed our way past them and got stuck in, like kids in a sweet shop with a week's pocket money to spend. We started at the Lockheed tent, right at one end of the row, with the intention of working our way right down to the other end at some unspecified time later on. Each of the tents has a little garden in front, just off the runway, prime viewing positions from which the guests can sit and watch the aircraft take off and land. Once we were in one hospitality tent, it was easy to progress to the next, we just nipped into the garden and hopped over the garden fence.

After a couple of beers with Lockheed, we worked our way steadily down the line, showing no mercy to any sponsor, as we shared a gin and tonic with Racal Communications and another one with Raynet, before reaching the British Aerospace tent. They quickly recognized us as unauthorized intruders and did not make us entirely welcome, which was a bit of a cheek, since the RAF are their biggest customers, but they did let us finish our drinks before they threw us out. Luckily the International Air Tattoo Patrons' tent was next door. If you want to entertain a couple of clients, but do not want to spend a fortune on your own individual tent, you can buy places in the IAT Patrons' tent. We were made very welcome there, despite the noise emanating from the air crew in the Lockheed tent, further up the line. Lockheed manufacture the Hercules, and were keeping the Hercules crews happy; so happy that several of them were already down to their boxer shorts.

Reluctantly we dragged ourselves away, for we were on a tight schedule; as well as the remaining hospitality tents, there was the VC-10 party bus, an Australian Hercules with so many cans of XXXX in the cargo space it appeared to have been sponsored by Castlemaine, and a cheese and wine party on a New Zealand Boeing 707.

We fitted in an afternoon tea and several more drinks and set off for our billet at about six o'clock, after a full and fascinating afternoon. We were billeted about twenty miles away, at Shrivenham, where we kept ourselves topped up with a few more drinks and a spot of dinner, before setting off to explore the fabled nightlife of Swindon. Lacking the services of a local guide, we failed to find any nightlife, fabled or otherwise, but no matter how bad your evening, you always manage to get back with kebab dribbling down your shirt and beer dripping off your trousers, and this night was no exception.

Our transport left at an outrageously early hour the next

morning, to get everybody into Fairford before the traffic started to pile up. There was a twenty-mile jam on the M4 later in the morning, and that was still thirty miles from Fairford. It was pouring with rain and looked set to be a horrible day. We slumped in the air crew tent and had some coffee, doughnuts and Danish pastries, which work much better than aspirin at clearing hangovers.

By about eight o'clock we had recovered enough to contemplate a change of scene and were wandering across the airfield when some Czechs hailed us and invited us aboard their aircraft for a drink. After the excesses of the previous day, a beer at eight o'clock in the morning was the last thing that I wanted, but in the interests of détente, we accepted, and spent an hour sipping beer and conversing in sign language with the pilot and his navigator, who knew no more English than we knew Czech.

Since it was still raining too much to do anything at our own aircraft, we were then forced to pop over to the VC-10 party bus for further supplies of coffee and doughnuts while waiting for the downpour to stop. Eventually we wandered back to our aircraft and spent the day chatting to people and selling Air Force 'gizzits' – pens, pencils, posters and other souvenirs – for the RAF Benevolent Fund.

Air show visitors range from families with children on a day out who have never seen a fast jet before, asking questions like: 'How fast does it go, Mister?', to professional air show goers – 'spotters' as we call them – who know more about the aircraft than we do. They read all the available technical literature and ask incredibly arcane questions, to which I invariably do not know the answers.

The rain cleared around lunchtime and it became a beautiful sunny day. One of the highlights of the afternoon was to be a display by two Fulcrum Mig-29s from the Russian Air Force. These were the planes that occupied most of our waking thoughts and a few of our nightmares during the latter stages of the Cold War. Day after day we practised against planes simulating their tactics, but we knew that the real Fulcrums were super-fast, very agile and quite deadly, and to be honest, we were scared stiff of them. The Soviet threat no longer exists and Germany has even bought some Fulcrums for its own air force, but the sight of them in English skies still gave me a momentary chill. I was watching with more than usually close attention as the two aircraft arced and swooped, crossing and recrossing above the airfield.

The Russian pilots were staging mock intercepts between their aircraft, like two sabre-wielding duellists, bringing gasps of excitement from the crowd, looping and barrel-rolling into screaming turns, then flashing past each other with what looked, even to my jaundiced eyes, to be little more than inches to spare. Such air displays require absolute precision; it is not like two tearaways playing 'chicken' in stolen cars on a housing estate – if they collide, the death toll, if any, will probably be limited to the two drivers. If two aircraft with a combined weight of over sixty tons, thousands of gallons of fuel on board and a closing speed of over a thousand miles an hour are brought into contact, the consequences could be horrific, not merely for the two pilots, but for the half-million spectators packed around the runways below.

Si and I were standing in front of our aircraft, doing the charity sales pitch to a small crowd of onlookers as the Ful-crums blasted overhead, with a deafening roar from their afterburners. It was their fourth or fifth pass, but this time something was different; against the roar of the afterburners, I heard a bang and then a faint pop. I looked up and froze in horror.

The bang had been the sound of the two planes colliding, slicing each other apart. The pop was the sound of the first pilot ejecting, the canopy blown aside as the rockets blasted him skywards. The next instant there was a massive explosion as his plane flew nose first into the ground. The other aircraft was in a flat spin, rotating as if in slow motion, while flames flashed from one end of the fuselage to the other. The cockpit disappeared from sight, engulfed inside a ball of fire. For a few heart-stopping seconds the plane seemed to hang in the air, spinning drunkenly. 'Eject, for Christ's sake, eject' breathed Si, knowing that the pilot would die instantly when the plane hit the ground.

Almost hidden behind the wall of flame, the pilot battled to right his stricken aircraft as it spiralled down. Unknown to him, his controls were not connected to anything except fresh Fairford air, because his plane had been cut in half by the other jet's wing, which had sliced through it like a cheese wire. With only feet to spare, the pilot ejected out of the middle of the fireball. His parachute opened and he began to drift down as his Mig ploughed into the ground with another massive explosion.

It was impossible to tell where the planes had crashed – into a safe area or into the heart of the crowd. One minute there had been the hubbub of half a million people and the roar of the jets overhead, the next there were the two huge explosions followed by a complete, deathly silence. That lasted a few moments, then all pandemonium broke loose. People were screaming, crying and running in all directions and sirens were wailing as the emergency crews raced to the crash site. Thousands and thousands of people were trying to get there too, just to see what was going on, like motorists rubber-necking at the scene of a car crash, but somehow the fire crews got through and were starting to put the flames out in less than a minute from the impact.

We were trying to clear people out of the fire lanes, but a lot of them just did not seem to be concerned. Apart from all the thousands scrambling over each other to get nearer to the crash site, there was one guy slap in the middle of the fire lanes, as if he was enjoying a pleasant stroll down a quiet country lane. As I asked him to get out of the way to let the emergency vehicles through, a group of policemen came rocketing through in a civvy car that they had obviously commandeered, but all the guy could say was: 'They don't look much like emergency vehicles to me'. I was absolutely staggered; there were two burning aircraft and an unknown number of casualties out there, and here was this guy, trying to be a smart-arse.

From the moment of impact, the two Fulcrums had both been completely out of control and it was only by the greatest good luck that they did not come down into the crowds. Two thirty-four-ton fireballs, ploughing into a densely packed crowd at five hundred miles an hour, could have wreaked havoc that would have left, not hundreds, but thousands of dead in their wake.

As it was, one Fulcrum came down in some woods just outside the airfield boundary and the other crashed next to the area where all the display aircraft were parked. There were no deaths, but some very near misses. A few guys were sitting on the wing of a Hercules when the burning wreckage of one of the Fulcrums hurtled over their heads and took the top clean off their tailplane, not more than fifteen feet above them. The crew of a Nimrod dived underneath their aircraft as bits of debris smashed into the ground all around it, and the canopy and ejection seat from one of the Migs came down right in the middle of the aircraft park. Debris fell on the *Patrouille de France* – the French equivalent of the Red Arrows – there was wreckage everywhere.

Three spectators sitting on a bale of hay had one of the closest escapes, as the trail of burning wreckage came up to within three feet of the bale. Unsurprisingly, they needed treatment for shock, but were lucky not to need treatment for something much worse.

Meanwhile the pilots were showing remarkable sang-froid. The second one floated down on his parachute, having just written off £30 million worth of aircraft. He landed, stood up, threw his helmet down in disgust, pulled off his harness and his life jacket, and then lit a cigarette, shrugged and started to walk away. What happened immediately afterwards, the television cameras did not pick up; the pilot of the other aircraft had obviously already held his own unofficial inquiry into the incident, because he walked straight up to the first pilot and punched him squarely on the nose.

Apart from the crash, the most difficult thing for me to come to terms with was seeing the Russians at Fairford. As well as the Fulcrum Mig-29s, the pick of the former Soviet bloc's fighters, there were Mig-21s and, above all, there was the Bear – the aircraft that has been the bane of the UK air defence for the last thirty years. From its inception as the Bear Alpha, through ten or fifteen different models, the Bear had been constantly probing the UK air defences. Yet here it was, a welcome and honoured guest at a British air show, having been given a conducted passage through those same air defences to get there.

By an irony, my own squadron was on Quick Reaction Alert that weekend. QRA is normally held by the squadrons at Leuchars, because they are the closest to the Greenland–Iceland–UK gap, through which the Soviet threat would have come, but Leeming had taken over the role while the runway at Leuchars was being repaired. We had guys sitting in the Q sheds in fully-armed aircraft, waiting for the Russian Bears to pour down the gap. Yet while those guys were sitting in all their flying gear, ready to scramble and be airborne at a moment's notice should any intruders probe our airspace, two other Tornados from Leuchars were escorting a Russian Bear straight through the air defence region to land at a British air show.

Si and I flew back up to Leeming on Monday morning and went straight back on to Quick Reaction Alert ourselves. We were sitting in the Q sheds, fully-armed and ready to go against the Russian hordes, when the Bear flew back out through our air defence region to go back to Russia. It was all somehow a bit too surreal for me. I had never done QRA before, so it was quite exciting for about the first ten seconds, and then it rapidly got very boring. I sat down, watched a video, wandered around, had something to eat, wandered around, watched TV, wandered around, had some coffee, wandered around, watched another video and found I still had eighteen hours to go.

Although we still hold the posture, we know – or at least we think we know – that nothing is going to happen, so I took the opportunity to take a shower. Of course, as it was my first time on QRA, the ground crew thought it would be jolly amusing to sound the siren, just as I was completely soaped-up. One minute I was soaping myself and singing a suitable shower song and the next the loudest siren in the history of the universe went off. I thought: 'Oh my God!' and ten seconds later was sprinting down the corridor, stark naked and covered in soap, trying to jump into my coveralls and get my immersion suit on. As I struggled with it, I began to realize that the siren was not the only sound audible. Someone, somewhere, was laughing. I turned round to see all the ground crew standing at the end of the corridor, doubled up with laughter, applauding.

QRA is still the most important commitment that the squadron can have, but it has obviously lost some of the urgency it had five years ago, when the Soviet hordes were a genuine threat. Back then, there were people ready to scramble and be airborne inside a few minutes. Now, if the scramble siren goes, we have a little more time to get airborne, although it's still pretty fast. It means that we have to live in most of our flying kit for twenty-four hours, including our G-pants and our immersion suit – the rubber suit that protects us if we eject into the sea. We have to wear that all the time, because it can take five minutes to get into all of our kit.

We take over the duty at eight in the morning and immediately 'cock the jet' – put it into the highest state of readiness possible without having the engines running. We leave our helmets connected up in the aircraft, so we can just pick them up, put them on and go, and the straps are already adjusted to us. Everything in the cockpit is switched on, so that if the siren goes off, while we sprint for the aircraft, the engineers already have the power on and the systems are starting to warm up, and obviously, the aircraft is fully-armed as well. We have two Q sheds at the end of the runway; when the blast doors open, we taxi twenty yards and are on the runway, ready to take off.

The air defence posture of the F3 squadrons used to be as long-range interceptors against hundreds and hundreds of Russian aircraft – Bears, Bisons, Badgers, Backfires – launching cruise missiles, iron bombs and nuclear bombs against the UK.

The job of the F3s was to get out as far and as fast as we could to the North, shoot down as many as we could, come back, load up and get back out again. We trained to do that for a long time, but the Gulf and Bosnia saw a complete end to it.

God knows what we will be involved with next, but the tactics change constantly now, so I am not really sure why we still hold QRA, living in the Q sheds for twenty-four hours, like coiled springs against a threat that, in all honesty, probably does not require that much springiness any more. Even if the threat of a mass attack over the former East German border has disappeared, I do not believe that we are in a better or more stable world, quite the opposite in fact. No one is sure where, when or what the next threat is going to be; the one thing of which we are certain is that there will be a threat from somewhere.

That threat will have to be faced by much reduced British forces, because the 'peace dividend' has been collected in full, by cutting back on the armed forces. Since the Gulf War, many Air Force squadrons have been disbanded and the Army has lost innumerable regiments through closures and forced mergers. It has been a difficult time for all of us, not knowing where the axe would fall next. What used to be regarded as a job for life now suffers from the same uncertainties and insecurities as every other job.

Resources are now as thin on the ground as manpower. There were very few serviceable tanks left in Germany during the Gulf War, because despite only a proportion of the tank regiments being deployed, every last tank had to be cannibalized for spares. The cuts have been so deep and so widespread that many people think that an operation of the scale that was mounted in the Gulf or the Falklands could never be attempted again.

The smaller-scale commitments have also grown in number. As well as the defence of UK air space and our commitments to NATO, we also have to maintain a presence in the Falklands, contribute to 'policing' actions in Bosnia and the Gulf, and be ready to react instantly to any fresh conflicts that arise.

Whereas we used to be away for two to three months of the year, it is now entirely normal to be out of the UK for six months out of twelve, putting a huge additional strain on our resources and our family lives.

John Peters: During my time in Germany, the Berlin Wall has come down, the Cold War has ended and I have been able to go to places like Colditz, Koblenz and East Berlin, which I would never have been allowed to visit before. One of the nicest experiences of all was to escort Hungarian Mig-21 'Fishbeds' across to the Fairford International Air Tattoo and then escort them back again afterwards. The Boss himself flew one of the escort aircraft and it was a great honour to be asked to fly the other, but it was also a very strange feeling to lead what until very recently had been 'The Enemy' into the heart of our own country.

The Mig-21s are old aircraft, which do not have much range, nor any navigation kit, and are also limited in height and speed. The Hungarian pilots could speak no English and had only very basic maps. We flew to the Czech–German border to pick them up and fly them to Fairford, an incongruous package of two Tornados, four Migs and an Andropov-26 with an interpreter on board, to relay instructions between us.

We picked them up on a gin-clear day, four Mig-21s high in the sky, the big red numbers on the nose and the outline of the aircraft familiar from a thousand briefings. Both sides just sat there for a while, gawping at each other, and then we persuaded them to fly in close formation while we got some photographs of an historic occasion.

As we got close to Brüggen, there was a thunderstorm and we had to divert to Norvenich, a German base about twenty miles away. A diversion under such circumstances is very rare; it was just our luck that it should have had to happen now. Since the Hungarians had such bad maps and could not talk the language, we already had plenty of problems and they were made worse when the interpreter called up to tell us that the

Migs were absolutely fuel critical. We split them up, with two hanging on me and two on the Boss, and they flew close-formation with us through the cloud. We expected them to fly in echelon on the wing, as we do, but their definition of close-formation is line astern, and they disappeared behind us, which was rather unnerving.

We also discovered, again via the interpreter in the Andropov, that their approach speed was a lot faster than ours, 220 knots, whereas we normally come in at about 170. As we got closer, the weather worsened. We flew in under the cloud, rejecting Air Traffic Control's requests to ascend for radar identification as we struggled to convince them of the seriousness of the situation. Eventually we led the Migs down, flew over the top of the runway as they landed and then circled around to come in and land ourselves. We taxied off the runway, pulled up alongside the alien Migs and went to meet the guys who flew them, the first time I had ever set eyes on any air crew from the Warsaw Pact.

I was staggered at how antiquated their aircraft were, even in something as routine as filling them up with fuel. We have pressure feeds which take only ten minutes to fill the aircraft with hundreds of gallons of aviation fuel, but the Migs just had a system like a car. A ground crewman had to sit on the top of the planes for hours, filling them up by gravity with a petrol pump, like you would fill your car at a service station.

The cockpit was also incredibly old-fashioned; all I could think was: 'How were you ever going to fight a war against us?' They had none of the kit that we have, and although a good pilot can mask a lot of technological deficiencies, no one could compensate for deficiencies on this scale; if it takes two Tornados to fight one F-15, it would take four Mig-21s to fight one Tornado.

The maps the Hungarians had with them were also unbelievably rudimentary. In the Cold War days, the Eastern bloc countries did not want to run the risk of having their pilots defect, so they never gave them any maps. They also stuck to fixed frequency radios, so that their pilots could not talk to each other without Big Brother listening in. The map the Hungarians had been given could have been drawn by a not particularly gifted child in primary school, an A4 sheet with a thumbnail map of Europe and a thumbnail map of England with lines drawn on it – no co-ordinates or anything. Those guys are awfully brave to fly like that, but I was staggered at the primitive state of their flying technology.

After refuelling, we set off for Fairford. The weather was not that good, all the way over, but the Hungarians insisted that they could hang on in formation with us. Both of us again led a pair of Migs up through the cloud, having told them: 'If you get lost, climb up to height and stick to your routeing and we will pick you up'. As we came through the top of the cloud, I saw the Boss, about four miles ahead of me, but he only had one Mig on his tail – we had lost the other one.

I was just trying to work out how the hell we would ever find it again when Humpo, who was navigating for me, pointed out that we now had three Migs flying line astern behind us. I do not know and I do not ever want to know how that third plane managed to lose the Boss, fly blind through 20,000 feet of dense cloud and somehow tag on at the end of my pair four miles behind him. Finding a needle in a haystack would be child's play by comparison. It was like driving along a single track road in thick fog behind a red Lada and then emerging from the fog to discover it directly behind me instead. If ever I was looking for evidence of a fifth dimension, I would ask the pilot of that Mig. The rest of the journey to Fairford was almost routine after that dose of excitement.

Air crew never lose interest in looking at other people's aircraft, but that was especially true at Fairford, where they had all the Russian aircraft, not just the Mig-21s we had brought with us, but Bears and Fulcrums as well. After looking on these as the enemy for so long, to sit in one and talk to its pilot was an incredible experience.

The displays by the Russians, flying the much more advanced Mig-29 Fulcrums, were again very aggressive and close to the edge; they looked as if they were trying desperately hard to impress, perhaps too hard. I missed the few vital seconds before the crash, but Humpo and the others told me that they could see that it was going to happen.

Humpo and I were sitting on top of our aircraft watching the Fulcrums, which were coming down towards the bottom of a loop, when I was distracted by someone asking for an autograph. As I leaned over the edge of the wing to reach the sheet of paper, I heard a bang and looked around to see the aftermath of the crash. It was as if everything was in slow motion, one plane diving straight into the earth, the other in a flat spin, rotating like a dinner plate. When it hit the ground, even the smoke from the crash seemed to be in slow motion, rising like oil in water.

Then the flames burst out and all hell broke loose. Everyone was running towards the crash site to get pictures and see what was going on and the firemen were going through the crowds, some at forty miles an hour. We could see the two parachutes coming down so we knew the pilots were alright, but we did not know what had happened to the spectators. I was convinced that people would be killed, and was astonished to discover that there was nothing worse than shock or minor injuries for the medics to treat. Looking at the film afterwards, we could see guys sliding off a Hercules, just a heartbeat before some wreckage crashed through the tailplane, while some guys from the Nimrod crew said that they did not know whether to run towards the crashing aircraft or away from it and in the end they just stood under the wings and prayed as debris rained down all around them.

All the air crew doing the static displays huddled together and the consensus was: 'That's it then, end of air show'. Within a couple of minutes, however, to our total astonishment, the Swiss aerobatic team of Hunters lined up on the runway and wound up their engines. We all stood transfixed as they took off, with what must have been a very immediate image of the consequences of a mistake imprinted on their minds, yet they produced a superb, tight, professional display. We were full of admiration for them; producing the goods under pressure is what all air crew are striving to achieve, but it takes great bravery to go straight up after a crash like that.

For an hour or so after the crash, air crew were wandering up and down saying: 'I feel a bit strange, I've got a real empty feeling in the pit of my stomach', because even though we live with the risk of death, to see that crash and realize how devastating it could have been, was terrifying. We were all imagining the horrific consequences of a burning hulk smashing into a crowded campsite, but once the news got around that miraculously no one had been hurt, the cynical air crew banter was immediately resumed – the 'Right Stuff' returned.

The Air Show really starts for the air crew when the public are heading for home. That is when we start cracking the tubes open and socializing with air crew from all over the world. There are parties galore, especially on all the Hercules transport planes, which are air show party wagons the world over.

I kept bumping into John during the weekend, as our paths invariably converged on the same party or 'beer call', but we did not spend the whole weekend together – you do not suddenly dump all your mates from your own squadron to go and spend time with someone else, no matter how good a mate he may be. Our aircraft were only split by a couple of hundred yards on the airfield, and people kept bouncing between the two of us, saying: 'I've got one autograph, can I have yours'. As soon as we actually got together, a crowd still formed, which was very surprising, so long after the Gulf.

On the Sunday night there was a huge party in a hangar for all the participants at the air show. Flying suits in every colour of the rainbow rubbed shoulders, 'banter' was high on every-one's agenda, delivered in what seemed like every language and accent in the world. The hangar, packed with several thousand bodies, was decorated with miles of bunting. A huge net full of balloons hung over the dance floor and there were giant video screens flanking the stage where a succession of bands kept the place rocking into the small hours. Behind the stage was a mini fair with switchback rides, bucking broncos and gladiator games. Just outside the main doors were rows of flaming hobs from which a battalion of chefs was kept busy producing omelettes to order. It was true air crew heaven: beer, promotions girls, loud music and flying all in one weekend.

I kept meeting old acquaintances and as usual, there were beery embraces and heartfelt promises to keep in touch, but we were all aware that we were lying. Air crew are notorious for it, because no matter what promises are made, no one ever keeps in touch. Eventually we will bump into each other at some airfield, or exercise, or some God-forsaken bar in the back of beyond, and pick up again from there. For an hour or two, we will be the best of mates once more, putting the world to rights, and then once more we will part, with yet more empty promises to keep in touch.

Flying back on the Monday morning, Humpo and I were again escorting the Migs. All the litter, cans and bottles from the previous day's air show and the previous night's parties had miraculously been cleared up overnight, so that the aircraft could taxi out. We briefed the Hungarians as well as we could, and then set off for Brüggen, where a reception had been laid on for them. Again, it was a strange feeling to go burning up through UK airspace with a pair of Migs on our wing. It was a beautiful day, blue weather all the way home, and the flight was reasonably straightforward, but it did not alter the strangeness of leading them into Brüggen. Fairford was one thing, but that was an air show. Brüggen is an extremely businesslike working base, secret and probably the premier front-line RAF base, and yet here I was giving two Mig-21s a scenic flight around it.

Only one of the pilots had a smattering of English, so there was not a lot we could say to them before we parted company. To say goodbye, we just nodded to each other, but the nod said a lot.

20

Reflections and expectations

AN ERA OF FRIGHTENING INSTABILITY

John Nichol: Although I did not spend all that much time with John at Fairford and I do not see him that often anyway these days, that is not particularly unusual, it is just the normal way of Air Force friendships.

In civvy street – civilian life – if you have a mate, when you move away you tend to write to each other, phone up regularly and make arrangements to see each other from time to time. In the Air Force, virtually nobody does that, because you are always moving away and making new friends. You are posted every three years, and each time you will make 200 new friends and acquaintances. If you are constantly trying to stay in touch with the friends from the last place, it will never work. So instead you just tend to say: 'OK, I'll see you around'. I was best man at a good mate's wedding and we even own a house together, but we still do not keep in regular touch. It would never occur to either of us to ring up and say: 'Hello mate, what are you up to?' When we have got something important to say or we want to arrange something, we will phone up and say: 'I'm passing through, let's get together', but that is it.

The next time we do get together, nothing will have changed and that seems to apply to all Air Force friendships. I met a couple of guys at Mildenhall Air Show I had not seen since basic training, when we used to be out every Friday and

Saturday night on the prowl together. We met up in the bar and picked up just where we had left off, having a brilliant night out, but then the next morning it was again just: 'Well, see you around sometime', and it may be years before we bump into each other again. The extended network of friends also means that if you are diverted to another airfield or end up somewhere by accident, you always know that a phone call will get you somewhere to stay and someone to share a few beers with. The structure of a good friendship is always there, but it is not the way that a lot of people in other walks of life would envisage a very good friendship.

The same holds true for my relationship with JP. I certainly thought at first that what we went through in the Gulf would change our relationship completely, but that has not happened. It has certainly not made us closer but it has not really driven us apart either. It is just something that happened, another part of life's rich tapestry in the Air Force. We do not make deliberate arrangements to meet up with each other, but when we happen to be in the same place at the same time, we will have a good time. I knew JP was going to be at Fairford, for example, and we arrived within a few minutes of each other. So we sat around, chewed a tube and chewed the cud and after I had gone off to prowl the hospitality tents, we met up again in the evening and we went around downtown Swindon together. We were together again the next morning, selling things for the RAF Benevolent Fund, when, as usual, people still identified us as a pair. They came up and said: 'Good to see that you are back together again' and it was not really worth trying to explain that we are not back together at all.

In the days when it was going to be Armageddon or nothing, we always had a sense of unreality about our work, especially in the GR 1 – the ground attack bomber – because it was going to be the final answer, the nuclear holocaust. If we ever went to war, that was going to be the end. Even if we survived our mission, there was going to be no airfield to come back to, we would have no family left, there would be nothing but death and destruction.

Then suddenly the Cold War was over and our role was transformed. Someone came up with the idea that we were going to fly to war and we were going to come back; we were going to do mission, after mission, after mission. It was going to be quite like the Second World War; we would go backwards and forwards over the lines, people would not come back from missions and people would die, but we would continue to do it. That was what happened in the Gulf. We went on day one all the way through to day forty-nine – well I did not, I went on day one all the way through to day one – but a lot of guys went all the way through. A few did not come home, but not that many.

We used to have a very defined enemy, we knew exactly who we were preparing to fight, but now we have absolutely no idea at all; we have not got an enemy. There are a number of conflicts around the bazaars of the world, but we have no focal point, and all the intelligence documents on the Soviet forces, piled as high as the Lloyd's Building, are suddenly not the most useful things to have any more. We still study Russian aircraft and Russian tactics, but we have to be prepared to fight against every other aircraft in the world as well.

The arms race has taken a different turn, because the superpowers are not buying from their own industries and as a result, the arms manufacturers are turning to the outside. The Americans are now selling their aircraft to many other countries. At the same time, it is even being mooted that the RAF might buy Russian aircraft to replace our maritime patrol aircraft, or Russian helicopters to replace our current attack helicopters; it is perfectly conceivable that we could do that. The German Air Force is already flying some of the most advanced Soviet fighters. Aircraft that we trained to fight and were absolutely terrified of, the Germans now have in their inventory; we can climb into them and fly them.

When you are in a war plane you can be remote from what you are doing, like the American B-52 pilots in Vietnam who dropped their bombs from three miles up and never saw them exploding; but even without facing nuclear or chemical weapons, once you have been on the wrong end of a bombing raid . . . well, I would be lying if I said I had not thought about it.

Being on the receiving end of 1,000 lb and 2,000 lb bombs, as JP and I were in prison in Baghdad, is the most horrific experience. For forty-nine days and nights we suffered continual bombing by our friends and allies. Bombs went off around us with monotonous regularity. We would see the flash and a few seconds later, we would hear and feel the rumble of the explosion. On two horrific occasions, the buildings in which we were being held were targeted for particularly close attention. Instead of seeing the flash and counting the seconds to the rumble, just as kids do during thunderstorms, the flash and the blast were simultaneous. Walls crumbled, ceilings caved in and debris flew everywhere. A direct hit from a bomb is not something that anyone would ever forget. We only knocked at death's door a couple of times, but there were troops down in the trenches, Iraqi conscripts, who were getting bombed every single night. It is inconceivable that anyone experiencing that would be unaffected by it.

Yet I honestly did not feel any personal trauma as a result of what we went through in the Gulf, perhaps because of the psychological care that we PoWs were given on our return. People probably thought we would be gibbering wrecks after our treatment by the Iraqis, but it just was not the case at all, none of the guys has had any adverse effects, as far as I know. The human mind and body have a remarkable resistance to hardship and torture and an extraordinary resilience when it is over.

Just the same, everyone who came back from the Gulf said they had been affected by the experience and were different in some way. Combat creates emotional stresses that are far in excess of those faced in even the most stressful civilian job. When you have been placed in a situation where your life is constantly threatened, it makes you re-examine your most basic values. You only have to look at the number of marriages that have failed, a couple from our squadron alone. The guys came back and said: 'That's it, there's no point in living a lie any more, no point in pretending to be what you're not, because tomorrow you might not be here at all'.

Flying has lost some of its excitement, or at least a little bit of its edge, since the Gulf. After being in combat, flying the aircraft to its limits and doing absolutely everything that we had been trained to do and everything that our aircraft was capable of doing, the return to civilian rules and regulations was a difficult adjustment to make. We suddenly had peacetime limits imposed on us again, albeit perfectly legitimate ones. We are not allowed to fly around the UK at 900 miles an hour, fifty feet over the top of towns; the public would be a tiny bit annoyed if we did. We went back to peacetime 'constraints', and as a result, we do not get the buzz from flying our planes that we had out in the Gulf.

Having said that, it is perfectly conceivable that in the next six months, six weeks or six days, somebody could just snap their fingers and call on us to go and do something very similar to the Gulf . . . or something very different. So nobody lets himself go and thinks: 'I can't be bothered to do this' or 'I'm not going to do it the best way I can', because there is always that chance that someone is going to call in their dues, point the finger and say: 'You, get ready, right now'

The Gulf experience has undoubtedly affected my attitude to life. I live and let live now, I really do not get bothered about as many things as I used to. I am not interested in trying to prove a point, nor in getting one over on someone. I live my life from day to day, I spend my money and I enjoy myself, because tomorrow could be my last day on earth. Yesterday could have been my last day and I would be really brassed off if I was looking down, wishing I had done something different. I am glad that I have a good lifestyle, friends, family, somewhere to live and food to eat. I am using what I have now and if I go . . . well, I will have no regrets.

John Peters: Although the business end of our training is often played out using computers and radar screens, there is never any danger of us becoming dehumanized, of seeing warfare as just a video game, rather than the reality – an activity that takes lives. We are made very aware that our weapons kill people, even without putting ourselves on the wrong end of the biggest air offensive in history, as John and I did in the Gulf.

The Air Force training does its job. After Advanced Flying Training, you go to the Tactical Weapons Unit, proudly wearing your gleaming new 'wings' – the badge of office, proving that you are now an RAF pilot. I and my peers arrived brimming with confidence and full of the glamour of flying, to be greeted by the Squadron Commander's words of welcome: 'You are nothing. You think you can fly jets? That is not what the Air Force is about. It's about dropping bombs and firing missiles. When you shoot an aircraft down, you don't take the aircraft out, you aim for the pilot – you kill the man. That is the weak spot. If you can't cope with that thought, you can leave now. You have to prove to me that you have the bottle to kill the man. If not, I will drop you like a stone.' It was a sobering start to a fast-jet career.

We spend a long time learning about weapons effects, such as the blast and fragmentation of a 1,000 lb bomb. We not only learn the effects of the weapons, but also how to plan their use, selecting the deadliest for each situation: air-burst 1,000 lb bombs for troops in the open, creating the maximum devastation from blast and fragmentation; cluster bombs against convoys, 147 bomblets, with a shaped charge that penetrates armour and fragmentation that blasts shrapnel over an area the size of a football pitch; 1,000 lb 'slick' bombs to penetrate concrete defences, varying the fuse settings and delays to ensure that the bomb goes off deep inside the structure. Watch it on television and all you see is a bomb going through a window or an air vent, followed by a few puffs of smoke, a couple of seconds later. Seeing only that, you have no conception of the havoc wreaked by 2,000 lbs of high-explosive detonating deep inside the building. I know, I have been there.

Bomber crew are also made very aware that there is an attrition rate for them in wartime. Whereas fighters know that if they cannot win a particular engagement, they can turn tail and 'bug out', before rejoining the fight, bombers have to grit their teeth and press on, regardless of the threat, knowing that some will get through, but some will be shot down, just as John and I were in the Gulf. Everyone with half a brain knows that reality, but we are not stupid; no one would go to war if they did not also expect to come back. Even after what happened in the Gulf, if I were back there now, I would still be thinking: 'It won't happen to me'.

Flying high above a conflict, like modern-day knights on high-tech chargers, does give air crew a detached view of conflict compared to other servicemen, even when the objectives are what we euphemistically call 'soft targets' – unprotected by armour or concrete, such as soft-skinned troop lorries . . . or soft-skinned troops. Yet you only had to read American press reports to see that the US air crew saw the full, massive destructive impact of their weapons on the Iraqis fleeing up the Basra Road.

Our experience of war is still far removed from that of a soldier, involved in a very personal, one-on-one conflict. The army still bears the brunt of the shock of violence, for its soldiers see, hear, smell and even touch the results of the weapons of war. Argentinian soldiers defending Mount Longdon during the Falklands War were softened up by air strikes and artillery barrages. Milan missiles, wire-guided 'tank-busters' normally used against armoured vehicles, were used to blast apart their rock and concrete bunkers, slaughtering the defenders inside. Yet despite all the firepower of their modern weapons, the British soldiers still carried out the final attack through a hail of bullets and cleared the trenches in ferocious hand-to-hand fighting, using grenades and bayonets – First World War trench warfare.

After the Gulf, the television documentaries again concentrated on the ground forces and the personal effects of the war upon them; what they saw and how they felt. The air war was portrayed very much in terms of a computerized war game; bomb-sight cross wires on infrared images. Yet controlling every cross was a pink, vulnerable body operating that aircraft, while seeing tracer searing up through the sky. Not one air crew crossed the border into Iraq without being shot at and locked up by Surface-to-Air missile systems, not one crew failed to see the destructive power and impact of their weapons, not one crewman did not know someone who failed to return from his mission. Nor was the air war the brief encounter that the ground forces experienced. As one American pilot said to me: 'What is this "100 hour war" shit? I did more combat hours than that myself. My war lasted seven weeks.'

Soldiers see people being killed at close range and have people shooting at them, but it is no less stressful to be locked-up on a radar, when you know that the radar lock is the prelude to you being destroyed with a missile. Being fired at by Triple-A, a barrage of multicoloured fireballs exploding around you to create a wall of death through which you must fly, or being targeted by a Surface-to-Air missile, a twenty-foot metal telegraph pole, packed with high-explosive and launched towards you at Mach 3, is as terrifying an experience for air crew as being bombed must be for soldiers.

There is one difference between war in the air and on the ground – aircraft can never take prisoners. Air crew can and do survive the loss of their aircraft, as John and I have reason to know, but at root, air combat is life or death every time. Once the focus of the air defences is upon you, there is no bush to hide behind. Only your acquired skills and your knowledge of radar and missile systems – plus a measure of luck and perhaps the courage to push yourself beyond the limits – will keep you alive. One of our squadron in the Gulf saw a white point of light streaking towards him. It took him seconds to realize that it was a missile; the realization and the explosion came simultaneously. We are trapped in our cockpits, desperately looking for a way to escape death. We do not fight our battles hand to hand, but the stress of combat is still there and the combat still pits man against man, even though the weapons are missiles and fast jets instead of grenades and bayonets.

Modern wars are fought by fully professional forces on the nation's behalf, whether or not the nation is unaniminously in support of its government. As a result, the population remains largely ignorant of the physical and mental demands that war makes upon combatants. The public experiences the spectacle of a 'television war' and shares a vicarious thrill in victory, but does not pay the emotional and physical price paid by those who have fought the conflict, although the letters that John and I received suggested that many people were genuinely moved by our experiences. The television film of the PoWs perhaps also reminded people that the war was not just a matter of crosses on bunkers and bombs in windows; there were men – and women – on the end of those crosses.

War remains a unique phenomenon, inexplicable to those who have never been in combat. There is no relevant comparison in civilian life; even disasters like Lockerbie, Hillsborough or the King's Cross fire are significantly different. As one Falklands veteran, Steven Hughes, put it in Hugh McManners' excellent book *The Scars of War*, going to war is like: 'willingly taking part in the disaster – all of you going to King's Cross, including setting fire to the place yourselves.'

None of us involved in the Gulf will ever forget what it is like to go to war, but although people seem to want to hear about a massive change in my life as a result of the Gulf War, I have really changed very little. John claims that the Gulf experience has made him more tolerant, but I disagree, he is still the same direct Geordie that I knew before, and he certainly still argues his point as vehemently as ever – essentially he has not changed!

We were very good mates before the Gulf, but the friendship is put under greater strains now that we are with separate squadrons in different countries. We have not really sat down, had a few beers and just chatted since we split up, and we certainly have more disagreements now than we used to. People expect, and even demand, that John and I be a lot more than just a couple of good Air Force mates, because of what we went through together, but I do not think that we will ever really be bosom buddies. People always want to hear superlatives; they want everything to be dramatic, but in real life, not everything is.

Helen Peters: John does not think he is a changed man, but I do. If anything, he is more stroppy, he does not suffer fools gladly and he is more prepared to stand up for himself. Books say that the psychological effect of such experiences is to undermine people's confidence, but I would say that it has had exactly the opposite effect on John. He is a bit uneasy about what people think of him, but generally speaking, he is a more confident person. He used to be a bit too self-effacing, but now he is more prepared to speak up with his opinions.

There have certainly been difficulties with relationships with other people as a result of the publicity that John received after the Gulf. The difficulties are dwindling a lot now, particularly since we have moved to a different station where there are fewer people who were involved in the Gulf, or who felt that their noses had been put out of joint. There was a fair amount of that initially, when we were still with the same group of people, many of whom had also been involved in the Gulf and felt a bit resentful about some of the attention that John was getting, but I think that is all by the by now. You get the odd comment, like one of the guys coming back after doing one sortie in the Gulf and telling John: 'I've done half a sortie more than you now'. Most of that sort of thing is just said as a joke, but sometimes you still get the odd comment that is definitely a little bit more than a joke.

I think John would like to feel that he has a slightly closer relationship with John Nichol than he actually has, but military friendships in general often seem to be quite transitory and superficial. The constant moving on inevitably means that friendships are picked up and put down easily, but I suspect that the price paid is that most service friendships lack true depth.

John Nichol is quite a softie underneath, but he would never, ever, let anybody think that he was. On the television documentary, my John came over as being much more emotional, but John Nichol had made a conscious decision that he was not going to allow his emotions to show, to the extent of breaking down on television. At one point, when talking about the effect that the broadcasts about the PoWs had had on his parents, it all got too much for him and he got up, left the room, went away and controlled himself before he came back. My John just did the whole thing straight through and whatever happened, happened; it was just different ways of wanting to deal with things.

Air Force life is always stressful for relationships, but the stresses were greatly increased in the aftermath of the Gulf conflict. There have definitely, very definitely, been a lot of problems and a number of marriages have broken up. I think some could have been avoided if the boys had stopped playing stiff upper lip, or if the powers-that-be had been prepared to be a little more understanding. Some research suggests that as many as thirty per cent of battlefield casualties are psychological, yet the forces remain very sceptical about psychological problems in their men. PTSD – Post-Traumatic Stress Disorder – is still regarded in some military quarters as little more than the modern equivalent of a white feather. Every time they go to war, the Army, Air Force and Navy try to get more sensible about the way they deal with the stress of combat, but it still seems to come down to an individual 'Boss' – a Station Commander in our case – deciding whether he wants his lads to see a psychiatrist.

I personally feel that a lot of good would have been done if all the men who came back from the Gulf had been given a fifteen-minute interview with someone who deals with stress-related problems, and who could then have decided whether any particular people needed help. We now know of several men on squadron who subsequently – up to two years later – needed to get that help, and I think a lot of us could have picked them out, almost from the day that they came back.

The PoWs that I have met are the most sane, stable and well-balanced of them all, perhaps because they had so much help in coming to terms with their experiences, but there are probably lots of lads who were doing sorties every day in the Gulf who could be helped tremendously even by just one session with a counsellor. They may have things that they cannot talk to their wives about and do not want to talk to their mates about, in case it is seen as a sign of weakness, but if they had all been ordered to have counselling, it would have removed that stigma. These are not people who have lost their senses completely, just those who might need a little help.

I am not sure if I have changed as a result of what happened. I am probably even less tolerant of people who make a hell of a fuss about fairly irrelevant things and get themselves in a heck of a state. I just think: 'Wait a minute, what are you getting yourself in such a paddy about?' I bite my tongue sometimes, because I can feel myself getting indignant and would probably end up being quite rude to them. It is a bit like my reaction to the early news flashes from the Gulf. Initially the media always seemed to find relatives of people who were going to be in the catering corps two thousand miles from the front line, but who were still wailing on: 'My son didn't join up for this, how am I going to cope, I can't sleep and I can't eat', and I was thinking: 'They're in the armed forces, for goodness' sake, you've got to accept what that entails'.

It is slightly different if you are married to air crew, however. I have lost – we have lost – a number of very good friends, only one of them while at war. The rest of them died during training exercises. We know several people who have walked out in the morning saying: 'Bye-bye dear, see you later', who never came home.

I have been to plenty of funerals of friends killed in routine sorties, and, although I do not sit down and brood about it, I try not to let John walk out of the door in the morning on a cross word, because he might not come back. You live with that all the time, and to a certain extent, a war makes no difference. It is just more likely to happen in wartime, but it is not something totally new.

John Peters: To be based on Germany, at the heart of 'Fortress Europe', watching the Berlin Wall come down, was an incredible experience. People were talking about 'The End of War' and all sorts of other wildly optimistic scenarios, but although the Soviet threat has been lifted, we still face an era of frightening instability. We are no longer expecting to be fighting from fixed positions in Armageddon – a general, all-out war. We have now become more of a large-scale, rapid-reaction force, expecting a limited war instead of a general war – a bad dream instead of a nightmare. That does not mean limited in size; the Gulf War was enormous in scale, but it was fought with defined, limited objectives.

Unfortunately, the 'decisive blow' of Desert Storm appears to have made very little difference. The Iraqis may be out of Kuwait, but the situation in the Gulf remains very unstable. My own squadron has already carried out further bombing raids against Iraq and a third involvement looks increasingly likely. The second was a very limited attack, but if Saddam Hussein provides any further provocation, I am sure that there will be a much larger air offensive next time.

Air power came of age in the Gulf, it proved to be the most flexible, quick and cost-effective way of enforcing political will rapidly and unanswerably. You do not have to mount a huge military campaign; if you want something specific destroyed quickly, air power can do it.

The success of air power in the Gulf may prove to be an albatross around our necks in the future, and whether air power could end a conflict like Bosnia is another question. The situation over there is just so volatile it could all go pear-shaped overnight. As servicemen, we are well aware that we can be put in life-threatening situations, but we plan and operate to limit them. What is scary about conflicts like Bosnia is that, however flexible you are, any sort of intervention is unlikely to achieve anything beyond scaring us witless and getting some friends killed. There are at least twenty solutions to the Bosnian problem, but all of them probably suck. Bosnia has the look of a European Vietnam – a scrappy, indeterminate, unpopular war.

Nor is Bosnia the only powder keg waiting to explode. Though the Cold War is over, the 'Soviet hordes' have not just disappeared into thin air. Russia and the rest of the republics of the old Soviet Union remain potentially explosive flash points; hungry people will go to war for food.

For much of my life, I have lived under the constant threat of nuclear Armageddon, and yet I was sure that I would never go to war. Now the world has changed. I have already gone to war once and I am far from certain that I will not be doing so again.

Glossary of Abbreviations

AMRAAM	Advanced Medium-Range Air-to-Air Missile
APU	Auxiliary Power Unit
ATC	Air Traffic Control
AWACS	Airborne Warning And Control System
BIF	Bomb In Face
BVR	Beyond Visual Range
CAP	Combat Air Patrol
CBU	Cluster Bomb Unit
COC	Combat Operations Centre
EMBS	Emergency Braking Speed
FLOT	Forward Line of Own Troops
FOG	Fuel On the Ground
HUD	Head-Up Display
IAT	International Air Tattoo
IMC	Instrument Meteorological Conditions
LHA	Liquid Hazard Area
MPC	Missile Practice Camp
NAPS	Nerve Agent Pre-treatment Sets
OCU	Operational Conversion Unit

OLF	Operational Low Flying
PBF	Pilots' Briefing Facility
PK	Probability Kill
PTSD	Post-Traumatic Stress Disorder
QRA	Quick Reaction Alert
RHAG	Rotary Hydraulic Arresting Gear
RHWR	Radar Homing and Warning Receiver
RVR	Runway Visual Range
SAM	Surface-to-Air Missile
SOP	Standard Operating Procedure
TACEVAL	Tactical Evaluation
TFR	Terrain-Following Radar
TLP	Tactical Leadership Programme
TOT	Time On Target
UXB	Unexploded Bomb
VHA	Vapour Hazard Area
VNE	Velocity Never Exceed

Index